Democracy,
Authority,
and
Alienation
in Work

John F. Witte

Democracy, Authority, and Alienation in Work

Workers' Participation in an American Corporation

THE UNIVERSITY OF CHICAGO PRESS
Chicago & London

The University of Chicago Press, Chicago 60637
The University of Chicago Press, Ltd., London

© 1980 by The University of Chicago
All rights reserved. Published 1980
Paperback edition 1982
Printed in the United States of America
89 88 87 86 85 84 83 82   2 3 4 5 6

Library of Congress Cataloging in Publication Data

Witte, John F.
  Democracy, authority, and alienation in work.

  Bibliography: p. 207.
  Includes Index.
  1. Employees' representation in management—
United States.   I. Title.
HD5660.U5W57   658.3′152′0973   80–16241
ISBN 0–226–90420–2 (cloth)
      0–226–90421–0 (paper)

For Mary,
who gave up so much for so long

Contents

List of Tables and Figures

FIGURES

Preface

This book is about industrial democracy in an American corporation. Throughout I will be referring to the term *democracy* in a somewhat extreme form in relation to the current usage of the word in American theories of organization. I have not considered workers' participation as merely a progressive management technique or a vague approach to a more "humanized" work place. Although I am not condemning these innovations for the ends they seek, it is nevertheless the case that most American experiments in this vein have taken advantage of the symbolic value of "democracy" while not applying the basic principles of democracy as it is conceived in political theory.

A serious conception of democracy implies a principle of political equality. Modification may be required in an organization that must accomplish an explicit purpose, but the ideal of equality must still be present. The promise of industrial democracy is that—given the limited scope of activity and the continuous attention of participants in close physical proximity in the work place—this ideal might be translated into meaningful participation by individuals in critical decisions that control their lives. The ideal is at once powerful and dangerous. It is powerful in that, if realized, it would fulfill the promise of direct participation impossible to realize in the larger and, for many people, less meaningful organizations of community or nation. It is dangerous in that democracy is a potent ideology that can be used to cover the worst sorts of elite manipulation while raising false expectations and demanding sacrifices from those receiving the fewest rewards.

In general these dangers are not of serious concern in the United States because only a few companies have attempted experiments bold enough to take real advantage of the symbolic power of democratic rhetoric. On the other hand, the rhetoric is prevalent in contemporary management theories, and it is important to understand how far short of a serious formulation of democratic principles these theories fall. Perhaps more important, this book may call attention to the severe problems in instituting a system of direct, meaningful workers' participation for those countries which have attempted—and in some cases are proclaiming the arrival of—true industrial democracy. In our appraisal of these systems, we must be very careful to distinguish the extent and form of that "democracy." To suggest that democracy exists when it is mere illusion is the cruelest form of authoritarian manipulation.

The number of people to whom I owe thanks is very large. Foremost among them are the employees of the corporation I will refer to as "Sound, Incorporated" (SI). They provided me the remarkable opportunity to study and work in the workers' participation project they initiated and have continued. I thank John B., Ruth M., Bob R., Andre K., Tom J., Peter M., Jackie M., Ray C., Hector M., Judy B., Jean S., George B., Bill G., Paul P., Ruby L., and all those on the L606, 6208, and lacquer-finish lines and in the Employee Relations Department. For their courage, foresight, and genuine concern for their company and, more important, their employees, I especially thank Sid, Arnold, Tony, Sterling, and my close friend Dave, who has borne more of the burden than anyone else.

During the time of study I received financial support from the National Institute of Mental Health, the Employment and Training Administration of the U.S. Department of Labor, and the Rockefeller Foundation. The generosity of these institutions allowed me to maintain the neutrality of a participant observer which was essential to the project.

My research and writing were aided by Nancy Z. from SI, whose efforts in documenting and analyzing all aspects of the project were of immeasurable value; by Nancy Berlin, Pat Kramer, and Steve Sauerman, who helped with the interviewing; and by Marilyn Henry for typing and Amy Kritzer, who reviewed the final draft of the manuscript. Finally, I thank Mary Witte, who has been involved in many aspects of this project: interviewing, participating actively at SI, editing, typing, and arguing.

Among those at Yale University, I am grateful to Victor Vroom, John Meisel, Douglas Rae, Sanford Berlin, and especially Robert Lane, who was involved in this project from the beginning and who has influenced my entire thinking about politics and how it should be studied. Finally, and most important, I am grateful to Robert Dahl, who provided the initial inspiration and supported the research financially as well as intellectually.

1. Introduction

"I see industrial democracy is the latest fad again," remarked the elderly professor before a 1974 conference of corporate managers who had paid a great deal to learn about participatory management techniques. He went on to pose a question for the audience.

"If industrial democracy is such a good idea, an idea that should appeal to the democratic instincts of one of the most democratic countries, why do all the experimental projects, fancy seminars, and idealistic books and articles not produce a ripple in the major institutional centers of power in the United States?"

A marvelous battle ensued. Liberal managers turned from attacking the professor to pin the blame on bureaucratic union leaders interested in protecting their own power. The few union leaders and academics present characterized management-run experiments as manipulative and fraudulent, intended either to combat union organization or to increase productivity. It struck me some time later that the arguments of both sides, while true to a degree, only obscured the real dilemma. The professor was questioning the basic premises of industrial democracy. He was suggesting either that the values to be realized are not widely held or that industrial democracy will not produce the results expected of it. His assessment of the potential for industrial democracy in the United States was bleak indeed.

I felt at the time that the professor's cynicism was excessive, especially in view of the growing publicity about the Lordstown labor protests, general concern for blue-collar alienation, and prominent projects in participative management by giant corporations like General Foods, Proctor & Gamble, and Texas Instruments.[1] Also on the stage that evening was the president of a $100 million corporation that had begun a program to "humanize and democratize work." His relatively radical position excited the audience. His remarks countered the reactionary position of his academic opponent, and he reassured the audience that industrial democracy was not just a passing fad. It seemed that surely times had changed when a wealthy American executive could endorse "the remarkable strides made in Norway, Sweden, and Yugoslavia to bring humanism and democracy to the economic enterprise."

Seven months later I joined one of his subsidiary companies, which will be referred to here as Sound, Incorporated (SI), as a participant/observer in a program intended as a dramatic demonstration of industrial democracy. This book presents an analysis of the first three years of that project; it focuses on the problems, promises, and potential of workers' participation in an American setting.

After working full time for several years trying to make workers' participation succeed, my initial enthusiasm has waned, and I have come to understand and, to a degree, share the professor's cynicism. In this study, I reach optimistic conclusions about some of the essentials of organizational democracy, particularly the competence of American workers to participate effectively in decision making. However, the principal message is that *meaningful* workers' participation will be extremely difficult to achieve, given the widely held American faith in meritocracy, with its concomitant beliefs concerning the purpose of the corporation, the structure of corporate authority, and distribution of influence and reward. It is this commitment to meritocratic norms that establishes the limits of democracy in the economic enterprise.

This judgment is based on the observation and study of a specific experiment in industrial democracy, but it is consistent with much previous research, as well as with commonsense notions of how modern organizations operate. To lay the foundation for the analysis to follow, this chapter outlines the two general sets of theoretical issues on which the potential for industrial democracy turns. The first, of interest to political theorists, is an examination of the limits to the democratic process at a very fundamental level. The second set of issues, addressed primarily by organization specialists, concerns the specific mechanisms and procedures for institutionalizing participation.

CLARIFICATION OF TERMS

The terms *participation, control,* and *democracy* will be used in a "hard" sense relative to some of the current usage in the participative-management literature. Throughout the text, the following definitions will be used:

> *Control:* The ability of an individual or group to determine unilaterally the outcomes of a decision-making process.

> *Participation:* Actions by an individual or group that affect outcomes in a decision-making process.

These definitions imply a hard use of terms in that actions must be directly related to decision outcomes. *Control* is used in an extreme form in order to ensure that, when a statement like "The president controlled the choice of plant sites" is made, there will be no confusion as to the distribution of power in relation to the decision in question. Similarly, when workers' participation or participative management is mentioned, it means more than a situation in which a manager asks for input, advice, or suggestions from workers. In the present context, *participation* implies a reasonable probability of affecting the outcome of a decision. In other words, it will not be used to describe a very asymmetrical power arrangement in which the powerful member seeks to secure the opinions of the weaker parties. The word *influence* will be used synonymously with *participation*, except that the latter will always imply an observable action (voting, discussing, etc.), while influence may occur passively (e.g., "Anticipation of the president's reaction clearly influenced the proposal").

In organizational theory, the word *democratic* covers a wide range of circumstances. The democratic organization described by Warren Bennis and Philip Slater—using such phrases as "full and free communication," "consensus decision-making," "emotional expression," and "human bias"—is far from the rigorously formal structure of elections, councils, and committees that composes the Yugoslav system of industrial democracy.[2] Use of the terms *industrial* or *organizational democracy* in this study will tend toward the Yugoslav definition. Industrial democracy implies more than a humanistic bias and an "open" system of management; it implies a set of decision-making mechanisms based on a reasonable assumption of political equality. These mechanisms might include decisions reached in mass assemblies; referenda; elections of representatives to councils, committees, or assemblies; and direct participation in the work unit itself.

There will be times, however—primarily when the word *democratic* is used as an adjective—that something less formal will be meant. Tannenbaum, who conceptualizes control, and hence democracy, disregarding formal procedures, defines the democratic organization as one in which "groups at the lower levels in the hierarchy (such as rank and file) have more control than groups at higher levels (such as executive board or president)."[3] Following this general idea, a decision-making process will be assumed to be more democratic if the influence of those lower in the organizational structure is increasing. This usage of the term permits discussion of the democratic character of management styles, approaches to problem solving, interpersonal relationships, and the conduct of routine tasks that may be divorced from formal procedural mechanisms such as elections or assemblies.

CONSTRAINTS ON THE DEMOCRATIC PROCESS

Twentieth-century political theorists have consistently outlined the limits to ideal forms of direct democracy for the larger geographical units that compose modern polities. The basic question is whether these same limits apply when the unit of analysis is the work place. Many have argued over more than a century that, because of the restricted size of the work place, the relatively narrow scope of decision making, and the importance of work in people's lives, direct forms of democracy in the economic enterprise can succeed where they are bound to fail in the larger society. But the problem of judging whether direct democracy "succeeds" is difficult indeed. We can anticipate that judging success will not depend on a simple measure or a single judgment but, rather, on an amalgam of factors. Thus one of my methods of inquiry will be to analyze the experience at SI in relation to factors that have been suggested as constraints on direct forms of democracy.

The most obvious and most frequently discussed limits are the physical constraints imposed by time, space, and communication.[4] Decision making requires meeting space, time for deliberation and study, and accurate and timely communication among those involved. Although the reduced range of decisions and the numbers and proximity of people in the work place suggest that barriers may be greatly reduced in organizations, we will see that in the economic enterprise, in which time and resources expended in decision making have a direct and immediate effect on both costs and individual responsibilities, these factors are far from inconsequential.

Physical limits to direct forms of democracy are by no means the only difficulties, and some would argue that, given modern techniques of communication, they may be the least of them. More far-reaching issues are the human questions: first, the belief in and desire for democracy and, second, the decision-making competence of the average person. Support for increased workers' participation, by workers and managers alike, is essential to the success of industrial democracy. This support may be even more important in the work place than in the larger political system, where decisions are made at a distance by a sometimes incomprehensible tangle of elites. In the latter case both political apathy and outright hostility to democratic procedures usually have little effect on the slow, constitutionally cautious policymaking process. The situation in an organization reverses this process. In the "close" ordered society of the industrial corporation, apathy, lack of interest, and resistance have an immediate impact. Worker representatives agonize over the lack of concern on the part of their constituents; enthusiastic participants in autonomous work groups become frustrated and angry over the lack of enthusiasm of some of their peers; and managers who feel the encroachment of democracy fight to preserve their authority. Since passive acquiescence tends to favor the current structure of authority, belief in the legitimacy of participation is an absolute requirement if that structure is to be transformed.

Thus the first questions to be explored concern attitudes toward worker participation. How much participation do workers believe they should have? In what types of decisions? How do these beliefs coincide with those of managers? What factors are correlated with a belief that participation is legitimate? And, finally, why do people hold these opinions? What explanations do they give? The answers to these questions, based on interviews conducted at SI before the participatory program began, provide a backdrop for subsequent events.

Final judgment on the question of support for participation requires more than a simple analysis of the expressed beliefs of workers. Marxists have long claimed that capitalist workers falsely perceive their own interests, in that they have adopted the prevailing bourgeois norms—in this case, support for the traditional form of corporate authority.[5] The keys to deciphering this claim are first, to understand the reasoning people use to explain their positions; second, to determine how certain they are about their attitudes; and third, to measure attitude changes, if any, once workers are given the opportunity to participate in the decision-making process. It seems reasonable to argue that, if workers are uncertain about the meaning and consequences of participation, and if they perceive themselves as relatively well off under the status quo, they will be initially conservative in their support for increased participation. However, as they begin to understand what participation entails and as their influence increases, it seems equally reasonable to hypothesize that attitudes will change in the direction of increased support. This hypothesis is only part of what Carole Pateman calls the educative effect of participation.[6] Pateman accepts it as proven, but I consider it one of the crucial questions on which the prospect for organizational democracy rests.

Beyond the belief and desire for democracy is the question of competence. The need at times to assign authority to individuals competent in a specific policy area is accepted by most political theorists. Doctors and pilots usually serve as convincing examples. Theorists differ significantly, however, when the argument turns to the range of decisions which must be made by competent authority.[7] Actually the competence issue implies several questions. One meaning of the word *competent* has to do with mastery of a technical area, evidenced by the knowledge of pertinent information and the acquisition of technical skills. The decision-making "competence" of doctors and pilots, to which I might add plumbers and electricians, suggests this meaning of the word. One of the questions to be explored here is to what extent technical considerations impede workers' ability to make reasonable judgments. This problem will be considered for company-wide joint worker-management groups and for participation at the shop floor level.

There is another important sense in which we must consider worker competence: that of the "competent" representative. The general question is whether worker representatives will adequately protect and promote the interests of their fellow workers. If the answer to this is no, either participation is limited to decisions at the work-group level, or it darkens into manipulation and a most hypocritical form of domination.

A final set of potential constraints, particularly when analyzing democratic processes within an organization, has to do with outcomes. The problems that have already been discussed are common to democratic systems in general, but the necessity of achieving specific ends to some degree adds a consideration for industrial democracy that is irrelevant to other forms. Democratic polities are judged more on the character of processes and procedures than on achieving some specific goal or purpose. The degree of openness, the right of opposition, and nonviolent resolution of conflict are some of the standards of judgment. Most contemporary theorists will argue that interests are diverse and goals are relative, the function of the political system being to reach compromise agreements, resolving divergent purposes according to procedures deemed legitimate by those involved. There is an obvious distinction between their emphasis on process and the emphasis in economic enterprises on achieving specific material outcomes.

In one sense, however, there are outcomes expected in a democratic polity which are similar to those that will be expected in an industrial setting. In both systems, participants will expect basic assurance of certain rights. Rights of speech, assembly (or "organization"), and due process (grievance procedure) will be important in both. Any attempt at democracy will falter if these rights are consistently overridden. However, in an economic enterprise, expectations of members of the organization will go beyond these conditions in at least two important respects. The first is maintenance and protection of adequate wages and salaries. Hugh Clegg, a sympathetic critic of industrial democracy for nearly three decades, argues that cooperative decision making will lead to worker co-optation with a resulting anemia in the pursuit of wage and grievance demands.[8] Whether these vital interests can be protected is a critical question. It will be a primary consideration in the chapters on joint worker-manager decision making.

A second important outcome, specifically associated with industrial democracy, is the effect of democratic procedures on the nature of work and the character of individual jobs. It is a consistent claim by all proponents of worker participation (in proposals based merely on management style as well as formal systems of industrial democracy) that participation will reduce alienation in work. A fundamental premise of workers' participation is that increasing control over the forces affecting one's behavior on the job will result in a parallel reduction of worker alienation. (The change-over-time results analyzed in chapter 9 will consider this claim for various forms of participation.)

A final constraint on industrial democracy, for which there is no direct parallel in democracy in the geographical unit, is the goal of profits. In the

United States, where most projects in "work humanization," "job enrichment," or "participative management" are administered by consultants working for management, there has been a long, arduous, yet incomplete effort to demonstrate that these progressive techniques increase motivation and productivity.[9] At SI, economic measures were also carefully analyzed. The results over time, presented with a caution inspired by a number of uncontrolled factors, are nevertheless optimistic on such measures as labor productivity and employee turnover. However, a critical phase in the analysis to follow will go beyond a mechanical discussion of these indicators to a closer look at how the pressured drive for economic success affects essential attitudes and structures behavior in a manner ultimately inimical to the realization of democracy in the work place.

Of specific concern will be the effects of individual ambition and competitiveness on democratic norms. I argue that, although the frustrated ambitions of employees provide workers with particularly competent leaders, the meritocratic system of reward, promotion, and accountability based on individual performance in relation to economic standards is at odds with a democratic model. Norms defining a meritocratic system are in direct opposition to principles that underlie a democratic organization. The extreme contrast between these existing, and widely accepted, organizational norms and those that naturally arise when democratic principles are introduced generates significant resistance within the organization and greatly limits the effectiveness of workers' participation.

Demonstrating that participation will not destroy profitability may affect attitudes somewhat, but fundamental beliefs in individualism, competition, and just deserts drive the modern corporation. Reconciling these beliefs with the communal, cooperative goals of organizational democracy is the challenge to be faced if serious attempts at industrial democracy are to flourish.

From a different perspective, these potential constraints can be considered as essential criteria which must be fulfilled if the democratic process is to succeed. The physical problems of time and communication must be overcome; there must be support for the idea of workers' participation; employees must be competent decision makers; and a range of outcomes based on the expectations of employees, managers, and owners must be realized.

Modes of Participation

Although theoretically the criteria described above are general, in that they can be discussed independently of the form or mechanism for introducing workers' participation, in practice any determination of the extent to which they are fulfilled depends on the way participation is organized. Different designs for industrial democracy contain different mixes of essential elements. Variations occur both in the degree to which the criteria must be met and in the exact form they will take. For example, competent participation in an autonomous work team is very different from the competence required of a worker representative on a high-level policymaking council. Similarly, although co-optation may be the critical question for worker councils, among workers at the shop floor level cooperation may be the essential element. We cannot judge the effectiveness of a democratic state by relying on abstractions concerning democratic character, political apathy, and elite responsibility without considering the structure of political parties, electoral laws, or local organizations. So we cannot judge the effectiveness of industrial democracy without considering the mechanisms by which such a system might be put in place.

Joint Worker-Manager Representation

Decision making occurs at many levels within a corporation. It is unrealistic to suggest that all employees should actively engage in discussion and resolution of all company-wide issues, and this has not been seriously proposed.[10] Ultimately, representation will be needed. At SI representation initially took two forms. The first and more important was an elected central council composed of workers and managers; this council had broad policymaking powers as well as control of other experimental groups. The second form of representative participation was special-purpose committees. These, like the central council, consisted of both workers and managers. However, in most cases members were appointed on a voluntary basis, and the functions of the special committees were always very narrow, being confined usually to a single policy area, such as communication, training, education, or the company newspaper.

Worker representation is very rare in the United States, where most participatory experiments have been conducted at the operational level.[11] The key theoretical issues come from European experience, particularly in Yugoslavia, Germany, and, to a lesser extent, Great Britain and Norway. From empirical study and theoretical speculation, a number of questions have arisen concerning the potential effectiveness of joint decision-making committees. The principal issue for those concerned with worker rights is the possibility of co-optation.

Most studies conclude that co-optation is a probable outcome of joint decision making. Clegg's arguments, which summarized studies in a number of countries, have been mentioned. Fred Emery and Einar Thorsrud, leading Scandinavian specialists in work humanization, come to a similar conclusion in describing Norwegian efforts toward shop floor participation.[12] The strongest negative evidence, however, comes from Yugoslavia, which has the most advanced formal system of work participation in the world. Empirical research conducted by Obradović, Rus, and others demonstrates that Yugoslav workers' councils are dominated by managers and professionals at the expense of lower white- and blue-collar workers.[13] Replication of that research at SI, which gives us the first hint of the capabilities of American workers in such situations, is a great deal more optimistic.

The problem of co-optation is only one of several potential difficulties with this method of workers' participation. Problems of communication between constituent and delegate caused by apathy, distortion, neglect, or constraints of time can lead to misrepresentation of interests even if the representative remains independent. Moreover, the power of joint committees may be limited either in terms of the policies considered or in the implementation stage, when it is necessary to rely on the existing hierarchical management structure. (Co-optation, misrepresentation, and what will be defined as structural impotence provide the framework for the discussion of joint decision making in chapters 5 and 6.)

Direct Participation in the Work Unit

Much research has been done on participation at the operational level, in both office departments and production work groups. The majority of these experiments, employing various schemes of participation in the work units themselves, were designed to test the effects of participation on job satisfaction and productivity. Surprisingly few of these projects in the United States have published precise results. These measures—job satisfaction and productivity—were obviously of interest to us in the experiments at SI. As it turned out, we were much more successful in measuring changes in alienation than in productivity for the autonomous and semi-autonomous work teams.

Experimental evidence is more limited when we venture beyond these traditional measures. For example, one of the basic problems of "shop floor" democracy is to determine which production techniques and job designs provide a setting in which meaningful decision making and participation are possible at all. Concern only for efficiency tends to produce simplified jobs (devoid of decisions of any kind) and a method of monitoring output geared to the individual rather than the work group. In this situation, can participation be anything more than a ritual, without real substance or effect? What will it cost to redesign existing modes of production to add components of human problem solving and the possibility for teamwork?

The dynamics of participative work projects (i.e., developments over time) raise another series of questions. In a fully autonomous group without a formally designated leader, how will the group solve problems of coordination and interpersonal conflict? Will cooperation grow or decrease over time? Will the interests of the workers in decision making change as they experience both the rewards and pains of added responsibility?

In an attempt to answer these questions, five experiments were conducted at SI in 1975 and 1976. The results of these experiments are both promising and disappointing—disappointing in that they were impossible to sustain over an extended period of time; promising in that, relative to representative forms of participation, shop floor participation seemed to have the greatest effect on reducing alienation and increasing support for further participation by workers. (The progress and breakdown of these experiments and the theoretical dilemma facing shop-floor democracy are discussed in chapters 7 and 8. The change-over-time statistics are presented in chapter 9.)

The changes at SI were unique both in scope and in the fact that an outside academic was allowed to participate and to report the results— both the successes and the failures. Reporting on a complex series of organizational changes spanning almost three years demands some latitude in emphasis and method. My emphasis throughout will be on the theoretical issues discussed above, combining the concerns of both political and organizational theory. This concentration on the problems of industrial democracy precludes much attention to "work improvement" or the "quality of working life" in general. Indeed, a treatise on those subjects might have focused on worker education, wages and benefits, working-hour schemes, or the design of work procedures and dealt only briefly with participation.

My methods vary; however, quantitative measures are used when appropriate. This reliance on "numbers" is necessary simply because there are very few objective data available on meaningful experiments in worker participation. In the great majority of these experiments, reliable measures have either not been made at all or have been released only as internal or external consultants have seen fit to release them. Thus, every effort will be made here to present results as rigorously and honestly as possible. I am quite certain that few of the individuals involved in the program at SI will agree with everything said in the pages that follow, but I hope they will all judge the evidence to be factual and the general themes at least a fair representation of what took place.

2. Background of the Study

Sound, Incorporated, produces high-fidelity equipment for both private and professional consumers. It is situated in Los Angeles, with the work force being distributed among five sites within fifteen miles of each other. The company's products are of high quality and are consistently at the top of their market in price. Profit margins reflect this position: SI is one of six subsidiaries of a publicly owned parent company, and, although five of the six are profitable, SI contributes more than any other unit, with sales grossing over $50 million a year. This position was reached by a program of very rapid expansion over the past seven years. In 1969, SI employed only one-third of its current work force and realized annual sales approximately one-sixth those of 1976.[1] This growth has been possible because SI products have the reputation of being the very best in the high-fidelity field. Thus the company places tremendous emphasis on quality in manufacturing.

The number of employees at SI varied from a low of 850 in January 1975 to 1,350 in June 1977, the dates covered in this study. There is no union, and no organizing activity of any kind was evident during the time covered here, although the question of the relationship between the participatory program and a union was brought up by several workers. To date there has been no serious attempt to organize the company. The absence of a union is an important factor in interpreting the outcome of the participatory experiments. It can be reasonably argued that without a union the test of industrial democracy is wholly insufficient. On the other hand, in the United States, where not even one in four workers is unionized and where almost all work-place experiments are conducted in nonunion plants, the SI experiment can be appropriately compared to other experiments and the results may generalize to a larger population.

Almost half the SI employees were women; 45% had Spanish surnames, and 5% were black. Despite a company policy specifying a minimum level of comprehension of English, 10%–15% had a problem with English. The mean years-of-education figure was 11.0 for nonsupervisory employees, 13.1 for supervisors, and 14.8 for managers. Characteristics of the work force as a whole, with parallel statistics for a random sample drawn for interviewing purposes and statistics for a second wave, are presented in appendix A.

Wages, salaries, and employee benefits were quite good. Wages were in the seventy-fifth percentile of the greater Los Angeles area. (They reached no higher than this percentile because the aerospace industry, working much of the time on cost-plus contracts, skewed the distribution.) The benefits at SI, which were very near the top for comparable industries in the area, included medical, dental, and life insurance; a pension plan; educational reimbursement; an employee stock-ownership plan; and an employee stock-purchase plan.

The manufacturing work was extremely varied. Approximately 40% of the jobs were light assembly work, requiring in most cases careful work and a high degree of dexterity. About 30% of the workers were engaged in furniture building and finishing. Another 15%–20% were machine shop operators, running production lathes, drill presses, and spray-painting equipment. The remainder of the work force were warehousemen, packers, quality control inspectors, office personnel, etc.

Work layouts were also varied. In Plant 1—the original site—the first automated belt was installed in May 1976. The rest of the work was staged in buffers (usually on carts), and there was no mechanized forced pacing. In Plant 2, a furniture factory, the majority of work was similarly staged and paced; the furniture went from department to department on either nonmechanized roller conveyors or carts. Plant 3, established in 1973, was the most automated. Here there were four belt-driven lines, but workers could alter the pace on these to some degree because several workers performed the same operation, and this enabled them to double up, take short breaks, etc.

The scope of work, defined by the range of responsibilities and the cycle time for jobs, was also extremely varied. In some places, particularly the machine shop and mechanized assembly lines, the scope was quite narrow (although operators set up their own machines in most instances). At the other extreme, there were several areas in the furniture factory where an individual or a group of workers was fully responsible for the entire construction and finishing of a large and complex piece of furniture. In terms of mechanization, forced pace, and task differentiation, there was much less of an assembly-line atmosphere than is found, for example, in an automobile assembly plant. However, during the period of this study, there was a continual movement toward more mechanized, fragmented, and forced-pace jobs.

The management organization at SI was conventionally hierarchical though less authoritarian in style than in most U.S. companies. Below the president was the staff, composed of the department heads of manufacturing, marketing, finance, engineering, and employee relations. The manufacturing units were organized in two shifts of about 150 workers each at the three plants. Each plant was run by a plant manager, to whom each shift superintendent reported; he himself reported to the vice-president for manufacturing. Three supervisors on each shift had "leads" reporting to them. Supervisors were salaried and constituted the first step on the management ladder. Leads were workers in charge of individual sections of six to fifteen workers; they were paid an hourly differential. Most face-to-face directives for workers came from leads. In general, the company had a tradition of relaxed and friendly supervision, although participation in group decision making was informal at best and varied widely from department to department.

Eighteen months after the participatory program began, the pattern of management was very close to a Likert pin model of group meetings encompassing all levels in the hierarchy.[2] Regular weekly meetings took place between the plant managers and the vice-president for manufacturing; plant managers conferred regularly with superintendents and supervisors; weekly meetings in each plant were attended by the manager, superintendents, supervisors, and—on a monthly basis—leads; supervisors and leads met every day and interacted continually. Initially the only regular meetings were between the vice-president and his staff. The Quality of Working Life Program (the name given to the participatory program) did not directly attempt to steer the management structure toward regular meetings at all levels except in the five experimental work projects. Instead, the movement toward the Likert model seemed to be inspired by the vice-president for manufacturing, who was continuously involved in the Quality of Working Life Program.

This pattern should be qualified in two ways. First, regular meetings among workers on the floor, except for the experimental work teams, were less frequent; however, this practice, too, was increasing by the time this study was concluded. Second, holding group meetings does not automatically ensure that in day-to-day situations supervisory style follows the humanistic/participatory approach. Although from the very beginning SI supervision at all levels was relatively liberal, styles varied greatly, and some leads, supervisors, and middle-level managers were very autocratic. This variation in the character of day-to-day supervision is inevitable, regardless of the formalized process of group decision making.

THE PARTICIPATORY PROGRAM

The original impetus for the program in industrial democracy came from the president of the parent company. He had been largely responsible for SI's rapid growth following its purchase by the parent company in 1969. His ownership or personal control of approximately 25% of the parent company's stock made him unquestionably the dominant force in the organization. However, he believed in decentralized management and left the subsidiary companies to be run to a large extent by local managers.

In the late 1960s the president became interested in work humanization and completed a doctoral thesis on the subject. He began a work humanization project in another (unionized) division in 1973. Outspoken in his idealism, he was fond of saying that these projects were possibly his way of saving his soul. However, he was not without ego, and he never shunned publicity; this publicity enhanced the image of a unique businessman, one the president felt was worth endorsing as a new breed of American executive. Because his headquarters were in New York and because he believed work improvement projects could not be imposed on an organization, his direct involvement in the project at SI was very limited after the initial discussions about it were concluded.

At SI itself, strong support and enthusiasm came from the president and the director of employee relations. In fact the latter had been hired with this program in mind. The president, who was politically liberal and both interested and experienced in the arts, initially freed the program from the constraints imposed on most similar experiments in the United States. At a meeting in October 1974, when I first met him, he summarized what he felt was the task at hand: "What we're really talking about is converting this organization from a monarchy to a democracy." Later in that same month, these two men, together with the vice-president for manufacturing, the head of manufacturing engineering, and another manager, formed what came to be known as the Steering Committee. After joining SI in December, I also became a member of this group. The purpose of the committee was to create a joint worker-manager system that could take over the subsequent design of the program. Officially labeled the Quality of Working Life Program, it came to be known throughout the company by its acronym, QWL (pronounced "quill").

From the beginning, the Steering Committee was guided by two ideas. First, the program was meant to be serious and continuing—a program that might include "experiments" but was primarily intended to produce permanent changes. Second, it was not to be a management-designed program, attempting to accomplish specified goals. Its only definite feature was to be maximum involvement by workers in decision making. The goal of the Steering Committee was to create a structure, ideally including employees from all levels, to guide the program. The first option, which was nearly adopted, was a type of plant-wide assembly made up of fifty to sixty individuals elected from each work area. Although we realized that a group of this size could not form policies effectively or work intelligently at devising solutions to individual problems, we hoped that a joint worker-management executive council would emerge from it. Theoretically, the general assembly would examine problems, discuss possible solutions, and vote on them; the executive council would develop detailed alternatives and recommendations.

The Steering Committee eventually concluded that three problems made the plant-wide assembly proposal unworkable. (1) The size of the group would make it very difficult to give everyone a chance to participate effectively. (2) The number of individual or section problems would be huge, and many of these could not be dealt with immediately. (3) Less important but still significant was the cost of holding such meetings, in terms of time lost from work and rental of faciliites in which the meetings could be held.[3]

The Planning Council

In March 1975 the choice was made to organize the direct election of a joint worker-management Planning Council composed of eight workers and five managers. The workers were to be elected in each facility and on each shift; management was to elect their representatives on an at-large basis.[4] Committees were formed on each shift at each facility to design election procedures for their areas. The procedures were identical in two major characteristics: nominations were open to anyone who wanted to run, and run-off elections were held when there were more than five candidates. In each case the runner-up became an alternate delegate to the council. After initial section meetings, first among supervisors and then among all employees, 15% of the nonsupervisory employees and 20% of management ran for election.

The Planning Council was the very center of the QWL program, and it provided the most significant degree of worker participation at the policy level. The council was not structured and was essentially given a blank check by top management. The original Steering Committee did not even stipulate the length of terms or the procedure for replacing members. Although one of the stated purposes of the council was to design additional forms of participation so that many more employees could become directly involved in decision making, no limits were placed on its authority to deal with problems on its own. Thus the precise formal role of the council was never specified. Its relationship with management was ambiguous. This troubled some members, who requested "more structure." However, as decisions began to be made, people gained confidence in the program and accepted informal boundaries. Since two of the president's staff were members of the council, many decisions required no outside approval. While in some instances decisions were submitted to the president or his staff for approval, they were never vetoed, and only infrequently was further consideration suggested.

The Planning Council discussed a wide variety of issues. The first series of meetings was devoted to the internal workings of the council. A tenure of one year was decided on, with all members eligible for reelection. The council agreed that it should strive for consensus whenever possible, but it adopted a majority rule voting procedure. For "important" issues eight votes (of the thirteen) were required for passage.[5] Three-hour meetings were held at first every week and later every other week. The chair was rotated among volunteers. A portion of each meeting was devoted to problems brought to the attention of individual representatives, usually minor issues affecting specific facilities. The remainder of the meeting was devoted to a standing working agenda of major items.[6]

Table 1, which depicts the percentage of time the council spent on various topics, displays the breadth of the discussions. The list ranges from physical problems (such as noise, music on the public address system, and plant security) to traditional union issues (such as grievances, wages, and benefits).

TABLE 1
Major Planning Council Issues

	Times Discussed	Percentage of Total Meeting Time Spent on the Issue
Communications from employees	25	17.6
Planning new facility	8	12.0
Structure of the QWL program	22	11.0
Training program	12	9.1
Experimental work projects	14	8.5
Wages and salaries	11	8.1
Communications	7	6.3
Orientation program	7	4.6
Working conditions	15	3.5
Grievance procedure	3	3.5
Working hours	5	3.2
Company newspaper	4	2.4
Job postings	1	1.6
Job classifications	2	1.5
Company financial conditions	2	1.0
Worker attitudes	2	1.0
Miscellaneous topics	23	6.3

SOURCE: Statistics were obtained from analyzing tape recordings of meetings from 5 May 1975 to 28 September 1976. Percentages are based on seventy hours of meetings.

NOTE: Each meeting began with suggestions, problems, or ideas that had been brought to council members by employees. These topics included many of those listed in the text. It was not feasible to classify each of these as a separate issue.

However, significant amounts of time were also spent on major policy areas, such as planning worker involvement in the design of a new facility, projects to restructure work along participatory lines, and the creation of numerous training programs at all levels in the company.

During the initial phases of the QWL program, for instance, SI was involved in an intensive search for a plant site which would serve to consolidate all its operations. When an appropriate site was found, the Planning Council began considering ways employees could participate both in planning the move itself and in designing work areas in the new facilities. In office areas and relatively self-contained factory departments, working from blueprints that had only section boundaries drawn in, work sections laid out their own areas completely. These prints were then reviewed by adjacent sections, maintenance people, and, if necessary, industrial engineers. In sections with a continuous flow of production from one work group to another, leads, plant management, and engineers first created a block layout depicting the product flow. This was followed by meetings to discuss the general layout and, finally, by section meetings in which the designs of individual work areas were discussed. The Planning Council created this system of participation and issued a series of policy statements formalizing the procedures.

In the area of training, the council's role in affecting policy was somewhat different. When the QWL program started, the company had no formal training programs. Early expressions of such a need led to the decision to hire a qualified training specialist who would report to both the director of employee relations and the council. When employee relations found a suitable candidate, he was interviewed by the council. From that point on, the council approved the basic plans of the training program and responded to reports from the training specialist. Most important, due to the way trainees were selected and the fact that the specialist was in part responsible to the council, the training program as it developed was, at least in theory, very democratic. Job training curricula and procedures were created by the leads in various sections; a group decision-making approach for all levels was stressed (groups usually including three levels in the hierarchy); and sessions with supervisors and managers concentrated on providing the groups with desired information or instruction. In other words, even though the council delegated major responsibility for the development and implementation of training functions, its role in selecting the administrator and overseeing the program ensured the continuous participation of those most affected by training decisions.

Special-Purpose Committees

The Planning Council was given responsibility for extending employee participation throughout the company. The first structures developed were special-purpose committees, usually called task forces. These were always joint worker-management committees but less formally organized than the Planning Council. (Traditional company committees such as the activity committee, the safety committee, and the credit union board are not included in this category.)

Membership on these committees was rarely elective; usually the council made appointments on an ad hoc basis. The criteria for membership varied, depending on the committee. Training committees were made up mostly of leads because of their expertise and the fact that they were doing most of the on-the-job training at the time. The standing committee on communications was organized on a geographical basis, so that all facilities would be represented. Some members of the committee on worker education were selected because of their special skills (e.g., as copy and technical writers), others simply because they were enthusiastic volunteers. The ratio of workers to managers varied widely as well. For example, the newspaper editorial board had one manager and ten workers, while the task forces in charge of experimental work projects had a majority of supervisory personnel.

Although most of these groups were permanent standing committees, some, like the groups that designed the Planning Council election procedures in each facility (see p. 15 above), were established on a temporary basis to complete a single task. All committees were responsible to the Planning Council.

Experimental Work Projects

In the initial meeting of the Planning Council, it was agreed that experiments in new forms of work organization should be a central aspect of the QWL program. These experiments became known simply as "work projects." After several months' deliberation, the council set up work project task forces in each facility to suggest appropriate areas for experiments.[7] On the basis of their reports, the council chose five projects in a variety of organizational designs. The number of employees ranged from ten to fifteen in each project.

The most radical and democratic were two fully autonomous work teams established without any designated leadership. The group was given responsibility for decisions on scheduling, job assignments, rotation, training, materials, etc. Two other teams were set up on a semi-autonomous basis. The existing leads in the areas were responsible only for day-to-day problems; the group set operating guidelines and discussed general problems in regular weekly meetings. The last project, in an office department, was intended to decentralize day-to-day decision making while formulating department policy in regular group meetings.

It is impossible to claim that any of these projects was a total success. In 1976, one year after they began, only the office project was still going. The two fully autonomous work teams had by far the hardest time, primarily because they had been set up to build new products—products that turned out to be extremely difficult to manufacture. Interpersonal conflicts, problems with coordination, and ambiguously defined roles for supervisors and support personnel also contributed to the groups' problems. One group finally elected to have a lead and then selected one of its members for that position. The other group was suspended by management after several months so that the product and manufacturing process could be redesigned. The two semi-autonomous groups had fewer problems but also much less room for meaningful participation by workers. One of these groups was run fairly autocratically by the lead, and the group meetings were not able to break out of this pattern. The other group, clearly the most successful of the manufacturing groups, began as a very democratic operation. Attempts to make this latter line fully autonomous were aggressively resisted by the group, who desired to keep their lead.[8] The office project continued with some success. Its major difficulty was a supervisor who was very reluctant to delegate responsibilities. While the group meetings had some clear effects on department policies, the day-to-day pressure and frustration of working under extremely close supervision limited the success of the project and produced a high degree of turnover in the department.

Surprisingly, the change-over-time statistics on these projects demonstrate improvement in a number of areas. Although this is somewhat perplexing, given the difficulties that were apparent to everyone, the statistics do suggest the potential benefits of direct participation at the operational level. Possibly more important, however, is what we learned about the limitations and constraints involved in the design of autonomous work teams. While these limitations were due in part to errors in the design and implementation of the specific projects, I am convinced that some of the critical factors restricting shop floor democracy are symptomatic of basic problems inherent both in the technical design of modern work processes and in requirements for and subsequent effects of centralized authority and responsibility.

Several concluding notes on participation are necessary. First, it is important to be specific about the type and level of issues considered in the various participatory structures. To simplify matters, we can think of decisions as falling into two categories: policy and procedure. *Policy decisions* are defined as relatively permanent, requiring a large commitment of resources and a long-range planning process. Quite often policy decisions affect a considerable number of people in the organization. *Procedural decisions* involve a small expenditure, can be implemented and changed very quickly, and affect only a restricted number of people. In these terms, the work projects were almost completely procedural; the special-purpose committees involved both procedural and policy questions; and the Planning Council dealt primarily with policy decisions.

The level of policy is revealed by table 1. Clearly a number of very important decisions were made without worker involvement. Pricing policies, new product development, retained earnings, selection of the new facility site, hiring of managers—none of these was, to my knowledge, ever mentioned in formal meetings. However, these are also some of the areas where workers desire to exert the least influence. Comparisons with other projects are difficult, since accurate and precise descriptions of issues, voting procedures, and the amount of actual worker influence are rarely provided. Nevertheless, there is no question that participation at SI was a significant departure from the normal process of decision making in American corporations.

RESEARCH METHODS
Participant Observation

At SI, where I spent eighteen months working full time on the QWL program, my role was unique. It was variously defined as "facilitator," "educator," "catalyst," "irritant," and "coordinator." In order to maintain neutrality, I received no remuneration from the company and had no official title. My regular activities included participation in almost all meetings of the Planning Council, work projects, and special committees. I was very active in these meetings, stimulating discussion, introducing neglected points of view, and at times vigorously arguing a position. I also coordinated activities, followed through on decisions, and documented proceedings. As time went on, my role expanded to encompass informal handling of grievances and working with numerous individuals on personal problems, mostly related to work but frequently stemming from other areas, such as finances, family difficulties, or encounters with the police.

This method of research has some clear advantages. First, as the decision-making process evolves, it is possible to gain a great deal of information about people's beliefs and rationalizations, as well as about cause-and-effect relationships. When the trust of workers and managers has been secured (and after a time the former were less suspicious of me than the latter), informal discussions at work and elsewhere give the researcher a much more precise understanding of people's attitudes than it is possible to gain through conventional interviews alone.[9] Similarly, participating in events as they occur, the researcher does not have to rely on reconstruction of events to determine what led to a particular outcome.

A second, somewhat more controversial advantage is that quality of information is improved when the researcher is very familiar with a situation and the individuals involved in it. Documents have more meaning in their complete context. Precise knowledge of a situation also aids in interpreting responses and probing for hidden meanings in an interview. And finally, interview responses are more honest if participants know and trust the researcher.

At the same time, the most dangerous threat to the reliability of data collected through participant observation is that people being studied may trust the researcher too much. I was visibly identified with the QWL program from the beginning, and this may have biased some responses in favor of what people thought was my position on an issue. For example, even though I personally conducted only twenty-one interviews on the second wave, employees knew that other interviewers were working for me, and this may have influenced their evaluation of the program or their comments about the possibilities of increased participation in the future. Unfortunately, as with almost all experimenter effects, it is impossible to gauge such bias or weigh it against the gains to be expected from the advantages listed above.

Another common objection to the participant/observer concept is that his own observations will be biased by his active role in the process. This problem is less severe if the researcher uses objective methods and analysis to supplement personal observations. The difficulty is that in many studies of organizational change, especially those reported in popular, semi-scholarly journals, objective measures either are not used or are used only to demonstrate success. Quite often, whether the researcher is actively involved in the program or not, he or she has a stake in the success of the project (e.g., insuring a future connection with the company or garnering consulting fees or academic plaudits). This widespread problem, which at times is nothing less than intellectual fraud, is one of the reasons why, in this study, I utilized quantitative measures and a rigorous level of statistical analysis whenever appropriate.

Research Methods

These sources of data were used in the analysis that follows:

1. *Interviews.* Interviews with a random sample (17%) of the workers and 60% of the managers were conducted before the program began and sixteen months later. Seven in-depth interviews with worker members of the first Planning Council were conducted either after their terms ended or, in four cases, prior to their leaving the company. Insufficient time precluded more interviews of this type.
2. *Company Statistics.* Statistics on productivity, turnover, and, where possible, absenteeism were collected throughout the company.
3. *Tape Analysis of Planning Council Meetings.* Utilizing tape recordings, I analyzed Planning Council meetings in detail, attempting to quantify a number of variables that would indicate the competence and possible co-optation of workers (Who spoke most often? Who responded to questions? Who made proposals? Whose proposals were accepted? Who made decisive speeches?) In addition, key portions of more than thirty meetings were transcribed for use in a qualitative fashion.
4. *Documents.* A full-time administrative assistant recorded meeting minutes, internal memos, voting statistics, a chronological history, a

full description of major blunders, and a cross-referenced copy of all minutes, summaries, or transcripts pertaining to major issues.

5. *Observations Log.* I kept a personal diary of more than 500 pages, covering every day I was at SI.

Of these sources, the most important are the two waves of interviews and the analysis of Planning Council tapes. The interviews formed the basis for chapters 3, 4, and 9 of this book; the tapes provided essential evidence on the successes and failures of joint decision making described in chapters 5 and 6.

Interviews are the primary source of information for understanding the jobs people do, their initial attitudes toward participation, and the authority structure of a company. Changes in interview responses over time form a basis for estimating the effects of various modes of participation on alienation and on belief in the legitimacy of worker participation. Although it would have been very useful to have a control population in another company, expense and access problems precluded that possibility. Fortunately, for some measures there are comparable baseline data collected in another company in another part of the United States. These allow some anchoring of initial attitudes, although they do not serve as a comparison for change.

The interview sample was drawn in January 1975 and consisted of 117 workers. Fourteen more individuals I approached could not be interviewed because of language problems, and one refused to participate. Additionally, workers who became active in various aspects of the program but were not included in the initial random sample were interviewed periodically until September 1976.[10] Regrettably, layoffs totaling 27% of the work force took place in November 1974 and in the first week of January 1975. Since these were done primarily on the basis of seniority, the work force at the time of the sample was undoubtedly biased somewhat by workers with higher seniority. However, the average number of months workers were employed at SI is still only sixteen. Sample characteristics are reported in appendix A.

The supervisor and manager sample was not random. I attempted to interview as many of the fifty-eight management personnel as possible and succeeded in interviewing twenty first-line supervisors and fifteen managers. Many other supervisors could not conveniently take off the one and one-half hours required for the interview. The logical assumption is that bias in the management sample would be against participation. In recognition of this, special efforts were made to interview some managers known to hold negative views.

The interview was extensively tested for face validity using group discussions with workers first and then individual discussions following test interviews. This extended process was inspired by the participatory nature of the program, and it proved invaluable in constructing the final interview. A number of the more ingenious questions are the result of worker suggestions.[11] In addition to the face-to-face portion, the interview included a fifty-item questionnaire.[12] The length of the interview was due to the large number of open-ended questions. For example, for ten questions (or sets of questions) people were asked to explain why they responded as they did. Here the interviewer was required to record verbatim responses.

Most of the first wave of interviews were completed in February and March 1975. The final sample of workers, including activists, totaled 145. The interviews were conducted the first time by myself and two assistants not employed by the company. The company was reimbursed for the time workers were interviewed. By the second interview, in May and June 1976, attrition had cut the original worker sample to 120, and two workers had been promoted to supervisors. Change-over-time figures are based on 118 interviews for workers and 35 for supervisors and managers. The second wave of interviews was conducted primarily by three assistants, one of whom also conducted interviews the first time.

3. Belief in Worker Participation

Whether or not workers actually want increased participation in decisions is fundamental to the question of industrial democracy. The level and distribution of support is important both in designing democratic mechanisms and in considering the question of free choice facing workers. The amount of influence people would like to exert in various types of decision may well point up the best alternative among systems of codetermination on corporate boards, joint worker-management councils, or autonomous work groups at the shop floor level. Additionally, if workers demonstrate a low level of belief in participation, the problem of forcing democratic procedures on an unwilling populace must be considered.

HOW MUCH PARTICIPATION IN WHAT DECISIONS?
Previous Studies

Very little is known about how much influence workers feel they should have in different types of corporate decision. Several studies are currently in progress, but the few conclusions available in published studies are based on such general questions as "Do you feel that you personally participate sufficiently in decisions made at your place of work, or do you wish to participate more in them?" or "Should workers participate in making important decisions related to their work (or to general plant problems)?"[1] Even less specific, although still of some use, are inferences that can be drawn from studies of union and political participation, which can provide a useful context for interpreting questions of participation in the work place.

Modern studies of political participation, citizens' interest in and knowledge of politics, and structures of political beliefs support the conclusion that the distance between citizens and leaders—in the United States, at least—is both physically and psychologically extreme. In the 1976 national elections, only half of all eligible voters went to the polls. In a recent study of political participation, Sidney Verba and Norman Nie reported that 53% of the respondents in a national sample had never done any of the six things considered standard measures of political participation (contacting officials, working in or contributing to campaigns, etc.) and that 24% had done only one. Only 31% of the respondents claimed to be "interested" in politics and national affairs; 42% could not name either of their U.S. senators, and 60% did not know the names of their congressmen.[2] The established academic position is that the general population knows little about current affairs, expresses almost random attitudes over time, and rarely organizes its political beliefs along any logical continuum.[3] Furthermore, a number of studies going back three decades conclude that political activists, especially those in leadership roles, know more, are ideologically more sophisticated, and tend to support democratic principles more fully than the average apolitical citizen.[4] In sum, while there is some evidence that the distance between citizen and leader may be closing,[5] it would be difficult to argue conclusively against the assumptions of mass apathy and political incompetence posed by Robert Michels more than sixty years ago.[6]

Studies of participation in unions suggest that, for many, political apathy extends to the work place. With the exception of special purpose meetings and one or two atypical unions,[7] active participation by the majority of union members is very low. For most, voting is their only union activity.[8] Furthermore, there is long-standing evidence that union leaders differ significantly from the rank and file in many of the same ways that political leaders differ from ordinary citizens. Union activists are more knowledgeable about union affairs, generally have higher aspirations, are more highly skilled and socially oriented, belong to more external organizations, and are generally more active in community functions.[9] As to the question of union involvement in decisions that affect plant operations, Arnold Tannenbaum and Robert Kahn provide the only quantitative evidence. A section in their questionnaire asked members of four locals to rank the goals they felt their union should pursue. "Increased say in running the plant" ranked fourteenth out of fifteen goals, with only 22% checking it as "something the local should do."[10] Thus, from what we know of union activism, there is little reason to suspect that most workers would either endorse the idea of participation or become actively involved if the opportunity arose.

Studies dealing more specifically with the desire for participation in decision making soften this bleak picture in some ways. Harriet Holter, reporting on a study done in Norway in the 1960s, found that the majority of workers in both blue- and white-collar companies wanted increased participation in decisions that concerned their own work and working conditions (56%–67%), but only a small minority (6%–16%) wanted more participation in decisions concerning the management of the entire company. She also discovered that the employees who desired participation for themselves were in more highly skilled jobs, were more interested in advancement in the company, identified strongly with company goals, and were significantly more efficiency minded than those who were not interested in participation.[11] Thus, while Holter found support for certain forms of increased participation, she also confirmed the inferences of political and union studies that activists may not be typical workers.

The conclusion that workers desire more influence in decisions than is allowed by their current jobs has been supported by a number of studies originating at the University of Michigan. Nancy Morse reported that 70% of the insurance company employees she interviewed said they would like to make more decisions than were possible in their present jobs.[12] Daniel Katz found that, of 5,700 workers in a heavy-industry plant, slightly more than half wanted to have more say about the way their work was done.[13] Of all research, however, the series of studies conducted by Arnold Tannenbaum over the past twenty years are the most convincing. Using general questions to measure perceived control, influence, or participation, Tannenbaum has demonstrated that desired control is consistently higher than actual control at most levels in the organization. Furthermore, the discrepancy between actual and ideal control increases as one moves from the top downward in organizations. This is not to imply that workers believe they should have as much control as managers (i.e., a flat "control" curve); only that, relative to the current distribution, their influence should be increased.[14]

Based on these studies, the following hypotheses can be posed:

1. Workers will not support a "radical" increase in participation, although the level of desired participation will exceed their present influence.
2. Workers will desire more participation in decisions directly related to their jobs and immediate working environments, and less participation in higher-level management decisions.
3. Workers who seek to become actively involved in decision making will be relatively more skilled, more ambitious, more company oriented, and more socially and politically inclined than others.

The first two hypotheses will be discussed in this chapter, and the third in the following chapter.

How Much Say?

The initial interviews at SI were conducted just prior to the first elections to the Planning Council. They included a section on how much influence people wanted in different types and levels of decisions. Several methods were used to measure how much influence workers felt they should have.[15] Managers and supervisors were also asked what they believed to be the appropriate level of worker participation.

The most comprehensive measure, which allows a comparison between beliefs in worker participation and actual influence as well as a precise ordering of specific types of decisions, was based on the following question: "How much say do you think you or your work group *should* have in the following decisions?" The interviewer then went through the decisions listed in table 2, recording responses in the categories listed in columns 1–4. After several intervening questions, respondents were asked, with regard to an abbreviated list of decisions, how much say they

TABLE 2
Belief in Participation by Nonsupervisory Employees

Q. "How much say do you think you *should* have in the following decisions?"

Decision	(1) No Say (%)	(2) A Little Say (%)	(3) Some Say (%)	(4) A Lot of Say (%)	(5) Mean	(6) r
Work procedures	10	8	34	49	3.21	.54
Work rate	11	15	34	39	3.01	.55
Planning new facility	15	13	32	41	2.99	.35
Setting and ensuring quality standards	19	10	36	35	2.87	.42
Grievances	15	16	36	33	2.86	.54
Wages	16	12	42	28	2.79	.53
Selecting leadperson	27	12	29	32	2.66	.39
Working hours	25	9	42	24	2.64	.36
Setting production levels	25	18	37	20	2.52	.48
Job assignments	40	13	29	19	2.27	.53
Selecting supervisor	41	15	24	20	2.23	.52
Deciding who is hired into work group	46	14	21	19	2.14	.51
Reinvestment of profits	50	17	22	11	1.94	.47
Deciding who is promoted in work group	51	13	28	9	1.94	.53
Deciding who is fired from work group	61	13	19	7	1.72	.55
Selecting management	65	14	16	5	1.62	.50
Management salaries	78	5	11	6	1.05	.59

NOTE: N = 145.   SCALING INFORMATION: Mean = 39.8; S.D. = 9.7; Cronbach A = .87; r = Pearson correlation of item with scale minus item

actually had at present. Table 2 contains the list of issues and the responses for the amount of say desired by workers; Table 3 reports the statistics on actual participation. The list of actual participation items was reduced because pretesting had made it clear that there was negligible worker participation in the excluded decisions. Their inclusion added unnecessarily to the length of the interview and increased the possibility of acquiescent response set.[16] Figure 1 is a graphic presentation of the averages for each decision for both workers and managers.

The most obvious finding is the variance in the belief in participation. Different decisions elicited consistently different responses from workers and managers. For workers, the difference between the means of the highest item (work procedures) and the lowest (management salaries) is 1.76, or 44% of the theoretical range. In the combined categories of "some say" or "a lot of say" (table 2, cols. 3 and 4), 83% of the respondents gave one of these answers in relation to work procedures, while only 17% gave either response for management salaries.

The grand mean (2.41) is very near the scale midpoint, interpreted as midway between "a little say" and "some say." While this is hardly evidence of revolutionary fervor, it is far from total apathy. "Moderate

TABLE 3
Perceived Actual Participation by Nonsupervisory Employees

Q. "How much say do you *actually* have in the following decisions?"

	(1)	(2)	(3)	(4)	(5)	(6)	(7)
Decision	No Say (%)	A Little Say (%)	Some Say (%)	A Lot of Say (%)	Mean	Mean Desire– Mean Actual	r
Work procedures	30	26	29	15	2.30	+.91	.49
Work rate	45	17	25	13	2.07	+.94	.47
Setting and ensuring quality standards	44	16	21	18	2.13	+.74	.53
Grievances	57	23	15	5	1.67	+1.19	.37
Selecting leadperson	94	3	4	0	1.10	+1.56	...*
Setting production levels	62	19	10	10	1.67	+.85	.58
Job assignments	60	18	15	7	1.69	+.58	.55
Selecting supervisor	97	1	1	1	1.08	+1.15	...*
Deciding who is hired into work group	78	9	11	1	1.35	+.79	.47
Deciding who is promoted in work group	88	8	4	2	1.18	+.76	.33
Deciding who is fired from work group	89	6	5	2	1.17	+.55	.37

NOTE: $N = 145$. Starred items were excluded from the final scale because of low item correlations (caused by lack of variance). SCALING INFORMATION: Mean = 15.3; S.D. = 4.9; Cronbach A = .77; r = Pearson correlation of item with scale minus item.

participation" is the best overall description. Although on none of the decisions did a majority believe workers should have "a lot of say," on nine out of seventeen items more than half believed they should have either "some say" or "a lot of say." These findings support the first half of hypothesis 1, to which I will return below.

The second hypothesis has to do with the types of decision in which workers desire the most influence. As shown in figure 1, the proposition that workers want more participation in those decisions that affect their own work areas is supported, but only for those decisions that tend to affect workers on an individual basis. There was little interest in participating in traditional management decisions like profit reinvestment or setting the salaries of supervisors and managers. For those decisions that directly affect workers at the operational level, there is a clear distinction between decisions that can be interpreted as affecting only the individual (work procedures and rates, grievances, wages, etc.) and those that directly affect other workers as well (hiring and firing, job assignments, promotions). This point amends the hypothesis in an important way, because it suggests the possibility that in an autonomous work group workers will shy away from making the more difficult personnel decisions that

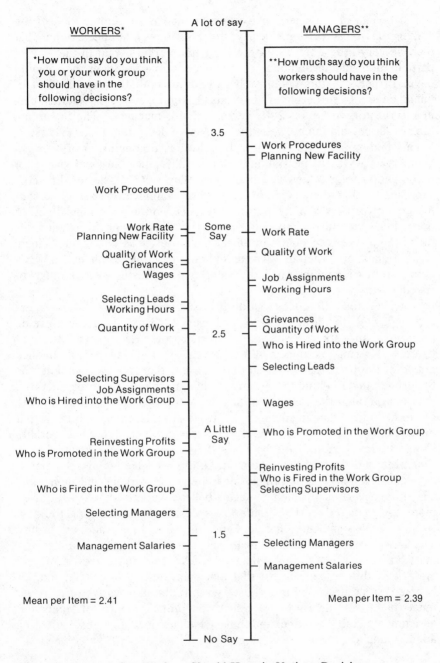

Figure 1. Average Say Workers Should Have in Various Decisions

might invoke interpersonal conflict. It seems that many workers would rather leave such decisions to leads and supervisors.

The beliefs of managers in workers' rights to participate in decision making may be surprising. Clearly, the most important conclusion is that there is very little difference between what workers want in the way of participation and the amount of influence managers think they should have. In general, this conclusion extends to both the overall level of influence and the ordering of decisions. Taken together, the average per-item score for workers is 2.41, versus 2.39 for managers. The Spearman rank order correlation between the respective decision rankings is .88.

This finding supports the more broadly based conclusion of Tannenbaum et al. for their five nations. Plotting differences in ideal visions of participation for workers and managers, they state, "The results show suprisingly flat gradients on most items. For example, lower-level personnel do not profess a more participative decision-making ideal than do upper-level personnel in any of the countries."[17] Although this result holds for different types of plants in all the countries, it is based on a single general question, whether "workers should have more influence." Evidence from SI demonstrates the same general result over a range of specific decisions.

However, the differences that do exist between workers and managers are intriguing. In the first place, managers tend to take more extreme positions than workers, especially on items at the very top and bottom of figure 1. This may be due in part to the fact that managers had advance notice of the participatory program and knew that top management was the prime mover behind the program. Thus, trying to appear democratic, they exaggerated the safe items they knew top management had already discussed (like "planning the new facility"). Another interpretation is that managers are more certain about the distinction between what workers should be involved in and what they should not. The few differences in rank orderings support this argument. Of the seventeen items, the means on eight decisions are extremely close between workers and managers. The three decisions in which managers believe workers should be allowed more say than the workers themselves desire are in planning the new facility, job assignments, and deciding who should join the work group. The areas where managers advocate less say than do workers are selecting leads, supervisors, and managers; grievances; and wages.[18] In general, these differences suggest that managers draw a somewhat sharper line separating decisions into those typically the prerogative of management (plant-wide decisions on wages and profits, control of leadership assignments, and discipline) and those which are local in nature, affecting an individual or, at most, a work group.

Ideal and Actual Participation

Table 3 presents the perceptions of how much say workers feel they actually had at the time of the interview. As is readily apparent from the differences in means of actual and ideal participation in column 6, the hypothesis that workers want more say than they presently have is clearly confirmed. The largest differences are registered for selecting leads and supervisors and for grievance procedures. However, if the six excluded items had been asked, assuming means near 1.0 ("no say"), planning the new facility and wages would top the list. As we will see in the next section, the discrepancy between desired and actual influence is even more dramatic in another company for which there are comparative data.

A second important feature of table 3 is the correlation between items in terms of actual and desired influence. The order of the items selected for the table is taken from table 2, which was arranged from highest to lowest actual participation. With two exceptions, the means in column 5 follow this order exactly. In other words, across the population, people desire greater participation in those areas where their present influence is already highest. We will see that the total amount of actual participation an individual has on the job is a primary factor in predicting how much influence the person believes he should have.

Concerning managers, the findings support those of several other studies: managers' perceptions of how much say workers actually have are consistently inflated. For each of the eleven items in table 3, workers believe they have less influence than supervisors and managers attribute to them. In seven cases, all either directly affecting the individual or the work group, the differences are significant at the .05 level. This result is not atypical. Several studies have found that superiors view subordinates as having significantly more influence than the latter feel they have.[19] The reason for this discrepancy is partly that superiors rarely "control" decisions (i.e., in the unilateral manner in which the term is used here). They perceive themselves as continually checking, discussing, and persuading, as well as being persuaded by others. While they may technically have the final say, they see workers as having some influence in many decisions, especially those directly affecting the workers themselves. Workers obviously fail to perceive their superiors as being constrained in this way.

Comparison with Another American Plant

A case study has inherent limits of generalization. Therefore comparable data from other studies are of considerable value. A quality of working life project at an automotive parts plant in Bolivar, Tennessee, is a useful source of comparison. This plant differs considerably from SI. The physical work at Bolivar is much more difficult because of the nature of the production (casting, assembling, and finishing automobile mirrors), extremely poor working conditions, and a comparatively high percentage of monotonous, narrowly defined jobs. The composition of the workforce is also very different in the two plants. Bolivar is a community of 7,000 people, located ninety miles east of Memphis in a relatively depressed farming area. Here 53% of the workers are black, compared with 45% Spanish at SI. Many of the workers at Bolivar are working at their first factory job; 24% run farms on the side, and 89% were raised on farms in and around Bolivar. Finally, the Bolivar plant was unionized in 1969 by the United Automobile Workers. The quality of working life project is thus one of a small number of participatory projects attempted in a unionized plant. The statistics reported in table 4 are from a plant-wide survey in August 1973, conducted as baseline data for their QWL program. Of the 983 employees, 300 volunteered to be interviewed.[20]

TABLE 4

Comparison of SI and Bolivar Automotive on Actual and Desired Participation (%)

Decision	Desired		Actual	
	SI	Bolivar	SI	Bolivar
Work procedures	83	64	44	27
Work rate	73	78	38	21
Setting and ensuring quality standards	71	72	39	30
Wages	70	76	...	...
Working hours	66	50	...	11
Setting production levels	57	62	20	8
Job assignments	48	69	22	...
Selecting supervisors	44	61	2	3
Deciding who is hired into the work group	40	40	12	5
Deciding who is promoted in the work group	37	66	6	...
Deciding who is fired from the work group	26	51	7	7
Management salaries	17	26	...	0
Average	52.7	59.6	21.1	12.4

NOTE: Entries are percentages responding either "Some say" or "A lot of say." These are the only figures available in the report on the Bolivar project. Blank entries indicate that the item was not discussed in the respective interview.

The comparative figures in table 4 are remarkably similar to those from SI, given the sharp contrast between the companies in terms of production, characteristics of the work force, and the general difference in lifestyles. Overall, Bolivar workers desire slightly more participation than workers at SI and have, on the average, less say in decisions as things stand. It should be noted, however, that on most decisions the two plants are extremely close. In some respects, given the essentially conservative tendencies in the Bolivar culture, the figures are surprising. It is quite possible that the self-selection method of interviewing at Bolivar produced a sample somewhat biased in the participatory direction.[21] It is also possible that the union could also be a stimulating factor, although there is little evidence from other studies to suggest this. At any rate, these rough estimates suggest that our findings at SI are reasonable.

Other Measures of Belief in Participation

Two other measures of attitudes toward participation were included in the SI interviews. The first is a single question: "SI has a board of directors of six members; do you think nonmanagement employees should be represented by a voting member of that board?" The answers were overwhelmingly positive. Of the sample of 145 workers, 107 (74%) replied in the affirmative, 21 (14%) said no, and 17 (12%) did not know. Of those responding in the affirmative, 32% believed workers should have one of the six board seats, 46% two, and 23% three. The percentage advocating worker membership on the board dropped off significantly for managers to 44% yes and 56% no. While there is some supporting evidence for the fact that Americans may be amenable to workers sitting as members of company boards,[22] the fact that almost three-fourths of the workers at SI supported the idea was somewhat surprising. The idea was not without its detractors, however. One employee explained his negative response with a textbook rationale for ownership control: "We don't have any money invested in this company. We have time invested. They have money to lose, and we don't have anything to lose." Still, it would appear that few workers agree with this basic capitalist reasoning.

It is important to note that, unlike the earlier questions on desired "say," this question contains no implication that the individual would be personally involved. This suggests the possibility that many more people would support the legitimacy of participation if the chances were slight that they themselves would be called upon to participate. It is conceivable that living in a republic, where direct participation for most citizens is limited to voting, produces a generalized response highly favorable to representative forms of democracy and at the same time creates minimal support for direct personal involvement.

The reluctance of workers to become personally involved is even more apparent when participation is perceived as a value that may be costly to the worker in terms of time, money, or security. In order to measure these trade-off effects, the following series of questions was asked:

1. Now we've been talking a lot about participation in deciding a lot of things. Let's imagine for a minute that there is another company somewhere nearby that would allow you to make more of these decisions than here at SI. If the pay, benefits, supervision, conditions, etc., were all the same as at SI, the only difference being a chance for you to participate more, do you think you would take a job there rather than at SI? Does participation mean enough to you to make the change?

2. [If the answer to (1) was yes,] As you can imagine, making decisions like those we've been talking about takes time. If this other company asked you to spend some extra time without pay, say two hours a

week, in order to get these decisions made, would you still do it?
3. What if the pay were less . . . say 10% less? [Use actual dollar figure.]
   Would you still take the job?[23]

The results are nearly as surprising as those registered for representation on the board of directors, although they move in the opposite direction. As shown in table 5, workers are very reluctant to trade a secure position, working hours, or wages for increased participation. Out of the total sample of 145, only 69 workers (48%) were willing to trade jobs just for increased participation. Of these 69, 46 would still take the job if they had to work extra hours, but only 24 (or 17% of the total sample) would take the participatory job if it meant a cut in pay. When the costs of democracy are introduced, enthusiasm for its benefits seems to drop sharply.[24]

TABLE 5
Trade-offs between Participation and Security, Pay, and Personal Time

Question	N			% of Total Sample		
	Yes	No	Don't Know	Yes	No	Don't Know
Willingness to change to a job offering more participation	69	67	9	48	46	6
Willingness to work more hours	46	23	. . .	32	16	. . .
Willingness to work for less pay	24	45	. . .	17	31	. . .

NOTE: Last two questions were asked only
of those responding yes to the first question.

The various measures of participation provide a complex picture. Workers clearly desire more participation than their present jobs offer but believe in a great deal of influence only in decisions directly affecting their jobs. Even in these instances, there is very little evidence that they would accept sacrifices in security, wages, or hours as a price for increased participation. Why? What leads workers to believe in increased participation on the one hand and hierarchical authority on the other?

ATTRIBUTION OF BELIEFS IN PARTICIPATION AND AUTHORITY

Social scientists have brought an array of methodological techniques to bear on the problem of explaining attitudes; however, they rarely use the simplest technique of all—asking respondents to explain their answers. This attribution process was a major concern in the present study. Since the procedure used for analyzing these attributions is somewhat unconventional, the interview questions and coding format must be explained.

A unique feature of the interviews was the balance between closed and open-ended questions. The latter were quite often associated with a set of fixed-choice questions. A number of these asked the respondent why previous responses had been given. To the extent possible, the interviewer recorded verbatim replies. These responses were then tabulated, eliminating only the most obvious redundancies. We then reviewed and grouped this list in terms of theoretical relevance. The responses were coded so that the first digit referred to the larger category and the second to the exact response. In this way some of the quantitative features of fixed-choice questions were retained, while, at the same time, it was possible to maintain some of the sensitivity, subtlety of interpretation, and understanding that are the primary advantages of in-depth interviews. The first example of this procedure is seen in the questions directed at individual reasons for advocating participation in some areas and not in others. Table 6 displays the results.

Why People Believe in Worker Participation

The most common rationalization is expressed precisely in this uncomplicated response by a young woman assembler: "I'm directly affected by a number of those things [work rates, work procedures, quality standards, etc.], and I know what needs to be done in those areas." Decisions directly affect workers; they have the expertise to make the decisions, and therefore they should be allowed to participate. This reasoning accounts for 60% of the responses given by workers and 64% by managers.

The tone of the responses is not always as neutral as that of the woman quoted above, however. Consider this from a very alienated furniture finisher: "We're not machines. We know what affects us, how to do the job...how fast we can work." Or this response from a tool-and-die maker who later became a Planning Council member: "This place is a multimillion dollar business that's run like a garage. Workers know easier and better ways to set things up—within limits, where they know what's what...especially their own areas."

The next most common explanation was based on a concept of the corporation as a community of interests, as a social organism in which all employees are mutually involved. This is particularly true among Spanish-speaking women, who are often secondary wage earners in their families and usually have little desire for participation. The most common analogies are to the home and family:

We should participate because the company is for all the workers. It's like a home away from home.

TABLE 6
Rationale for Participation or Nonparticipation

	Workers (%)	Managers (%)
In general, why do you feel workers should be allowed to participate?		
It directly affects us (them)	35.4	30.9
Workers have the knowledge/information	18.8	27.3
Mutuality—workers part of the company, etc.	11.6	12.7
Increased productivity	8.3	7.3
It is right/just	7.2	9.1
Workers have the competence	6.6	5.5
I like to make decisions/have authority	5.5	0.0
Personal growth/development	2.8	7.3
Miscellaneous	3.9	0.0
N responses	(181)	(55)
In some areas you don't think workers should have much say. In general, in those areas why don't you feel workers should be allowed to participate?		
Acceptance of authority structure	38.1	33.3
That's management's job	(18.8)	(12.8)
Management knows best, has knowledge	(15.6)	(5.1)
General	(3.7)	(15.4)
Workers lack knowledge/information	31.2	35.9
It would create conflict	14.8	10.3
It does not affect us (them)	10.6	.0
Workers lack competence	3.2	15.4
Limits to decision making (time, etc.)	1.6	2.6
Need for authority/supervision	.0	2.6
Miscellaneous	.5	.0
N responses	(189)	(39)

NOTE: These questions immediately followed the seventeen separate decisions listed in Table 2. In most cases individuals were asked why. Only if the prior responses were overwhelmingly onesided was this question omitted. Up to three responses were coded for each question.

Why? Because we should work like a family. Make all the decisions together, and then if we agree we will all do a better job.

The remaining categories account for very few responses. It is worth noting that the arguments one would most probably get for participation either from management consultants (increased productivity) or from radicals (worker rights) have little relevance for either workers or managers.

Why Not Participation?

The explanations given for more worker influence suggest a separation of decision-making authority based on direct effect and worker competence. Reasons given for not supporting participation confirm this basic separation but from the other point of view. Many workers simply feel some decisions are the job of management:

These are different problems that don't belong to me. They belong to management.

Those are things supervisors and managers have to deal with—it's their business. I wouldn't want any part of it.

In addition to what appears to be unqualified acceptance of management's role, many respondents premised the lack of involvement by workers on the superior expertise of managers in certain types of decisions. While the numbers in the second half of table 6 strongly support this interpretation, the table cannot demonstrate the naturalness and unhesitating brevity with which these feelings are expressed. The following responses are typical.

An angry, alienated cabinetmaker: I don't feel qualified where management is concerned. It's none of my business where peers are concerned. I have to work with them; I wouldn't want the responsibility of firing them.

A highly skilled cabinetmaker: It's up to management to have the say. That's up to them—they know what they want.

A college graduate working in the sanding department: Company policy is based on data gathered by the company and their experts, and I don't have any intelligence or knowledge about those things.

A long-term employee and leadman (after a moment's hesitation): We wouldn't have the knowledge. If you had more information [pause] maybe, but that's a little over our heads. We wouldn't fit in, anyway. We're not in the policy business.

A sixty-year-old employee with eighteen years' seniority: The company has qualified supervisors, and I firmly believe they know what they're doing. They should be the ones who make all the decisions. The company hires experts to oversee. It'd be like building a building without an architect.

Nearly all the responses pointing to a lack of expertise as the limiting factor viewed this lack as a matter of fact but did not explicitly exclude the possibility that workers could become effective decision makers if given the necessary information and training. In a number of cases, the "closeness" or direct effect of decisions was seen as an intervening variable mitigating the lack of expertise. This response of an electronic assembler is a good example of this connection:

We don't know anything about those policy things. How would we? We don't have any experience with them. They don't affect us very much, anyway. In those other things, they're in [our] ball park, and we know . . . hell, we know better than their experts.

The only way in which managers' responses significantly differed from workers' was that they doubted the ultimate competence of workers more often. However, of the thirty-nine supervisor and manager responses, only six fell into this category.

The only remaining rationale commanding a large share of the responses was fear of conflict. While the number of cases is limited, there appears an approximately equal split between people who saw conflict created between workers and management (usually referred to specifically as "they") and those who referred to tensions between workers. One woman suggested that "it's just like politics—too much hassle with them. *They* wouldn't listen to you anyway." From a completely different viewpoint, a young black furniture finisher saw management as a neutral arbitrator of intergroup hostilities and felt that participation would upset the balance among these groups. "That would create conflict, especially since I work with the people. Management deals with cold facts and is accepted as nonconflictual in these situations."

These explanations help to clarify people's beliefs in hierarchical authority for certain types of decisions—specifically, decisions that imply conflict, require specialized expertise, or are simply accepted as management prerogative. However, they tell us little about why the overall level of desired participation is at best only moderate. Two factors are critical in explaining the general reluctance of workers to support radical democratic changes.

The first is workers' natural acceptance of hierarchical authority and their perception that obedience to authority is an integral part of one's job. The pretest of the interviews contained the following question in the section devoted to studying authority relationships in the plant: "Have you ever refused, either directly or indirectly, to do something your supervisor told you to do?" All the pretest subjects (eighteen) answered no. We decided that, if the question was to measure any variation in acceptance of authority, it would have to be softened somehow. Therefore the final question was phrased projectively: "Can you *imagine* a situation where you might, either directly or indirectly, refuse to do something your supervisor told you to do?" Over two-thirds of the workers (68%) could not even imagine such a situation. Authority is accepted naturally; for the majority, disobedience is unthinkable.

By itself, this conclusion need not be at odds with a belief in increased participation. For example, obedience could be coerced, in that the workers see their option as obeying "or else." Similarly, workers may see a supervisor as having personal characteristics that make his directives acceptable even if there is no participation in their development. In fact, however, the largest number of workers attributed their obedience to what we might call the "job contract rationale." The breakdown of attributions appears in table 7. Forty percent of the responses directly link obedience with the individual's job. A machinist put it succinctly: "It's my job to do what I'm told." Beyond that, 17% responded in terms of

TABLE 7
Why Workers Obey Authority

	Worker Responses (%)
Job contract rationale	40.0
It's what I'm paid for	(11.0)
It's my job to do what I'm told	(18.0)
It's my responsibility	(7.0)
It's necessary/has to be done	(4.0)
Have to, implied threat (will lose job; need money; get in trouble)	17.0
Natural acceptance of authority (automatic; programmed; he's boss)	14.5
Character of supervisor	7.4
Personal attributes (dislike conflict; like to obey; etc.)	6.0
Don't necessarily obey	3.5
That's what the company wants	1.3
N Total responses	(228)

NOTE: The question asked ran as follows: "Most of the time, even if we disagree, we do what we're told to do on our jobs. But people do things for different reasons. On your job, when you're told to do something, why do you do it?"

coercion or implied threat, while 14.5% of the responses fell into the general category of natural (automatic or programmed) acceptance of authority.[25]

These answers do not provide information on whether employees consider the traditional authority structure ideal, but it is fairly clear that they readily accept authority and that many make a cognitive link between their jobs and the authority structure. Thus, for many, a significant part of doing one's job is doing what one is told. The evidence further suggests that in most cases there is an element of choice; obeying superiors is not perceived as overwhelmingly coercive but, rather, as part of the contract between the worker and the company. In a very concrete way, workers perceive themselves as selling not only their labor but also a significant portion of their freedom. Although it is logically possible for acceptance of authority in this form to coexist with strong beliefs in democratic procedures (such as electing supervisors or democratically delegating powers to supervisors), it seems far more likely that acceptance of a superior's control implies limited involvement of employees in most decisions. Peter Blau makes this point explicitly in discussing the effective authority of subordinates:

Typically a strict definition is given to the limits of this effective authority. Subordinates can often be heard to remark: "That's the supervisor's responsibility. He gets paid for making those decisions." This does not mean that operating employees shirk responsibilities, as indicated by their willingness to shoulder those they define as their own.

But the social agreement among the members of the group that making certain decisions and issuing directives is the duty of the supervisor, not merely his privilege, serves to emphasize that following them does not constitute submission to his arbitrary will but conformity with commonly accepted operating principles.[26]

A second factor that helps to explain the moderate interest in participation is simply that most people have never conceived of, much less had experience with, any form of direct democracy. For both workers and managers, the idea of applying democratic principles to an organization produces confusion and uncertainty. Jim Gibbons, president of IGP, Inc., and prime mover in the most democratic corporation in the United States, proclaims that "democracy is about as foreign to most Americans as an African tribal rite."[27]

It became clear in the interviews that very few people had ever considered the idea of employees being involved in the decision-making process. Many people reacted with blank hesitation to early questions about selecting leads and supervisors or hiring and firing fellow workers. The responses in many cases consisted of head shaking and muttering, "No" or "No, that's none of our business." In a large number of cases, respondents asked the interviewer for further explanation. It was apparent both to me and to the other interviewers that this was the first time most of those interviewed had ever thought of the idea of decisions being made outside the traditional hierarchical chain.

This problem carried over to the Planning Council in a somewhat different fashion. Although they took the basic fact of participation as a given, council members found the extent of participation, the structure and internal workings of the council, and its role vis-à-vis the existing management structure to be an initial and (to a lesser degree) continuing source of confusion and debate. The evidence from the content analysis of the tapes (table 1) indicates that these discussions occupied more council time than any other single topic. Although such issues partially resolved themselves over time, and the learning that resulted from muddling through them proved valuable, the council's lack of experience delayed the process and frustrated those involved. If organizations approach attempts to democratize decision making as a learning process, as was the case at SI, they should expect to start from a base fairly near zero.

In retrospect, both the natural acceptance of authority and the fact that democratic procedures applied to an organization seem foreign to most people should not surprise us. The major institutions which provide socialization in the norms of the work place are inherently hierarchical in that they define clear levels of authority and rarely provide training in social decision making. Liberal theories aside, family units are structured with a fairly rigid demarcation between children and parents. Although individual norms of tolerance and obedience vary greatly from family to family, one suspects that the number of families seriously attempting any form of group decision making is very small. Schools maintain the pattern. Teachers and administrators are, in one child's words, "the bosses." Attempts in high school and college to teach democratic procedures through student governments and participation in various committees are notoriously transparent. Membership in organizations, often theorized as a foundation of democratic society, comes later in life, if at all (73% of the workers at SI had no organizational affiliation). Even then, it seems questionable that most organizations can be said to train people in the norms or procedures of democratic decision making. For some, the military adds a further, rather obvious mechanism for insulating the individual from experience which might foster a commitment to democratic norms in private institutions.

All this is not to say that our system creates compulsive adherence to authoritarianism. One can find a similarly strong trend reinforcing the idea of individualism and personal freedom in many decisions. The problem is that these decisions are usually personally based (where to live, whether to continue in school, life-style, choice of companions, career, etc.). Lack of experience comes in decisions which affect *groups* of individuals. Except for "public" (government) decisions, we learn to defer group decisions to prearranged, usually institutionalized hierarchies. This distinction is clearly reflected in workers' desire for participation: they desire the most participation in decisions that apparently affect only the individual, less in those that directly affect other workers in their area, and least in decisions that affect the organization as a whole.

The notion of false consciousness, defined earlier as uncertainty that biases beliefs in favor of the status quo, is relevant here. Workers lack experience in group decision making; they also readily accept and feel secure with a norm of obedience. Suggestions of democracy are confusing and somewhat discomfiting. Thus for most the status quo represents an acceptable state. The critical question is whether the practice of democracy will reduce this uncertainty, producing a more liberal attitude toward participation.

Who Believes in Worker Participation?

Advocates of industrial democracy have generally not been primarily concerned about the desires of workers for increased participation. Consequently, very little is known about the relationship between individual characteristics of workers and their belief in participation. Although a number of theorists have speculated on the effects of age, education, job satisfaction, etc., the relationship of these effects has rarely been tested. It is important to identify those who believe in increased participation in order to improve our understanding of why people accept or reject the idea. Furthermore, since changes in the work force are somewhat predictable, knowing the characteristics of those who support participation will aid in future speculation concerning changes in support for participation.

Variables Included in the Model

The literature on union and political activism, as well as research on democratic norms, suggests a wide range of variables that could be hypothetically related to belief in participation. A multiple regression model is used here to discriminate the effects of a number of sometimes closely interrelated independent variables.[28] The primary dependent variable in this analysis is a "belief-in-participation scale" composed of the unweighted sums of the seventeen different decisions listed in table 2. As can be seen in that table, the reliability of the scale (Cronbach A) is very high at .87. The lowest item to scale correlation is .35, while the average is .51.

The independent variables in the final statistical model are listed in table 8. This table gives a brief description of each variable and, when possible, specification of the expected relationship with the scale of desire for participation. Appendix C contains the exact interview questions, frequency distributions of the appropriate independent variables, and scale information. Each set of independent variables will be briefly discussed before the findings are presented.

The first set of variables is fairly straightforward. The literature on union and political activism suggests that younger, more highly educated males are more likely to want increased influence in decisions. Of the two measures in the second set of variables (external influences) political activism is probably more familiar. It is measured using a standard set of political activities (voting, campaign activities, contacting officials, etc.), scoring the respondent one point for each activity in which he has taken part. Belief in democratic values is a measure of the individual's belief in basic rights like freedom of speech, the right to run for office, and majority rule, when they are applied to somewhat contentious specific situations. Examples are "If an admitted Communist wanted to make a speech in this city favoring Communism, he should be allowed to speak" and "A member of the American Nazi Party should not be allowed to run for mayor of this city."[29] The hypotheses are based on the assumption that political activism and support for democratic norms in the larger community will spill over and produce a belief in increased worker participation.[30]

The third set of variables (job characteristics) consists of (1) the official OEO job classification of the individual (ranging from 1 to 10, with 1 defined as the worst job); (2) the respondent's perception of how much

TABLE 8
Independent Variables Predicting Belief in Worker Participation

Variable Set	Reliability (Cronbach A)	Definition of High Value	Hypothesized Effect of High Value (Participation)
Background characteristics:			
Education	...	More educated	More ($b > 0$)
Age	...	Older	Less ($b < 0$)
Race	...	Minority	?
Sex	...	Female	Less ($b < 0$)
External influence:			
Belief in democratic-values scale	.85	Democratic	More ($b > 0$)
Political-participation scale	.66	Active	More ($b > 0$)
Job characteristics:			
Job classification	...	High-status job	?
Job-attributes scale	.73	Satisfied	Less ($b < 0$)
Scale of present participation on the job	.81	High participation	More ($b > 0$)
Alienation in work			
Alienation scale	.83	Low alienation	Less ($b < 0$)
Ambition			
Ambition scale	.62	Ambitious	More ($b > 0$)
Evaluation of supervisor			
Relationship with supervisor	...	Negative evaluation	More ($b > 0$)

participation he actually has in his present job (the sum of nine of the items in table 3); and (3) a measure of the individual's assessment of his job in terms of required equipment, enough time to complete the job, and general enjoyment of the work. The hypotheses for these particular variables are somewhat more controversial than those for variables previously considered. The a priori relationship with present participation is simplest: assuming that democracy is to a degree a learned process, present participation should lead to desire for increased influence. Hypotheses concerning job classifications and job characteristics are more difficult to argue. As Holter implies, higher-level jobs, which allow more freedom and enjoyment, may stimulate the individual to support worker influence in a wide range of activities.[31] On the other hand, a number of theories suggest that lower-level jobs, hierarchically controlled and inherently unenjoyable, will stimulate a reaction from workers in the form of demands for more say in decision making. The widely read HEW report *Work in America* consistently supports this position.

Alienation in work, the fourth variable set, is also vulnerable to the same contradictory arguments. This scale consists of four subscales modeled after the "powerlessness," "normlessness," "isolation," and "self-estrangement" dimensions of alienation described by Seeman.[32] The following definitions were adopted, with some revisions, from Seeman:

Powerlessness is a low expectation that one's own behavior can control the rewards and sanctions in work.

Normlessness is a state of perceived social disorder based on a lack of or confusion between behavioral norms.

Isolation is low expectancy of inclusion and acceptance expressed as loneliness or rejection.

Self-estrangement is taken to be engagement in activities that fail to fulfill the goals an individual defines for himself.

While the bulk of research on alienation has considered it as a broad cultural concept, the measures employed here refer strictly to work. The exact questions for these subscales are included in appendix C. As a means of examining the relationship between alienation and the desire for participation, the effects of each dimension were studied both separately and in a combined scale. For brevity and to alleviate the substantial statistical intercorrelation between the subscales, the combined scale (which has a reliability of .82) is used in this chapter and the next.

The index of ambition employed for this study is a combination of two questions, one measuring ambition over a long period of time and the other desire to get ahead at SI. The first measure was created by coding the open-ended responses to the question "What would you like to be doing five years from now?" with a 2 if a status advance was indicated and a 1 if not. The second question was simply whether the respondent would like to be a supervisor at SI some day. It seems reasonable to assume that, since advancement in modern organizations usually implies decision-making responsibility, personal ambition should be positively related to an individual's belief in participation. What is less clear is whether ambitious people believe *all* employees should participate or are making a special argument for their own position. This question will be discussed in some detail in the next chapter when we will consider the characteristics of those who sought to become activists in the QWL program.

Finally, the variable set labeled "evaluation of supervisor" is an attempt to measure the relationship between a worker and his immediate supervisor. A full section of the interview was devoted to authority and included questions on the scope of control, style of supervision, and degree of conflict present in various supervisor/subordinate relationships, as well as a general evaluative measure of the supervisor's capabilities.[33] Again, as with some other variable sets, a number of combinations of these factors were tried. The final measure used in this analysis combines the frequency of disagreement with the supervisor and an overall evaluation of the supervisor based on the characteristics the respondent felt an ideal supervisor would possess (for a description of this technique, see chap. 2, n. 12, or app. C). Assuming that participation will be perceived as a way to get around or to control a supervisor, negative evaluations of supervision should lead to increased support for worker participation.

Findings

The results of the analysis regressing the independent variables listed in table 8 on the belief-in-participation scale are presented in table 9. The regression is based only on the worker portion of the sample.[34] The results suggest a number of interesting conclusions. The fact that the variables explain 44% of the variance is in itself a good indication that we have located at least some of the more important factors contributing to support for worker participation. The second conclusion is that, in terms of the direction of the coefficients, the hypotheses suggested above were supported. However, in a number of cases, the ratio of the coefficients to standard errors (t values) suggests that the estimates are highly unreliable. Sets of variables are separated in the table, and the constrained F tests in column 9 represent the simultaneous effects of the variables in each set. Results will be reviewed in terms of these groupings.

Background variables appear to have a significant effect on the desire for participation ($F = 2.05, p < .05$). This is primarily due to the effect of age, which can be seen in column 5 as having the highest single bivariate correlation with the dependent variable ($r = -.37$). The remaining background variables appear to have very little relationship with the desire for participation when controlling for the full set of variables in the model. Education has a bivariate correlation with the belief-in-participation scale of .34, but the effect is completely eliminated when controlling for age and job classification. Thus youth and higher-level job categories are statistically more important than higher education. The external influences of political participation and support for democratic principles have surprisingly little effect on desire for participation.

Clearly, for this sample, characteristics that define one's job are very important determinants of belief in worker participation. Job classification, the degree of influence a respondent currently has in his job, and his evaluation of its physical attributes and enjoyment inherent in the job are all very significant. Naturally the simultaneous effect of this cluster of variables is significant at the .001 level. What may be more important, however, is the pattern of these relationships, especially if we include alienation in work and ambition, which also have significant effects on belief in participation.

An expectation model affords a possible explanation of these findings. The basic proposition in expectation models, though at times elaborated

TABLE 9
Regression Estimates on Belief-in-Participation Scale

Independent Variable	Actual Range	Mean	S.D.	r with Dependent Variable	b	Standard Error	t	Constrained F Test
Education	10	11.76	2.21	.34	.31	.43	.72	⎫ $F = 2.05$
Age	48	31.70	10.45	-.37	-.15	.08	-1.88	⎬ $df = 4,132$
Race	1	1.52	.50	-.17	-2.24	1.45	-1.54	⎭
Sex	1	1.44	.50	-.14	1.24	1.58	.78	
Belief in democratic values	20	16.97	4.24	.18	-.15	.18	-.83	⎫ $F = .38$
Political participation	8	11.30	2.36	.12	.15	.33	.45	⎬ $df = 2,132$
Job classification	7	2.81	1.57	.20	1.19	.59	2.01	⎫ $F = 11.01$
Job attributes	10	10.89	2.27	-.25	-1.47	.43	-3.42	⎬ $df = 3,132$
Present participation on the job	22	15.20	5.06	.36	.63	.16	3.94	⎭
Alienation in work	32	53.62	6.89	-.21	-.30	.12	-2.50	⋯
Ambition	3	2.48	1.25	.26	1.34	.67	2.00	⋯
Evaluation of supervisor	6	4.29	1.47	.27	.06	.55	.11	⋯
Constant	⋯	⋯	⋯	⋯	73.72	14.54	⋯	⋯

NOTE: The dependent variable, belief in participation, is an index constructed of the sum of responses to the decisions listed in Table 8.
For this sample size, $|t| \geq 1.65$ is significant at the .05 level, and $|t| \geq 2.33$ is significant at .01.

BELIEF-IN PARTICIPATION INDEX: Range = 36; Mean = 40.9; S.D. = 0.6.
EXPLAINED VARIANCE: R^2 = .40; F = 7.26; df = 12,132; N = 145.

with complex extrapolative trend factors and other complicating assumptions, is that, in situations where satisfaction is not attuned to expectations, antisystem behavior such as industrial conflict, civil strife, or rebellion will ensue.[35] Furthermore, some theorists pose that the likelihood of this occurrence is greater in situations where expectations are rising, either because of an inherent lag in satisfaction or because higher expectations create the possibility for an extremely wide gulf between aspirations and satisfactions.[36]

In whatever form, two variables are embedded in this model: expectations and satisfactions. Our data clearly indicate that each factor has an independent effect on belief in participation. If we assume that a higher job classification, ambition, and a relatively high level of present participation imply a high level of expectation, there is little doubt that expectation is related to the desire for participation. Similarly, a general feeling of alienation and negative evaluation of one's job and supervisor tends to produce a higher level of belief in the legitimacy of participation. But various statistical attempts fail to demonstrate that the gap between expectations and satisfactions is related in any way to a desire for greater influence. One of the primary reasons why this relationship failed to appear is that in fact expectations and satisfactions tend to be positively correlated. Those in higher-level jobs are significantly more satisfied ($r = .43$) and less alienated ($r = .21$). Present participation has a similar, although weaker, relationship.

What these results suggest is not that the model is incorrect, for a more specific application is decisive in analyzing the behavior of activists. Instead, the results indicate that desire for participation is not solely a protest activity. It is reasonable to assume that two forces may be at work. Those who are in higher-level jobs, are ambitious, and have had previous experience with decision making view participation as a personal opportunity to develop skills, assume further self-control, and possibly fulfill ambitions by demonstrating a capacity to handle increased responsibility. On the other hand, for the alienated and dissatisfied individual, participation may be viewed as an opportunity to reduce a grievance or at least to protest one's alienated state. Thus both expectations and alienation are related to a belief in participation. The negative correlation between these components suggests a fairly broad base of potential support. The individuals most likely to support participation are those with high expectations and high alienation. These individuals are surely in a minority, but they are very important in maintaining a non-co-optive system of joint decision making.

4. The Activists

There is a tendency to assume that if workers are permitted to select representatives from within their ranks to share decision-making responsibilities with managers, these representatives will accurately reflect the views of employees. Unlike political elites, workers' representatives are supposedly very similar to their constituents in status and concerns. This assumption should be challenged. I argue that employees who seek participation differ from the rank and file in a number of characteristics, and these characteristics have a significant effect on the likelihood of achieving adequate representation of workers' interests in systems of joint worker-management decision making.

FACTORS PREDICTING ACTIVISM

To determine what types of employee are most likely to seek active roles in decision making, a voluntary selection procedure must exist. The Planning Council elections and, to a lesser degree, membership on the special-purpose committees met this self-selection criterion. The election procedures for the Planning Council were based entirely on self-nomination. Thus, comparing those individuals who placed their names in nomination with the random sample of the work force establishes one distinctive category of activism. In the following analysis, "running for the Planning Council" will be a dichotomous variable, coded 1 for no participation and 2 if the individual ran for election. A second measure of activism, more broadly based and accounting actual participation as more significant than simply attempting to get elected, is an index based on Planning Council activity and/or special-committee participation. This participation index ranges from 0 to 3, with one point given for running for council election, one for election as a member or alternate, and one for membership on one or more special committees. These two measures serve as dependent variables in the analysis to follow.

Participation in shop floor work projects is not included, simply because it was not really spontaneous activism. While participation was meant to be voluntary, existing sections were used as experimental projects in three out of the five groups; and the people working in these areas were approached first about participating. In all cases, the employees agreed to take part; but it was clear that group pressures and desire to please a supervisor motivated some workers. This pressure was never overtly coercive, but the self-initiated spontaneity that characterized participation in joint committees was lacking.

Multivariate Analysis

The set of independent variables used to explain the variance in our measures of actual participation is identical with that used to predict belief in workers' participation (see tables 8 and 9). The rationale for using the same model is, first, that it is a priori difficult to separate hypotheses predicting beliefs from those predicting actual behavior. Second, by using the same model comparisons can be made, with appropriate caution, between the effects of the independent variables in each case. These comparisons provide some theoretical insight into differences between activism and support for democratic norms.

The results of the regressions on the activism measures are presented in tables 10 and 11. There is some built-in overlap between these two scales, because participation in the Planning Council is included in both measures. In spite of this, the similarity in results is striking. In addition, the results of a separate regression, in which the dependent variable is a dichotomous variable representing membership on special committees, is not included because the findings so closely parallel those in table 10. Since tables 10 and 11 lead to very similar conclusions, they will be summarized together (see chap. 3 or app. C for definitions of the included variables).

The profile of the activist in interesting in several respects. In the first place, activists are much more politicized than the typical worker. They have a higher level of political participation and are significantly more committed to specific democratic norms applied to the external political system.[1] There is little doubt that some people interpreted the program in political terms. When asked during the second wave of interviews why they had or had not run for the Planning Council, a number of people emphasized its "political nature." A young Chicana woman summarized the feelings of many workers: "All that talking and arguing...that's too political for me. I don't like political things. They make me nervous." At the other extreme were those who relish the political aspects of decision making. A fiery lead, reflecting on his Planning Council experience, remarked, "I liked those meetings....I'm not sure they liked me very much, but they were exciting and lively. We made some good decisions, too. I just wish some of the others had more guts. You see, I learned my politics in prison." Although not all committee members came from the same political training ground, they did have a much higher level of political experience than did the work force as a whole.

TABLE 10
Regression Estimates on Running for the Planning Council

Independent Variable	Actual Range	Mean	S.D.	r with Dep.	b	Standard Error	t	Constrained F Test
Education	10	11.76	2.21	.20	−.015	.019	−.79	
Age	48	31.70	10.45	−.14	.005	.035	.14	$F = .63$
Race	1	1.52	.40	−.23	−.086	.063	−1.37	df = 4,132
Sex	1	1.44	.50	−.15	−.041	.069	−.59	
Belief in democratic values	20	16.97	4.24	.34	.019	.008	2.38	$F = 7.05$
Political participation	8	11.30	2.36	.31	.032	.014	2.29	df = 2,132
Job classification	7	2.81	1.57	.14	−.023	.026	−.88	$F = 1.36$
Job attributes	10	10.89	2.27	.04	.033	.019	1.74	df = 3,132
Present participation	22	15.20	5.06	.12	.006	.007	.86	
Alienation in work	32	53.62	6.89	−.02	−.004	.005	−.80	⋯
Ambition	3	2.48	1.25	.41	.092	.029	3.17	⋯
Evaluation of supervisor	6	4.29	1.47	.23	.067	.024	2.79	⋯
Constant	⋯	⋯	⋯	⋯	1.187	.631	1.88	⋯

NOTE: The dependent variable, running for the Planning Council, is a dichotomous variable coded as 1 for "no participation" and 2 if the respondent ran in the Planning Council election. See table 7 for definition of the independent variables.

For this sample size, $|t| \geq 1.65$ is significant at the 0.5 level, and $|t| \geq 2.33$ is significant at 0.1.

RUNNING FOR THE WORKER COUNCIL: Range = 1; Mean = 1.21; S.D. = .41.
EXPLAINED VARIANCE: $R^2 = .32$; $F = 5.17$; df = 12; N = 145.

TABLE 11
Regression Estimates on the Participation Index

Independent Variable	Actual Range	Mean	S.D.	r with Dep.	b	Standard Error	t	Constrained F Test
Education	10	11.76	2.21	.25	-.039	.040	-.97	$F = .52$
Age	48	31.70	10.45	-.19	-.002	.008	-.25	df = 4,132
Race	1	1.52	.50	-.21	-.122	.136	-.90	
Sex	1	1.44	.50	-.18	-.156	.149	-1.05	
Belief in democratic values	20	16.97	4.24	.42	.059	.017	3.47	$F = 10.8$
Political participation	8	11.30	2.36	.33	.071	.031	2.29	df = 2,132
Job classification	7	2.81	1.57	.21	-.013	.055	-.24	$F = 2.28$
Job attributes	10	10.89	2.27	.08	.081	.040	2.03	df = 3,132
Present participation	22	15.20	5.06	.20	.022	.015	1.47	
Alienation in work	32	53.62	6.89	.02	-.007	.012	-.58	…
Ambition	3	2.48	1.25	.43	.182	.063	2.89	…
Evaluation of supervisor	6	4.29	1.47	.21	.139	.052	2.67	…
Constant	…	…	…	…	1.768	1.364	1.30	…

PARTICIPATION INDEX: Range = 3; Mean = 1.50; S.D. = .91.
EXPLAINED VARIANCE: $R^2 = .37$; $F = 6.53$; df = 12,132; n = 145.

NOTE: The dependent variable, participation, is an index composed of the sum of Planning Council participation (coded: 0 = none, 1 = ran for council, 2 = elected to council) and participation in special-purpose committees (coded: 0 = none, 1 = member of a committee).

For this sample size, $|t| \geq 1.65$ is significant at the .05 level, and $|t| \geq 2.33$ is significant at .01.

Even more significant in a statistical sense is the effect of belief in democratic values. For both measures of participation, a strong correlation exists between activism and support for majority rule, minority rights, and freedom of speech. The highly significant t-tests in the multiple regression demonstrate that this relationship persisted even after controlling for education and political participation (which are often theoretically linked to support for democratic values). In other words, external influences—experiences outside the factory—were key factors in drawing the line between active participants and casual observers.

Another important result, particularly when compared with the findings in the last chapter, is the significant relationship between activism and satisfaction with job attributes, as well as the lack of correlation between activism and alienation in work. Positive evaluation of one's specific job is significantly related to both measures of participation. Unlike the hypothesized relationship which predicted that the most dissatisfied workers would support and participate in decision making, it appears that in fact the activists are relatively more satisfied with their present jobs. On the other hand, alienation, measuring a much broader set of emotions, has absolutely no effect either in a bivariate or multivariate configuration.

The last two significant variables add to the complexity of what motivates people to become active in plant decision making. While we have seen that the activist is more politicized and on average more satisfied with his job, he would appear also to be much more ambitious and much more likely to be in a conflictive relationship with his immediate supervisor. The latter finding implies that whatever dissatisfaction exists among activists may result from and be directed at the authority structure—at least as it impinges upon them directly. Statistically, the effect of supervisory evaluation is very important in predicting activism. The individual who rates his supervisor lowest and has frequent disagreements with him is 40.2% more likely to run for the Planning Council than the worker who rates his supervisor excellent and never disagrees with him.

The question of whether the individual is ambitious or not also plays an important role in determining the likelihood of activism. Ambition explains the most variance in a bivariate analysis ($r = .41$ and $.43$ for the respective measures of activism), while remaining highly significant in the regression model ($p < .001$). Ambitious workers are far more likely to become activists than those who have no desire to move up to supervisory positions in the company or who have little interest in longer-range upward mobility. This finding holds for both measures of participation. If we consider going from the least ambitious group of individuals to the most ambitious, the probability of running for the Planning Council increases by 27.5%, and the error associated with this estimate is only 8.7%.

The results taken together confirm that activists are not likely to be typical workers. But we should remember that the characteristics of activists are very different from the characteristics of those most likely to profess a belief in the idea of worker participation.

Beliefs and Actions: The Models Compared

The same statistical model will be applied to predictions of activism as that used for testing the hypothesized factors associated with an expressed belief in participation. Theoretically it might seem more logical either to include in the model belief in participation as an independent variable predicting activism or, by making more complex causal assumptions, to pose a simultaneous equation model. However, attempts at the former method fail empirically, and the latter is rendered inappropriate by the difficulty of establishing a convincing set of structural equations separating beliefs from actions. In the first place, the bivariate relationship between the belief-in-participation scale (table 2) and our two measures of activism are very weak. The correlations are, respectively, .14 and .12 with participation in the council election and the participation index. Also, when the belief-in-participation scale is included in any of several regression models predicting actual participation, it has no significant effect.[2] In other words, there is strong evidence that for this sample there is little relationship between stated beliefs and actions. The reason for this is clarified by considering jointly the results presented in table 9 and those in tables 10 and 11.

Comparisons between the characteristics associated with a stated belief in industrial democracy and the factors that appear related to actual participation are dramatic. In terms of statistically significant variables, the overall pattern creates a waffle effect: variables significant on the belief-in-participation scale are insignificant in predicting actual participation, and vice versa. There are only two exceptions to this pattern: (1) ambition is strongly related to belief in the legitimacy of participation and also serves to stimulate actual participation; and (2) evaluation of the physical job attributes is significant in all equations, but the direction of the effect is reversed. In other words, those who are lowest in their evaluation of the overall enjoyment and physical aspects of their job are most likely to support increased worker participation verbally but least likely actually to participate in the election, the council itself, or special-purpose committees.

For the remaining variables in the regression, youth predicts support for participation but has almost no effect in predicting who actually participates. The same pattern holds for job classification, present participation on the job, and alienation in work. On the other hand, external influences such as belief in democratic norms and political activism, as well as evaluation of one's immediate supervisor, do not predict a high level of belief in participation but are strongly related to predicting who actually becomes involved. There can be little doubt that those individuals expressing a belief that workers should have more say and those who become activists and leaders differ in their prior political experience, the types of jobs they hold, their perceptions of those jobs, and their relationships with their immediate supervisor.[3]

THE ACTIVIST AS AN ATYPICAL WORKER

A final task is to consider not the multivariate effects of various characteristics on activists but the gross differences in these characteristics when comparing the work force at large with those who serve as their representatives on joint work-management councils. Although multivariate analysis reveals which characteristics are most relevant when considering the constellation of variables, actual behavior may be more a function of the characteristics of the council members vis-à-vis the constituents they are supposed to represent. Since the relevant question here is whether those who serve as representatives differ from the rank and file, I will concentrate on actual participation—those who won elections, not those who ran.

Table 12 provides either differences of means or, for dichotomous variables, differences of percentages between Planning Council or special-purpose committee members and the work force at large. Because there is great similarity between the two types of participants and the Planning Council was both more powerful and more exclusive (with membership solely by election), I will focus on figures for the council, noting only exceptions for other committees.

The overwhelming evidence is that those elected or appointed to these councils and committees were not typical members of the work force. Concerning the Planning Council, for all but two measures—evaluating job attributes and alienation in work—the differences are significant at the .05 level ($t = 1.65$). Whereas socioeconomic variables in the multiple regression model were relatively insignificant, there are clear differences in the bivariate relationships, as table 12 demonstrates. Representatives had an average of one year more education than their peers, were more than five years younger, and were predominantly white males. They were also significantly more democratic in their values ($p < .001$), and had at one time or another engaged in (on average) two more political activities than their fellow workers. In relation to their jobs, even though they evaluate the attributes of their jobs about equally, members were somewhat higher in job classifications and in the amount of participation they then had. Additionally, rather than being more alienated, they were in fact slightly more satisfied (although the difference is unreliable). In terms of ambition, the differences are dramatic. While 23.3% of the work force had long-range goals that indicated a desire to improve their status, 60.9% of the

TABLE 12
Characteristics of Activists Compared with the General Work Force

	Members of Planning Council			Members of Special Committees			
	Planning Council	Work Force	t	Committees	Work Force	t	N
Education (mean years)	12.6	11.6	1.74	13.1	11.5	3.30	145
Age (mean years)	27.1*	32.3	2.00	27.7	32.4	2.06	145
Race (% white)	72.3	45.0	2.26	58.3	45.5	1.15	145
Sex (% male)	77.8	52.9	2.01	70.9	52.9	1.62	145
Democratic values (means)	21.5*	16.3	4.85	20.0	16.4	3.26	113
Political participation (means)	13.1	11.0	3.61	12.4	11.1	2.58	145
Job classification (means)	3.5	2.7	2.02	3.6	2.6	2.71	145
Job attributes (means)	11.2	11.0	.21	11.8	10.9	1.47	114
Present participation on the job (means)	17.1	14.9	1.67	17.9	14.7	2.91	145
Alienation in work (means)	54.5	53.5	.60	54.1	53.5	.39	145
Ambition (means)	2.53	3.73	3.82	2.50	3.80	4.70	122
Long range (% status advance)	60.9	23.3	2.96	68.2	39.0	2.54	122
Supervisor? (% yes)	83.3	38.3	3.33	87.5	40.1	4.19	145
Evaluation of supervisor (means)	4.91	4.20	1.93	4.72	4.21	1.57	145
Frequency of disagreements	2.63	1.83	3.26	2.46	1.83	2.97	145
General evaluation	2.30	2.37	.32	2.26	2.38	.62	145
N	(18)	(127)	(...)	(24)	(121)	(...)	(...)

NOTE: For this sample size, $|t| \geq 1.65$ is significant at the .05 level, those who ran for the Council but were not elected was significant at and $|t| \geq 2.33$ is significant at .01. the .05 level. Thus those elected are younger and more democratic than those not elected.
For these items a comparison between Planning Council members and

Planning Council members professed similar goals. Moreover, 83.3% wanted to be supervisors some day, compared with 38.3% in the rest of the sample. Finally, there is a marked difference between activists and nonactivists in the frequency of disagreements with supervisors.

The differences between the work force and members of special-purpose committees are very similar to those described for the Planning Council, although somewhat weaker in a number of cases. The only variables that fall near or below a .05 level of significance for special-purpose committee members are race (minority members are underrepresented by 12.8%) and evaluation of supervisor.

These comparisons bring to mind the differences between activists and followers in both unions and politics in general. Excepting the finding on age, educated white men in higher job categories are more likely to become union and political leaders. Similarly, high levels of political activism and support for democratic norms have long been regarded as a distinction between political leaders and followers. Finally, although reliable data on the aspirations of political leaders are lacking and data available on union leaders are mixed,[4] many inferences suggest that, like the members of these committees and council, they also are decidedly more ambitious than the average man. Thus the empirically undeniable distinction between *homo civicus* and *homo politicus* (made by Robert Dahl in describing urban politics) seems to carry over to organizational attempts at democracy.[5]

INFERENCES AND INTERPRETATIONS

The relationship between the factors that seem to explain activism and those explaining belief in increased workers' participation is paradoxical. Although I have concluded that a belief in democracy seems to be associated with both alienation and a high level of expectations, activism seems to be related primarily to expectations. Signs of the upward aspirations of activists can be indirectly inferred from higher education, youth, outside activism, and higher job levels that include more say in decisions. The strongest evidence is of course the direct relationship between our measure of ambition and activism. On the other hand, the only sign of overt dissatisfaction was the highly conflictive attitude toward immediate supervision.

Considering the last point first, the proposed benefit of participation as a cure for alienation will at best be indirect for those most disaffected, since activists tend not to be the most alienated members of the work force. This problem is compounded by the fact that those most alienated in their work were also most likely to support the idea of workers' participation. If their exclusion from participation produces a cynical reaction, this may in turn reduce the overall level of belief in the legitimacy of increased participation.

Second, the higher levels of political participation and participation on the job, as well as activists' belief in democratic procedures, could also have a negative effect. Our political system's stress on negotiation and nonviolence could result in a tendency for worker representatives to compromise and cooperate too much with management in situations where conflictive confrontation is needed to support the claims of workers. This proposition suggests a co-optation of process rather than of goals. Political theorists from John Stuart Mill to Robert Dahl have commented on the importance of decentralized decision making as a method of training people in democratic practices; however, in a situation where one group may have inherent power disadvantages vis-à-vis another group, compromise and cooperation may well serve only the interests of the powerful. The importance of the strike in labor union power is the most obvious and relevant case in point. The absence of a union at SI makes this an even more important consideration.

Finally, and most important, employees who supported participation, especially those who became activists, were much more ambitious to move up in the organization than the average employee. For activists, who also tended to evaluate their immediate supervisors negatively, participation may be seen as a mechanism for interacting with higher-level management, displaying their abilities as rational decision makers, and demonstrating their basic loyalty to the company. Less formally, activists might have viewed participation as a corporate escalator—insulated from the interference of a hostile supervisor. Carrying this interpretation further, the activists, attempting to impress managers, might have been willing to renounce goals of their constituents, especially when confronted by firm management resistance. It could also be argued that in fact these representatives did not even share the goals of other workers, having already projected themselves into a management role and thus having internalized management norms.[6] Furthermore, since advancement is still controlled by the traditional hierarchy, constituency ties were thin, and the reelection motive provided a weak incentive for representing the claims of workers forcefully.

The problem of the ambitious, management-oriented labor leader has been alluded to by a number of researchers and theoreticians. Holter found in Norway, for example, a strong relationship between personal desire to participate in management decisions and supervisory ambitions. She also found that those who want to participate personally already have a higher level of participation, come from technical and administrative fields, have a relatively high level of support for work changes, and are much more favorably inclined toward attempts to increase efficiency.[7]

Although somewhat less direct, evidence from several other studies has shown that union leaders are more likely than rank and file members either to be in semimanagerial roles already or to aspire to management positions.[8]

More direct and persuasive evidence comes from studies of actual participatory systems. Studying Norway's experience with worker membership on corporate boards, Thorsrud and Emery discuss the role of ambition, based on the assessment of representatives they interviewed. One of these concisely summarized his motivation: "To come on the board means for a worker a way up and out."[9] More quantitative data comes from Yugoslavia, where Obradović and his colleagues report a strong relationship between ambition and membership on workers' councils. Although the authors inexplicably define responses to the question "How much do you want to be a manager?" as measuring a "need for participation" rather than ambition, the relationship with council membership is fully supported in table 13, the results of which are very close to those at SI.[10]

TABLE 13
Ambition and Membership on Yugoslav Workers' Councils

	Desire to Be a Manager	
	High	Low
Council member	142	78
Nonmember	137	163

NOTE: $X^2 = 18.19$.

Finally, an earlier British experience with joint consultation was also somewhat susceptible to the problem of worker representatives using their positions as individual stepping stones. A National Institute of Industrial Psychology report on joint consultation contains the following caution:

> Men of outstanding personality amongst workers often find satisfactory outlets through taking up work as representatives of one kind or another. But in one or two factories we visited this had created a difficult problem, for it is only to be expected that such men should attract a good deal of attention when selection for promotion is considered. If, however, promotions are frequently made from the ranks of shop stewards and worker representatives, such offices may come to be regarded as a step in promotion and representatives suspected of working to please the management rather than to maintain an independent position.[11]

Thus the relationship between activism in joint decision making and desire for promotion from the rank and file seems to hold over time and across national boundaries.

There are no directly comparable data in the United States. However, one of the most intriguing theories about the American labor movement, presented in a 1928 volume by Selig Perlman, describes a picture very close to the problem created for industrial democracy by individual ambition. Perlman saw the psychology of "job opportunity" as integrally related to unionism. He argued that unionism in America was delayed by the fact that nineteenth-century workers were raised not with an idea of job scarcity but, rather, with a belief in the abundance of opportunity. This "resulted in a social philosophy which was more akin to the businessmen's than to the trade unionists' or the guildsmen's." Union leaders were affected both by the ideology of opportunity and, disproportionately, by actual opportunities to advance either into management or politics. Although this spirit ignited ideas of "cooperative individualism" and led to numerous experiments in producer cooperatives in the 1870s and 1880s, the same spirit in the end destroyed the movement. The basic problem, according to Perlman, was that the cooperators, attempting to succeed as individuals, became either pitted against each other in attempts to cheapen labor or, in the case of successful cooperatives, began to expand, thus employing noncooperative labor and in fact acting much like capitalists. In Perlman's words, "Thus in the end the whole labor movement had bled and toiled for the sake of the elevation to the status of capitalists of a few workingmen."[12] Perlman viewed the stabilization and advance of labor unions in America, following the decline of the Knights of Labor in the 1890s, as the result of renouncing the premise of abundance of opportunity and replacing it with a "communism of opportunity" in which unions concentrated on controlling jobs either entirely (as in the case of printers) or through agreements on seniority, advancement and layoff, apprenticeships, "equal turn" rules, etc.

It may be that labor's present negative position on cooperative worker-management decision making is rooted in an understanding of the still powerful pull toward individualistic cooperation. It is very possible that Perlman underestimated the staying power of this individualistic philosophy. While he lived through a period of great expansion by labor, he also lived to see unionism stagnate at a level below that of any other major western industrial country. The continuing importance of upward mobility in industry for American workers was aptly demonstrated by Tannenbaum and his colleagues in their recently published five-nation study. Using five different measures of mobility costs (added responsibility, additional training, etc.), they found that for both large and small plants, U.S. workers were much more likely to absorb the costs to achieve advancement than were workers from Italy, Austria, Israel, or Yugoslavia. They also showed that U.S. workers not only desired greater upward mobility but also saw it as the central reward or punishment for doing exceptionally good or bad jobs. The authors concluded, "In Ameri-

can plants great prominence was given to the opinion and praise of supervisors as well as the opportunity for advancement, hinting at the importance attached to upward mobility in these plants."[13] In other words,
there is strong evidence that the conflict between aspirations for individualistic upward mobility and collective labor action remains unresolved.

5. Joint Decision Making: The Problem of Co-optation

In the first chapter, the issues underlying arguments about the effectiveness of joint worker-management decision making were discussed in general terms. The primary question was whether the interests of rank and file workers could be adequately represented by delegates selected through democratic procedures. From the point of view of workers, the danger is that decision-making mechanisms will be fraudulent, giving apparent legitimacy to decisions that may not be in their own best interests. As Clegg has argued, the costs to workers may be viewed in terms not only of short-run issues but also of long-run consequences for union power.[1] American labor leaders have taken similar stands on most participatory schemes. In order to understand the complex mechanisms that can lead to what I will call illusory democracy, definitions must be much more explicit than they have been so far.

ILLUSORY DEMOCRACY

Democracy is an illusion when procedural mechanisms intended to reach and implement decisive judgments in accordance with a rule of political equality fail to do so. In organizations, illusory democracy can result from three basic problems: co-optation, misrepresentation, and structural impotence. The first condition is based on management domination, the second on the failure of representatives to present the views of their constituents adequately, and the third on restrictions placed on the decision-making body itself. The following definitions apply.

Definition 1. *Co-optation:* A condition wherein a disaffected faction is brought into the decision-making process but fails to advance its preferences, because the process is controlled by an opposing faction.

Three forms of co-optation will be relevant to our discussion.

Definition 1.1. *Hegemony:* Achievement of consensus by the controlling faction made possible by persuading the leaders of other factions to accept their preferences.
Definition 1.2. *Incompetence:* Domination of the decision-making process by the controlling faction because of its superior skill, knowledge, and information.

Definition 1.3. *Coercion:* Domination of the decision-making process by the controlling faction through the use or threat of sanctions.

Definition 2. *Misrepresentation:* A condition wherein those selected to present and argue for the preferences of a specific faction fail to represent those preferences.

A distinction must be made between two forms of misrepresentation.

Definition 2.1. *Optation:* Failure of representatives to present the preferences of their constituents because they do not concur in those preferences.

Definition 2.2. *Isolation:* Lack of communication between representatives and their constituencies, with a resulting inability to ascertain or agree on the position of those being represented.

In the case of optation, the delegate consciously misrepresents the desires of his constituents, whereas in isolation the delegate attempts to present their interests adequately but is thwarted by a number of possible circumstances (technical communication problems, apathy, etc.).

Definition 3. *Structural impotence:* A condition wherein the decision-making body itself is powerless either to consider a crucial range of issues or to affect behavior in accordance with the judgments it reaches.

I do not claim that these definitions are fully distinctive, defining mutually exclusive categories of behavior. The differences in emphasis should be clear, however. Specifically, co-optation emphasizes the problem of worker leaders controlled and dominated by managers; misrepresentation, the problem of worker representatives knowing adequately and being willing to present the interests of their followers (whether managers are in control or not); structural impotence stresses the conflict between democratic and hierarchical sources of power within an organization. These distinctions form a dividing line as precise as I can present between the failures and successes of joint decision making at SI.

The evidence suggests that worker representatives at SI, under the right conditions, could successfully avoid co-optation. In contrast to the European experiences, management did not significantly dominate the committees and councils at SI. Problems of misrepresentation and structural impotence were not so successfully avoided.

THE CHARACTER OF PLANNING COUNCIL MEETINGS

Since the Planning Council was by far the most important committee at SI, I will rely heavily on the experience of this committee.

We can easily distinguish forms of co-optation analytically. However, as seems to be the case in much social science, our empirical tests are not so precise. In one of the first analyses of workers' councils in Yugoslavia, Sturmthal based his conclusion that the councils were dominated by management upon a verbatim description of a single meeting.[2] That description was very convincing, but it did not allow the reader to judge adequately the competence of workers or the coercion or hegemony of management. Later, the quantitative content analysis of meetings by Kolaja and then Obradavić and his colleagues confirmed the degree of domination but again left readers somewhat confused about mechanisms.[3] By combining these two forms of analysis, as well as arguing from the vantage point of an observer at hundreds of meetings, I hope to be somewhat more successful. The following section consists primarily of meeting transcripts and is intended to convey an idea of what Planning Council meetings were like. These transcripts will be referred to extensively in succeeding pages presenting more explicit arguments regarding levels of co-optation and rationales for the successes and failures of joint decision making.

Planning Council meetings were attended by three to five managers and six to eight workers, plus myself (or my replacement) and an administrative assistant who took minutes. Guests attended periodically, but numbers were limited by the size of the meeting room. The chair was rotated among a list of volunteers, many of whom were workers. Meetings were held approximately every other week and usually lasted three hours. Several special meetings that included members, alternates, and additional managers were held at a local club.

The character of meetings varies a great deal. This was evident in the more than fifty Planning Council meetings I either attended or heard on tape recordings. Some meetings seemed to follow the Yugoslav pattern: reports, made mostly by managers or the QWL staff, followed by questions and limited discussion. Others, however, were freewheeling, lively discussions, debates, or brainstorming sessions interjected occasionally with humor or anger. There were polite and not so polite arguments, sometimes splitting along worker-management lines, sometimes not. We witnessed openness, honesty, enthusiasm, moments of self-reflection and compassion, and usually in the end a cooperative resolve. Although it is difficult to portray these phenomena adequately, meeting dialogues provide a number of graphic examples. Even within individual meetings there were dramatic shifts: calm cooperation following a heated conflict; jokes and laughter following a period of nervous tension; or, as in the first transcript, concerning the drug problem in the plants, an active, enthusiastic explosion of participation following a tedious, disastrous hour-long attempt to construct a memo by full committee. On 11 June 1975, following some references by workers to the drug problem within the company, this dialogue ensued:

SALES MANAGER: Well, we should remember we're on tape; but if people are out there smoking grass at break times, or shooting drugs or whatever....

TOOL AND DIE MAKER: Christ, you have no idea!

Q/A [Quality Assurance]: Wait a minute.

FURNITURE INSTALLATION LEAD: Well, there is a certain amount of that thing.

SALES MANAGER: But it defeats the attitude of those that are really dedicated.

Q/A: Let me tell you the problem. The problem is we are building a craft product; it's a craft, but it is on the assembly line. Production, production, production, more, more, more, where people don't have time to sit back and do a good job on it. They don't have any idea what they're building; they don't care what they are building! So what do they do ... they just say fuck it.

SALES MANAGER: The company is growing bigger....

Q/A: We'd be better if we had ten little factories rather than one big one.

FURNITURE INSTALLATION LEAD: Exactly. There are jobs that people do that I could do stoned out of my mind. I mean on whatever drug you want to shoot into your arm. So a lot of people think I might as well be stoned out of my mind as not.

FURNITURE ASSEMBLER: A lot of people don't care.... [*Cites several examples.*]

FURNITURE INSTALLATION LEAD: [*Loudly, over three voices.*] I can cite you example after example of sheer depression that I see on the line. I mean, I see things that happen that I say Jesus Christ! I've seen people take hammers to things. There are certain needs out on the line that this company is not meeting, and they are hurting themsleves by not meeting them.

As often happened when the debate wound down, a "rational" management approach now took over; a list of problems was drawn up for the manufacturing engineer to investigate further.

There were also times when arguments became hostile—sometimes between workers, and sometimes workers against managers. The following transcript (17 June 1975) suggests the frankness of discussion and reveals one tough factory worker pitted against the whole council. For review, priorities for council projects were set first by listing the problems members wanted the council to work on (in a brainstorming session); then discussing each of the twenty-two items for about twenty minutes to define the problem; then voting on the list, with each council member allocating twelve votes across the twenty-two items. This process led to the four-day work week (the subject of this argument) being ranked sixth. Two weeks later, an unofficial poll was taken in one of the plants, and the fiery lead of the rework section (which repairs products that failed inspection) brought the results to the council. These are the highlights of the thirty-minute discussion that followed:

REWORK LEAD: I'd like to find out about this four-day work week. At least why we aren't going to talk about it.

FURNITURE INSTALLATION LEAD: It seems to me it was stated that we are working on it. I don't think we can let a certain group of people dictate to us what we should and shouldn't be doing.

REWORK LEAD: If we're not here to respond to the people, what are we here for? Are you a representative or what?

FURNITURE INSTALLATION LEAD: [*Angrily.*] We keep going over the same thing.

REWORK LEAD: Yeah, we've been going over the same thing, whether to issue something like this.

FURNITURE INSTALLATION LEAD: There is no way we can satisfy each little community in each plant, you know; everyone has specific things that are bothering him . . . We are trying to take this in an orderly way. If we get off the track, we'll never solve anyone's problem.

REWORK LEAD: What little community? We're talking about 95% of the plant. What I want to know is what I'm going to tell my people.

MANAGER OF MANUFACTURING ENGINEERING: I haven't attended all the meetings, but I thought we agreed this was down the list. Of all the things on the list, the four-day work week is the most complex and would take the longest time; therefore, it was decided to consider something else first.

TECHNICAL WRITER: To me this is evidence of something we discussed before. If we made a decision, were we willing to stick by it? Now we set up a list of priorities . . . we voted . . . O.K., those three top priorities have been set up, and we have to stick to them.

REWORK LEAD: You already. . . .

TECHNICAL WRITER: Wait a minute. . . .

REWORK LEAD: You already changed the list.

FURNITURE FINISHER: [*Sarcastically.*] No, we didn't.

REWORK LEAD:How may times? My point is that those people want us to work on the four-day week, and no one seems to be willing to do anything about that.

Q/A: [*Loudly.*] That is why we set priorities—so we could work at these things in order.

REWORK LEAD: I thought we also decided that we could change anything we decided on at any time.

TECHNICAL WRITER: Sure, so let's take a vote.

REWORK LEAD: I don't want to take a vote, since I know right away it would be defeated.

DIRECTOR OF EMPLOYEE RELATIONS: The problem I see with what I think to be your point of view has to do with the whole question of priorities.

REWORK LEAD: Yeah, that's what this is. [*Waves petition.*]

DIRECTOR OF EMPLOYEE RELATIONS: But [*raising his voice*] the employees didn't vote on any priorities—the numbers you're citing are strictly one issue, employees saying they would like or not like that issue. We have no idea what might come up if we asked the same question about all those other things. Trying to take the data. . . .

REWORK LEAD: [*Breaking in.*] Well, I. . . .

DIRECTOR OF EMPLOYEE RELATIONS: [*Sharply.*] If I may . . . trying to take the data on how employees feel about one issue and translating that into what our priorities should be seems to me totally fallacious.

REWORK LEAD: I'm responding to my people. I think people are afraid to talk about this issue.

FURNITURE FINISHER: I think this is ridiculous. We decided on a way to work. I can't see us regressing and going over and over it.

[*Another fifteen minutes of frustrating discussion followed.*]

DIRECTOR OF EMPLOYEE RELATIONS: I asked if you had any specific recommendations or if you intended to raise our general consciousness about that issue.

REWORK LEAD: No, raise your general consciousness, but. . . .

DIRECTOR OF EMPLOYEE RELATIONS: You've succeeded in that. Now, can we move on!

The director of employee relations was chairing the meeting. His last remark was not a question.

As an example of worker-management arguments, consider this single episode in a whole series of discussions on worker-supervisor relations and the inadequacy of the grievance procedure (24 September 1975):[4]

TOOL AND DIE MAKER: There is so much that can be done to improve the quality of working life at the department level, but supervisors don't want to take it upon themselves, or whatever, to do it.

TECHNICAL WRITER: I don't know if they can, though.

TOOL AND DIE MAKER: Why can't they?

ADMINISTRATIVE SERVICES MANAGER: In my area. . . .

Q/A SUPERVISOR: [*Breaking in, loudly.*] You've got to sit down and do it. If you don't have that openness between the hourly worker and supervisor, if you don't have that, you got problems.

TOOL AND DIE MAKER: One of the first things I brought out, meeting one, page one, there isn't that openness between an employee and his supervisor.

Q/A SUPERVISOR: [*At the same time.*] There should be.

TOOL AND DIE MAKER: And there never will be! [*Voice rising.*]

Q/A SUPERVISOR: [*Loudly.*] There should be. Any time I want to walk into [vice-president's name] office or [president's name] office, I call them and walk in there and talk to the guys.

TOOL AND DIE MAKER: Where are you on that ladder?

Q/A SUPERVISOR: It doesn't make any difference.

TOOL AND DIE MAKER: It makes a difference to the guys down here.

Q/A SUPERVISOR: No, sir, any time any of my employees want to talk to me, I come down here at 11:00 at night and talk to them.

WITTE: [*Angrily.*] All right, [Q/A supervisor's name], I—I. . . .

Q/A SUPERVISOR: So that openness is out there. Any time you want to talk to your boss, does he turn you down?

MARKETING CLERK: It does depend on your supervisor.

TOOL AND DIE MAKER: That depends on your supervisor.

WITTE: In my interviews I asked people about major disagreements with supervisors, and then I asked them what they did when they disagreed.

Q/A SUPERVISOR: O.K.

WITTE: Thirty percent said nothing! Nothing: I don't do a damn thing.

ADMINISTRATIVE SERVICES MANAGER: How many of that percent would do something, even if QWL did some magic thing?

WITTE: No, I don't know if they would, but there is something causing 30% of the people to not go and do anything when there is a major disagreement between themselves and their supervisor.

Q/A SUPERVISOR: There is always a way.

WITTE: [*Breaking in.*] There's something causing that. I don't know how much you can reduce it—maybe you can't—but also to say everyone has this great faith and openness with their supervisors is just not true.

ADMINISTRATIVE SERVICES MANAGER: [*Angrily.*] Well, not everyone.

Q/A SUPERVISOR: Not everyone, but the opportunity is there. You can have it. If you're not satisfied with what your supervisor said, you can go one step higher and. . . .

TOOL AND DIE MAKER: O.K., wait a minute here; what if you're an assembler out here and you have an argument with your supervisor?

Q/A SUPERVISOR: Sure.

TOOL AND DIE MAKER: Now, you don't like what your supervisor said. O.K., now you go to [inaudible] office or whoever's next up the line; O.K., so you go to superintendent's office; you don't like what [superintendent's name] says, so you go to [plant manager's name], right?

Q/A SUPERVISOR: Right, right.

TOOL AND DIE MAKER: What are your chances with supervisor X and [superintendent's name] from that day on?

Q/A SUPERVISOR: Sooner or later you're going to get an explanation. . . .

TOOL AND DIE MAKER: [*Breaking in loudly.*] Sooner or later you're going to get it!

[*Laughter.*]

Q/A SUPERVISOR: No, no, you're not going to get it. . . .

ASSEMBLER: Yes, you are.

SALES CLERK: Right.

[*Meeting broke up into side conversations, loud talk, and some laughter.*]

Q/A SUPERVISOR: Sooner or later, you're going to get an explanation that it's totally justified, that. . . .

[Laughter.]

TECHNICAL WRITER: I've heard that before.

ADMINISTRATIVE SERVICES MANAGER: Unless it's way out.

MARKETING CLERK: What if you feel it's not way out, and they keep telling you it *is* way out? Where do you go?

TOOL AND DIE MAKER: You go over a supervisor's head with something, and you're on thin ice from that day on. You're on the shit list, number one.

MARKETING CLERK: And it's something that's not written; it's something that's not said; it's just there; it's like that invisible curtain, you can almost reach out and touch it.

MANUFACTURING SUPERINTENDENT: Look, I've heard this before, and I've been here two years; and I don't think there's that much of it. . . .

TECHNICAL WRITER: I could actually sit here and name some names of people who do it. They don't have to necessarily can you; they can just make it; they can give you the crap job. And—and it'll get to a point where you'll want to quit. And that's all it takes; they don't have to can you; they can make it so rough that you'll want to quit, and I've seen it happen. I could name names, but I don't want to do it; I'll keep my mouth shut.

FURNITURE FINISHER: Where I'm at, it's been going on for two years. Anyone who's been there two years or more will not go to their supervisor. They're not going to go . . . they don't trust them, and they don't like them.

Q/A SUPERVISOR: I think the company overall has given *total* respect for the hourly employee and his craftsmanship. . . . And I'm not giving you some line out there; I'm just telling you exactly how I feel about it.

FURNITURE FINISHER: Well, that's what you feel about it.

Q/A SUPERVISOR: Yeah, sure.

FURNITURE FINISHER: But when I go to work, I don't work for SI; I work for [supervisor's name]. I work for him and not SI.

TOOL AND DIE MAKER: That's right!

Finally, let us look at this bitter discussion [4 February 1976] of the council's involvement in planning the design and move into the new SI facilities. There had been five minutes of argument on unconfirmed rumors about moving. The focus was a task force set up independently by the president to coordinate the move.

TOOL AND DIE MAKER: This move has been in the wind for the three or four years I've been here. We were told that when the move gets down the line, we were going to have a lot to do with it. Now they've set up another committee. We were never advised who's on the committee, what their function, or anything else; but the rumor's out, and we have to explain this committee.

ADMINISTRATIVE SERVICES MANAGER: That's not true.

TOOL AND DIE MAKER: I was never—we were. . . .

ADMINISTRATIVE SERVICES MANAGER: Last week [manager of manufacturing engineering's name] and [director of employee relations' name] went through the committee.

TOOL AND DIE MAKER: I never heard who is on the committee, never heard what their function is, what they do, who they represent.

[A chorus of voices that are indistinguishable.]

Q/A SUPERVISOR: Well, we're not involved.

ADMINISTRATIVE SERVICES MANAGER: Well, what do you want? There are representatives from each department.

TOOL AND DIE MAKER: Who are they?

FURNITURE ASSEMBLER: Who chose them?

ADMINISTRATIVE SERVICES MANAGER: Well, the committee's only met once.

[A number of indistinguishable voices.]

TOOL AND DIE MAKER: Wait a minute, can I say something! Who, how were they chosen? Who do they represent? How are they going to work?

[More indistinguishable voices.]

TECHNICAL WRITER: O.K., hold it. Can I say something? O.K., I have nothing against the committee being formed, regardless of who formed it; but... you've said you can't give somebody an obvious choice of what they want [in laying out the facilities, etc.] because it hasn't materialized yet; it hasn't been totally confirmed that we are moving. And if that hasn't been totally confirmed, then start a task force. That in itself is saying we are anticipating the move... it represents that idea; it presents that idea.

ADMINISTRATIVE SERVICES MANAGER: You have to start somewhere. The task force was started because they have expertise in those areas. It began with proposals; they aren't going to go in there and lay out the whole area.

TECHNICAL WRITER: I know, I know, I realize that; but the thing is it was done.

ADMINISTRATIVE SERVICES MANAGER: *[Breaking in.]* QWL hasn't been involved yet. *[Voices come in, then over the voices.]* I mean, at what point do you jump in? At what point do you bring in 1,300 people? What do you use as a vehicle to communicate with them?

INDISTINGUISHABLE SPEAKERS: Great. All right. Hold it. That's ridiculous.

TECHNICAL WRITER: O.K., maybe the QWL Council isn't involved; but we're faced, as representatives, with having to answer questions.

MARKETING CLERK: *[In the background]*. Right, we are involved.

TECHNICAL WRITER: And without even knowing why, who, and when the task force was appointed.

ADMINISTRATIVE SERVICES MANAGER: If it wasn't clear last meeting, I would have imagined you would have asked.

TECHNICAL WRITER: I wasn't here.

TOOL AND DIE MAKER: Last meeting that committee was. . . .

ADMINISTRATIVE SERVICES MANAGER: [*At the same time.*] That committee has met once.

TOOL AND DIE MAKER: [Manager of manufacturing engineering's name] said there's been a task force to look into it; that is all that was said. Nobody said who was on it, how they were chosen, what their function was, or anything else. It's here in the minutes.

Q/A SUPERVISOR: It says from six departments in the minutes.

DIRECTOR OF EMPLOYEE RELATIONS: Let me add some information now that'll resolve some of the questions. [*Five-minute speech follows.*]

These transcripts hardly portray workers as docile incompetents, passively ratifying the proposals of managers. The workers challenge, they fight, and they are not easily fooled. In all transcripts they stuck to their positions, sometimes to the point of stubborn recalcitrance (e.g., the four-day work week battle). For the most part, positions were supported with logic, many times with logic superior to that of the managers (e.g., the grievance procedure debate). These transcripts reveal some of the more lively discussions, but they are not entirely atypical; and they clearly indicate the basic competence and perseverance of workers as well as the sense of equality that characterized most discussions.[5]

CONTENT ANALYSIS OF PLANNING COUNCIL MEETINGS

The preceding transcripts demonstrate that the Planning Council allowed healthy, honest debate and even obstinate clashes at times, and it stimulated openness and enthusiastic participation. However, although these dialogues suggest the style of the meetings and the limited nature of management control, it is reasonable to question whether in fact they were not special cases and whether, over the long run, management was dominating participation, setting the agenda of discussion, and initiating most activities. To resolve this question over an extended period, we carried out a detailed content analysis on all available Planning Council tapes covering the first two years of the program.[6] We examined (1) frequency of participation; (2) time of participation; (3) who made proposals; (4) whose proposals were accepted; (5) who supplied information as factual data; and (6) who made reports to the council. By recording these variables quantitatively, we are able not only to compare the participation of workers and managers at SI but also to gauge the degree of management control in comparison with earlier studies.

The results, displayed in terms of management/worker ratios, are presented along with comparable data from Yugoslavia in tables 14 and 15. The first table shows the absolute values, not considering the number of people present at a meeting. This gives us the overall ratio of management advantage (or disadvantage) in the meetings themselves. Table 15 takes

TABLE 14
Content Analysis: Absolute Ratios of Management Advantage

| Measure | Kolaja Study | | Adizes Study | | Obradović Study | SI Planning |
	Factory A	Factory B	Factory ABC	Factory XYZ	(20 Company Av.)	Council
Frequency of participation	1.94	.58	4.5	2.45	2.63	1.08
Time of participation	NA	NA	NA	NA	4.47	1.53
Number of proposals	2.55	1.51	.83	2.44	4.00	1.15
Proposals accepted*	NA	NA	NA	NA	3.33	1.70
Supplying information	NA	NA	15.5	5.67	NA	3.91

SOURCE: The figures for the Yugoslav studies are from Jiri Kolaja, *Workers' Councils: The Yugoslav Experience* (London: Tavistock, 1965); Ichak Adizes, "The Effect of Decentralization on Organizational Behavior: An Exploratory Study of the Yugoslav Self-Management System," Ph.D. dissertation, Columbia University, 1968; and Josip Obradović, "Distribution of Participation in the Process of Decision-Making on Problems Related to the Economic Activity of the Company," *Participation and Self-Management* 2 (1972): 137–64. For each measure, the entries represent management totals divided by worker totals. Thus, e.g., Kolaja found that managers as a group in Factory A talked 1.94 times as often as workers.

NOTE: "Proposals accepted" is the ratio of the percentage of management proposals accepted to the percentage of worker proposals accepted.

TABLE 15
Content Analysis: Per-Person Ratio of Management Advantage

| | Kolaja Study | | | | Adizes Study | | Obradović Study | SI Planning Council |
| | Workers' Council | | Management Board | | Workers' Council* | | Workers' Councils† | |
Measure	Factory A	Factory B	A	B	Factory ABC	Factory XYZ	(20 Company Av.)	
Frequency of participation	6.0	.90	4.85	9.71	14.0	3.79	3.94	1.77
Time of participation	NA	NA	NA	NA	NA	NA	6.71	2.51
Number of proposals	7.9	2.33	7.16	..‡	2.59	3.77	6.0	1.90
Supplying information	NA	NA	NA	NA	48.3	8.76	NA	6.41

NOTE: For each measure, the entries represent the totals per manager divided by total per worker; e.g., Kolaja found that, for Factory A, each manager spoke on the average 6.0 times more often than each worker on the Workers' Council.

*Council membership was estimated from Kolaja's study. This is appropriate because Adizes in fact replicated Kolaja's study ten years later. Factory ABC is A and XYZ is B.

†Computed using an estimate of 40% management, 60% workers. These estimates are conservative, because the percentage of worker members is usually higher.

‡Ratio not computable since managers made all thirty-one proposals over the year.

into consideration the number of people attending meetings (or estimates, in some of the Yugoslav cases) and is intended to judge participation on a per-person basis, thus giving us a better idea of individual capabilities. For all entries, a figure of 1.0 represents equality; those below 1.0 indicate worker advantage; those above, management advantage. Of the Yugoslav studies, Obradović's is more recent and far more extensive than those by Adizes and Kolaja.[7]

Several conclusions are self-evident. First, to a varying degree, managers clearly display an advantage in all the crucial aspects of decision making in all the companies studied.[8] Managers talk more often and account for significantly more time in discussions;[9] they make more proposals and have a higher percentage of their proposals accepted than do workers. Additionally, based on the SI study and the factories studied by Adizes, managers appear to have a very large advantage in supplying information in meetings. Second, the apparent advantage of managers at SI is much less than in the Yugoslav factories. With one exception, the ratios are lower in every category across all the factories, considering either absolute values or per-person ratios. Some of the differences are extreme. For example, comparisons with the Obradović study are impressive. SI's managers as a group spoke almost exactly as often as workers, but Yugoslav managers participated 2.63 times as often. The ratio is even greater for the total time of participation; SI managers spoke about one and one-half times as long as workers, but the comparative ratio for Yugoslav managers is nearly 4.5:1. Both the number of proposals and the ratio for acceptance of proposals show similar patterns: although there was near parity in making proposals at SI, managers made 80% of the proposals in Yugoslav worker councils. The same trends hold in relation to the per-person ratios in table 15. Thus for all measures, managers have something of an advantage in most cases, but joint decision making is much closer to equality at SI than in previous experiences in Yugoslavia.

These tables also reveal another important point, however: the management/worker ratios for contributing information in discussions. At SI, over a two-year period, managers contributed 3.91 times as many facts overall; and on a per-person basis, the average manager provided 6.41 times as much information as did the average worker. The comparable ratios in the Adizes Yugoslav study (the only other study that has measured this variable) are significantly higher. It appears that access to adequate information is a general problem of joint decision making.[10] At times the difference was great, the issue crucial, and the gap decisive in determining the outcome. Consider this discussion of Planning Council involvement in the annual wage review the first year (2 July 1975):

> REWORK LEAD: Does anyone know exactly what our role is? I guess I asked this last week, but I'm not really sure anybody knows what our role is, as far as the wage survey goes.

TECHNICAL WRITER: [Director of employee relations' name] did explain to us that maybe at some time, if things work out in that particular manner, that we may get involved in it.

REWORK LEAD: What? This year or next year?

TECHNICAL WRITER: Well, it would have to be next year. This one because there isn't enough time and because our understanding of it is, you know, really not enough to get involved in the short time to do it. They have a plan.

REWORK LEAD: [*Breaking in.*] Oh, I don't know, I understand my paycheck pretty well. I know I put in forty hours for a paycheck every week, and I'm sure everyone here does occasionally.

TECHNICAL WRITER: But actually grasping the understanding of how to do it. It would be a rather short period of time to learn exactly how to do it and do a good job of it. And we could really make a mess of it. It was made pretty clear by [director of employee relations's name] that maybe next year we might get involved if we start early.

REWORK LEAD: ...I don't know, maybe we should have some information in which to go on, you know, to look at. Maybe we won't be able to do anything, who knows?

FINANCE CLERK: It's not something you get into halfway.

VICE-PRESIDENT OF MANUFACTURING: Let me ask you a question, [rework lead's name].

REWORK LEAD: All right.

VICE-PRESIDENT OF MANUFACTURING: Do you understand all these things that are on this sheet today?

REWORK LEAD: No, not really.

VICE-PRESIDENT OF MANUFACTURING: Well, that's the whole program. If you don't understand that, then there's really no chance at making a contribution.... It could do more harm than good.

The resolution was never really carried through. Although in the next year's wage and benefit review the council's role was clearly increased, the expertise was still supplied almost solely by the Employee Relations Department. There is no question that workers' lack of information and expertise is a problem that requires further comment.

The knowledge required of workers in joint decision making takes two forms. The first is mastery of required practices, theories, and data, either in specialized functional areas or on specific problems. The laws on working hours, the procedures of a time-and-motion study, and the curing times of various epoxies are examples of this type of information. The second form of knowledge is less specific, more theoretical, and closer to what we might call "general business knowledge." It is usually the product of years of experience and study. It is the type of knowledge that is crucial in decisions concerning new ventures, where precise facts and figures provide only partial data; it is the ability to draw parallels to past events, and to suggest that this or that factor needs to be taken into consideration. This knowledge goes beyond intelligence or logical capability; it consists of the ability to draw on events and information that have been stored in the brain over a period of many years.

Workers are much more likely to be able to master specialized information than to match managers in general knowledge. At SI, there is evidence that workers took advantage of their experience on the council to reduce the information gap over time somewhat by acquiring specialized expertise in specific project areas. The trends over time depicted in table 16 (see p. 80) show a clear decline in the advantage held by management. This decline was the result of workers' involvement in subcommittees and, in some cases, assignment of responsibility for following up on problems brought up in meetings. In this way the workers began to acquire some specialized information. However, in most instances follow-up on proposals and projects was assigned to managers, because of their rank and centrality in the organization. The fact that the ratios measuring who supplied information in table 16 never drop below 4.25 reflects this limitation, as well as the continuous mangement advantage based on differences in generalized knowledge.

Further use of special-purpose committees and greater equality in assignments would tend to decrease the differences in specialized information. On the other hand, generalized knowledge is impossible to equalize and gives management an inherent advantage, especially in those areas most removed from the employee's experience. The only solutions are education and increasing the length of committee terms. However, even if these remedies were applied, policy-relevant information would never be equally distributed between workers and managers.

Although differences in knowledge affect the competence of workers somewhat, the general conclusion should not be forgotten. One doubts that even the most idealistic proponent of industrial democracy would predict that the participation of the average worker would be equal to that of managers. Managers will almost always have greater experience in public speaking and group dynamics and more practice in the formation of logical arguments. What the experience at SI shows is that these differences may not be overwhelming and that, over time, managers may not dominate joint decision making to the degree previous studies seem to indicate.

Unfortunately, since special-purpose committee meetings were not recorded, the detailed analysis derived for the Planning Council could not be replicated for other committees. However, observation of special-purpose committees over an eighteen-month period leads to the conclusion that there was even less co-optive behavior in most of these groups. Several factors support this contention. First, in most instances the ratio of workers to managers was greater than in the Planning Council (one group had no manager at all). More important, the narrower scope of responsibility made it possible for workers to accumulate and master the required knowledge and information. This same narrow, specific scope of responsibility also made it easier for these committees to fit into the existing organizational structure, thereby generating little management resistance. As I will discuss in more detail, this was not the case for the Planning Council, whose potentially broad (but not precisely specified) authority created a degree of opposition in the existing hierarchy. The drawback here, affecting both the council and special-purpose committees, was that in most cases these responsibilities were added to existing jobs, thus making it difficult to schedule meetings and to keep well-meaning but busy employees involved.

Explaining the Success of Joint Decision Making

Most of the inferences at the end of the last chapter—regarding the analysis of beliefs in participation and the characteristics of those who sought to become activists in the program—were negative in relation to the potential success of workers' participation. However, the experience at SI reported so far does not seem to warrant the degree of skepticism implied in those inferences. The task at hand is to explain the lack of co-optation and reinterpret some of the inferences based on the data in this chapter. Four factors are important in this explanation: (1) the range of cooperative goals between workers and managers; (2) the capability of workers to take initiative; (3) the capabilities and learning of worker representatives; and (4) the effects of what I will call frustrated ambition (perceived failure to meet advancement goals).

Cooperative Goals

All too often, scholars of industrial relations, particularly if trained in political science or sociology, treat the relationship between workers and managers as one of inevitably opposing forces struggling to obtain divergent goals. This situation was clearly noticeable at SI on certain subjects. On the other hand, for a large number of issues, either unanimous agreement was reached and cleavages did not form at all; or the cleavages were not along worker-management lines. The cooperative relationship resulted primarily from two factors, overlapping interests and empathy. For the majority of issues raised at SI, there was a great deal of common ground on which to base policy compromises. Some examples were drug use, plant security, inadequacies in the facilities, production difficulties (e.g., heavy lifting or other physical strain), and lack of training; these were problems concerning both workers and managers. Even on the issue of wages and benefits, there were strong incentives for lower- and middle-level managers to fight for increases on behalf of their employees.[11] I am not suggesting that workers and managers approached these problems from exactly the same point of view or with the same emphasis on potential solutions; however, it is important to realize that few issues led to battles between diametrically opposed forces divided along worker-management lines.

In cases in which either goals conflict or one party does not have a well-formed position, empathy can also lead to a cooperative outcome. This is particularly true for first-line supervisors, who in many cases have more in common with workers than with upper-level managers. Managers who have worked their way up from the shop floor are also sensitive to the problems of workers. At one point, the head of manufacturing engineering brought up the problem of unequal participation in some of the Planning Council meetings; several people were not saying anything at all. He concluded his comments with several stories that reflected his own fears about speaking before groups. His understanding of how the others felt had a noticeable effect. Several workers, one of whom spoke only broken English, began to talk much more often. In another instance, after a long argument over the relationship between workers and supervisors, in which the vice-president of manufacturing (who started at the company as a shop worker when there were only ten employees) had supported the supervisors as best he could, he finally broke down and said, "They need training. They come from within and don't know very much about supervising. That's why we're trying to get this training going. Hopefully, that will resolve some of these problems Paul and Manuel are talking about." One of the most vocal workers responded, "We understand that, Tony, and we agree; we were only trying to explain the fears people have sometimes." Even though the problem reemerged several times, an angry argument was defused; and the discussion turned to the cooperative goal of supervisory training.

Worker Initiatives

One of the most prominent characteristics of Planning Council meetings was the ability of workers to identify problems and convince the rest of the council that action was required. Analysis of the process by which this took place is instructive in that it exemplifies a specific set of advantages that workers have over managers; it also highlights the critical hurdles that must be overcome. In the usual sequence of events at SI, a worker, usually during "council interaction with employees" (see pp. 15–16), would present a problem that had been brought to him and sometimes make a specific proposal concerning it. If the problem was picked up, a discussion would ensue. Once the discussion was under way, the employees were very skillful, particularly in areas related to their own job experience, in persuading managers that the problem was real and deserved serious attention.

In issues precisely of this kind workers have access to information unavailable to managers.[12] They understand special conditions, know better what people are thinking, and comprehend the informal norms and behavior that govern the work site. As the transcripts on the drug problem and the grievance systems have shown, workers are skilled at turning this sort of knowledge to their advantage. Once this happens, a natural action orientation of managers takes over. Managers, particularly in manufacturing, are geared to "doing," to "solving," to making things happen. Although they may still have reservations about the severity of a problem or the likelihood of various solutions, once they agree that there *is* a problem, the stimulus for action leads at least to an investigation and quite often to proposals and solutions. These proposals may or may not lead to concrete changes. However, even when no changes result, the legitimacy of the process is maintained, at any rate in the short run, as long as a significant discussion and investigation have taken place.

Two factors were critical to the success of this process. First, the issue had to be considered an *acceptable agenda item*. Acceptability did not mean that positions on an issue were compatible or that goals were cooperative—only that the issue was appropriate for discussion within the decision-making group. The wide and informally defined scope of responsibility of the Planning Council, although leading to problems in other areas, ensured an initially broad interpretation of what was considered acceptable. In addition, several early procedural council decisions institutionalized this open format. That section of each council meeting devoted to interaction with employees was designed to maintain an open agenda. Also, the method used by the council to select and order major projects gave all members a fair chance to contribute to the working agenda.

The *style of presentation* was the other crucial factor in successful worker initiative. Demands, blunt refusals, or outward hostility usually led to defeat for either a manager or a worker. In one case, the assertive rework lead who was the center of attention in the discussion concerning the four-day work week questioned a policy of rehiring laid-off workers before the company was certain of an upward trend in sales. He suggested that management should maintain more flexibility through the use of overtime. However, in his address he used phrases like "the stupidest policy I've ever heard"; implied that the managers present were lying about the recovery in sales; and accused his fellow workers, who suggested that he wanted overtime for himself, of being cowards. As one might guess, the proposal never got off the ground. The issue was not really argued until a month later, when the corporate staff came to the same conclusion independently of the Planning Council proposal. An exactly opposite approach is seen in this proposal by a drill press operator, made in May 1976: "This suggestion may sound kind of wild; I'm not sure what we can do; but a group of people came to me and suggested we switch working hours in our plant to 7:00 A.M. I don't know what we have to do to look into this, but I think we should consider it." This low-key, conciliatory introduction enabled members to discuss the item and gave the drill press operator and several others a chance to present persuasive arguments. The results over the next five months included referenda in each plant leading to changes in hours on all but one shift (which voted it down), serious consideration of flex-time for office areas, and the beginning of a serious study of the four-day work week. The latter two proposals were still opposed by top management; but once the question of working hours had been opened up, pressure from the council and the work force expanded the discussion.

The fact that most workers either naturally accepted this diplomatic style or learned to accept it was useful to the council. This environment also allowed management to be persuasive on items they initiated. It is not unlikely that the high levels of political activism and commitment to democratic values which characterize activists are partly responsible for this style. This association would tend to counter the negative inferences that such characteristics might lead to excessive compromise when opposition is required.

Capability and Learning

Given the workers' initial confusion about and lack of experience in any form of organizational democracy, managers will very probably dominate joint decision-making groups at their beginning. The question is whether worker representatives can learn decision-making techniques and increase their knowledge sufficiently to participate on a relatively equal footing with managers. For the experiments at SI, the answer is yes. Trends over time in the statistics on participation derived from the content analysis of Planning Council meetings demonstrate a clear learning effect on worker members. The results, expressed as per-person ratios of management advantage and aggregated by quarters over the two-year period, are presented in table 16. Both measures of participation (frequency and time) reveal an interesting pattern that is repeated independently for each council.[13] Surprisingly, initial participation by workers is quite high, but the second quarter shows a great deal more participation by managers than by workers. This trend then reverses, and participation by workers increases; so that for both years the ratios in the last quarter are lowest. The same pattern is evident in the ratio of proposals made by managers and workers, respectively.

Essentially, what happened was that workers were very excited at the beginning of their terms, and participation and suggested proposals were very high. At the same time, realizing the democratic intent of the council, managers would hold back for fear of dominating discussions. However,

TABLE 16

Changes over Time in the Ratios of Management Advantage in the Planning Council (by Quarter)

Measure	First Council, 1975–76				Second Council, 1976–77			
	1st	2d	3d	4th	1st	2d	3d	4th
Frequency of participation	1.59	2.02	1.87	1.46	1.42	2.58	1.75	1.36
Time of participation	2.09	2.82	2.53	1.86	2.39	3.21	2.67	2.11
N proposals	1.66	2.05	1.85	1.40	1.49	3.58	2.33	1.49
Acceptance of proposals*	2.96	1.83	1.84	1.71	1.61	1.17	.75	.82
Supplying information	9.84	5.83	5.25	5.91	6.03	9.40	4.37	4.25

NOTE: With the exception noted below, all entries represent per-person ratios; i.e., the averages per manager divided by the averages per worker. E.g., in the first quarter of 1975, each manager supplied information 9.84 times more often than each worker. Entries for "Acceptance of proposals" are the ratio of the percentages of proposals accepted by managers divided by the percentage accepted by workers.

as the initial enthusiasm of the workers subsided and they began to realize that things would take longer to accomplish than they had initially expected, managers began to take charge both because they began making proposals of their own and because they began reporting on projects that had been set in motion.[14] The fact that this domination did not last is extremely important. Over time, workers acquired adequate background information (see the trend in table 16), lost their inhibitions about public speaking, and grew less dependent on management reporting. The workers also refined their skills of rational discussion and presentation.

The initial difference between workers and managers is critical here. The problem is one of style and logical construction. Managers are continually involved in discussions of what should be done, how, and for what reasons. Discussions among workers are quite different. A good example of this difference can be found in the heated discussion about the four-day work week (see p. 65). The style of the rework lead was rough, and the whole council reacted to it. Additionally, he was never quite able to tie his petition to an argument that priorities should be changed. Notice also that in the end the decisive speech made by the director of employee relations undermined the validity of the lead's evidence by suggesting that a poll on one issue is not equivalent to setting priorities among several issues. By the end of the year, workers were more likely to present proposals that had been carefully thought through and to propose them in such a way as to minimize implications of direct self-interest and emphasize benefits for the company. As can be seen in table 16, management's advantage in having proposals accepted declined dramatically over each year.

Education was an important factor both in the relatively equal initial participation ratios and in the learning process that took place. In Yugoslavia, which provides the only available comparative quantitative data, the difference in education levels between workers and managers is six to ten years. At SI, in most cases it was less than two years. It would appear that, from the point of view of ensuring balance in quantity and quality of participation, this education differential was beneficial. As one woman put it in an interview, "We elected people who could handle the job."

An important benefit of joint decision making was that the process proved to be an excellent training mechanism for leaders within the company, workers and managers alike. It offered workers a chance to learn about the company, gain experience in policy making, and acquire the managerial skills essential to group interaction. Much the same applied to supervisors and middle-level managers who, in a company the size of SI, had very little prior experience in policy formulation. Joint decision making gave more senior managers an opportunity to overcome the inevitable isolation that comes with top-level positions. By interacting with employees from all levels in the company, they were able to obtain a more balanced view of company operations. Upper-level managers were also able to get a firsthand look at individuals who might later be considered for promotion. Thus joint decision making both provided a possible advancement opportunity for the elected representatives and aided the company in identifying and developing potential leaders.

Frustrated Ambition

I have stated that workers who became activists at SI were a great deal more ambitious than the ordinary worker. I also emphasized the ominous potential of a situation in which workers, ambitious to get ahead in the company, engage in joint decision making with managers who will be involved in deciding their promotions. This inference, however, seems to contradict the conclusion that at SI managers did not dominate workers critically. The question is why joint decision making was as successful as it was, given that the workers on joint committees and the Planning Council were nearly all aspiring managers. The answer is simple; evidence for it is striking; and its implications are very important.

Although activists were consistently ambitious, they were sharply divided about their expectations of realizing their ambitions. Specifically, those individuals who were frustrated in their ambitions, frustrated by the prospect of not moving ahead in the organization, were critical actors in the QWL program. Because of basic differences in attitudes toward authority and democracy and in their behavior in joint decision-making sessions, these activists accounted for the vigorous debate and steady opposition to management that limited domination by the latter.

The first interviews conducted at SI made us realize the powerful effects of high ambition and low expectation of success. The interviews allowed the respondents numerous opportunities to vent their emotions. Individuals who desired strongly to get ahead and saw SI as a dead end were never reticent about their dissatisfaction. Their bitterness was most apparent in discussions of company management. This was primarily because those people who felt frustrated usually blamed specific superiors for blocking their own advancement. This frustration was central to their entire outlook, affecting views of their job and attitudes toward the company as a whole. The ambitious individual who disliked his current job but who also viewed his future in the company with promise would perceive his present job as temporary and therefore tolerable. The frustrated individual, ambitious as he was, usually also wanted to get out of his present job but saw no way of doing so.[15] The level and pervasiveness of hostility varied, of course, but was unmistakable. Nearly every person who vehemently expressed bitter dissatisfaction was at one time or another a victim of frustrated ambition.

The first wave of interviews demonstrates the differences in attitude for various combinations of ambition and expectations. A quantitative view of these differences is presented in figure 2. Since the measurements are somewhat limited and no linear multiplicative function is being proposed,[16] the nominal categories are appropriate. Because expectations

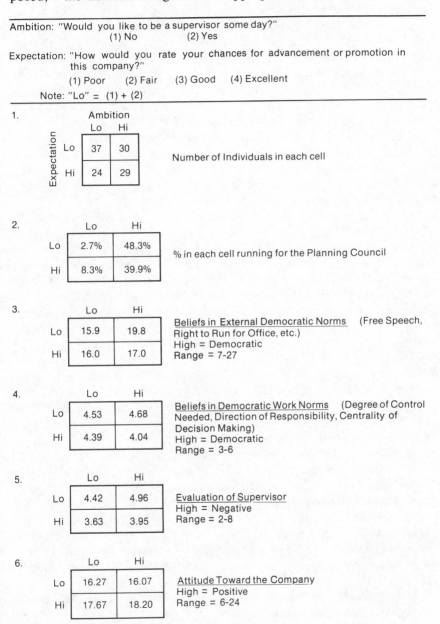

Ambition: "Would you like to be a supervisor some day?"
             (1) No   (2) Yes

Expectation: "How would you rate your chances for advancement or promotion in this company?"
             (1) Poor   (2) Fair   (3) Good   (4) Excellent

Note: "Lo" = (1) + (2)

1.   Ambition
                  Lo   Hi
        Lo | 37 | 30 |
        Hi | 24 | 29 | Number of Individuals in each cell

2.   Lo   Hi
        Lo | 2.7% | 48.3% |
        Hi | 8.3% | 39.9% | % in each cell running for the Planning Council

3.   Lo   Hi
        Lo | 15.9 | 19.8 | Beliefs in External Democratic Norms   (Free Speech,
        Hi | 16.0 | 17.0 | Right to Run for Office, etc.)
                                   High = Democratic
                                   Range = 7-27

4.   Lo   Hi
        Lo | 4.53 | 4.68 | Beliefs in Democratic Work Norms   (Degree of Control
        Hi | 4.39 | 4.04 | Needed, Direction of Responsibility, Centrality of
                                   Decision Making)
                                   High = Democratic
                                   Range = 3-6

5.   Lo   Hi
        Lo | 4.42 | 4.96 | Evaluation of Supervisor
        Hi | 3.63 | 3.95 | High = Negative
                                   Range = 2-8

6.   Lo   Hi
        Lo | 16.27 | 16.07 | Attitude Toward the Company
        Hi | 17.67 | 18.20 | High = Positive
                                   Range = 6-24

Figure 2. The Effects of Expectation on Ambition

were to be measured specifically in relation to the individual's job, the measure of ambition used was desire to become a supervisor rather than the combined ambition index used in previous chapters.[17] The results demonstrate clearly the difference effected by expectations in worker attitudes. The first two boxes of figure 2 show, respectively, the number of respondents in each cell (missing data points are excluded) and the dramatic effect of ambition on activism. The figures show a somewhat greater tendency to run for the council among those with frustrated ambitions than among those ambitious individuals who rated their chances of advancement as "good" or "excellent." This percentage difference in running for the council was also reflected in the final composition of the first council. In the second council, the percentage of frustrated workers was even higher. Nine of the eleven council members interviewed were in the "high ambition–low expectations" category. Thus there is a strong tendency among frustrated ambitious individuals to become activists in a participatory program.[18]

The difference that expectations make in attitudes is shown in boxes 3–6. For "beliefs in external democratic norms," frustrated ambitious individuals were not only significantly different from satisfied ambitious people ($t = 2.00$, $p < .05$) but also significantly higher than the entire population ($t = 2.72, p < .008$). On the scales measuring beliefs in democratic work norms,[19] evaluation of supervisor, and attitude toward the company, the relationship among all four cells varies somewhat; but in every case the statistical differences between frustrated ambitious and satisfied ambitious respondents is significant at the .01 level.

The fact that low expectations correlate with low evaluations of supervisors and negative attitudes toward the company needs little explanation. However, it is more difficult to explain why frustrated ambitious individuals tend to be more democratic in their orientations to both the external world and the organization of work. Several theoretical relationships are possible. It may be that a democratic outlook clashes strongly with accepted beliefs held by managers concerning appropriate organizational norms. This leads to conflict or at least to a superior's appraisal that the democratic individual is too unreliable or radical for a supervisory position. The individual is denied promotion, and his expectations drop.[20] On the other hand, it is also possible that the individual may endorse democratic forms of work organization as a vehicle to ensure his personal success. For example, several respondents stated that they would like to see workers elect supervisors, because they felt they themselves would be elected.

Unfortunately, after a number of attempts, we were not able in our analysis to distinguish between these motivations. It is probably inconsequential for this experiment, since the combined attitudes of hostility toward authority and belief in democratic values produced the required psychological mix to ensure fairly tough-minded, outspoken representation by workers. However, the question remains as to what would happen to these individuals if in fact they became leaders in a more democratic organization in the future. A primary commitment to democracy suggests one result, but perception of democracy as a vehicle for realizing one's personal ambitions leads to a totally different conclusion.

Since nearly all the activists in the program (with the exception of autonomous work groups) were ambitious, the differences in attitude suggest the possibility of fairly radical differences in behavior among activists. The first Planning Council, whose membership was evenly split between those with high and low expectations, provides some insight into behavioral differences. The statistics based on content analysis yield several interesting comparisons. Specifically, frustrated ambitious members spoke almost twice as often as their satisfied counterparts. Perhaps more important, frustrated members accounted for thirty-nine proposals made during the year, while members with higher expectations accounted for only twenty-two (with approximately equal rates of acceptance).

More significant than the numbers, however, was the style and tenacity of those representatives who saw themselves as victims of the meritocratic system. They participated with toughness when they felt it was necessary; they brought up nearly all the delicate issues; they were tenacious to the point of obstinacy in some instances; and when a situation was especially tense, they were usually the only ones who challenged management. A glimpse of this style is provided by the rework lead in the 17 June transcript or the tool and die maker in the transcripts from 24 September and 4 February. These ambitious council members all had low expectations about getting ahead at SI.

It is impossible to judge whether this behavior is based on hositlity born of frustration, boldness resulting from a belief that one has little to lose, or commitment to the role of democratic representative. However, there is little doubt that the toughness and anger brought to the sessions by these individuals were crucial in maintaining balance in the Planning Council. We may easily imagine that frustrated ambitious employees, sure byproducts of a pyramidal organization structure, may become increasingly numerous and vocal as rising educational levels produce rising expectations. The implications of this hypothesis will be discussed in chapter 10.

6. Joint Decision Making: Structural Impotence and Misrepresentation

Evaluating joint decision making is like working one's way through a complex maze with multiple entrances and exits. It is easy and tempting to exit by the shortest means, leaving a portion of the structure unexplored. The potential for joint decision making is apparent, and the drive for intellectual closure and symmetrical argument tempts one to leave it at that. However, to overlook the problems not only distorts the picture but also invites future failures that affect workers, managers, and the company as a whole. The problems discussed below vary in their significance and, most importantly, in their solutions. Several can be either eliminated completely or greatly reduced, while others appear to define the limits of joint decision making.

Structural impotence is a form of powerlessness within an organization. At SI, it took the form of transferring some decision making within the organization to democratically constituted committees but then restraining their influence, rendering them powerless on certain critical decisions. If this outcome had been engineered in advance by management, it would be a devious example of democratic illusion, but it could be overlooked as a quirk of another sham management experiment. That these problems were not intended but, rather, developed naturally is in many ways more devastating, because it suggests that such difficulties can be expected to recur in future experiments in industrial democracy.

Restraints came in two forms. The first was the limitation placed on discussions and actions in the Planning Council itself. I believe that this problem would have been much less acute in a unionized company. Union leaders, especially those with organizing experience, would recognize in the Planning Council management's arguments against formal grievance and wage committees as common tactics in the struggle to retain unilateral control over these crucial decisions. The second limitation placed on joint committees came not from within the committees themselves but out of the relationship between the traditional day-to-day structure of authority and the democratic committee structure. This problem is not so easily resolved as that of restricting discussions of certain "union type" issues.

STRUCTURAL IMPOTENCE
Restrained Issues

I have suggested that joint decision making is a useful mechanism for implementing innovations initiated either by workers or managers. I also argued that at SI the key to involving workers in that process lay in maintaining an open agenda, so that almost any item would be considered acceptable for discussion. Once the agenda had been opened up, workers were successful in demonstrating the validity of various problems, which in turn encouraged managers to support action in those areas. Although the general effectiveness of this process and its considerable potential in joint decision making must not be forgotten, for certain issues this process was severely limited. In several critical areas—most notably wages and grievances—there was no doubt that alternatives were controlled by the managers on the council, although discussion was open and lively, and workers were rarely persuaded to management's view.

Grievances   The formal grievance procedure at SI, specified by law, was a sequence of appeals up the management chain of command. It had only been used a few times in a number of years. Both the first and second Planning Councils experienced problems with grievance issues. During the very first sessions, representatives would bring to the council, among other things, individual problems raised by one employee in their areas (discrimination claims, wage and promotion problems, vacation scheduling, etc.). The council would discuss the problem briefly; at this point, one or another manager would usually suggest quite firmly that it was not the council's business but, rather, a matter between the supervisor and his employee, to be handled through the regular management chain of command. There would be dissent and argument by workers, which would lead to a general discussion of supervisor-employee relationships and the inadequacy of the existing grievance procedure. This process is exemplified quite well by the transcript from 24 September 1975 on page 66. Our content analysis shows that this sequence occurred five times in the first council and four in the second. These discussions were always lively, probably enlightening for managers; and they usually brought the individual's problem to someone's attention. However, they never led to the obvious solution of a specialized joint worker-management grievance committee, which was proposed on three separate occasions. The proposal was sidetracked each time for "future consideration" and never has been seriously considered.

As a result, employees remained at the mercy of an all-management grievance procedure; valuable meeting time was lost; and the council encountered hostility from supervisors and middle-level managers who felt the council was itself acting as a grievance committee. The last two effects tended to aggravate already deeply rooted problems. The fact that the most obvious alternative was never really considered was disappointing. However, without a union, it would have been very difficult to legitimize such a grievance committee in any case. Many grievance issues are sensitive for managers, and even slight management dominance of a joint committee would have destroyed its credibility.[1] Union grievance machinery, with all its cumbersome formality, remains the only real alternative for adjudicating fairly these types of conflict.

Wages   Wage, salary, and benefit increases composed the other area where decisions, open in theory, were in practice confined to a restricted set of alternatives. In the first year, it was suggested by managers on the council that, "due to lack of expertise," the council should review only the proposed changes and aid in communicating the changes to the work force. As in most decisions, this proposal was offered in "suggestion" form, not precisely defining the powers of the council. This vagueness was clarified abruptly when the rework lead I have cited before asked the critical questions point-blank, on 17 June 1975.

> REWORK LEAD: Does this council have some power as to the say-so of the rates of increases?
> DIRECTOR OF EMPLOYEE RELATIONS: Well . . . that really hasn't been decided one way or another.
> REWORK LEAD: But if we decide, then we do have the power?
> DIRECTOR OF EMPLOYEE RELATIONS: [*Quickly and firmly.*] No!
> REWORK LEAD: No? O.K., that's what I wanted to know.
> DIRECTOR OF EMPLOYEE RELATIONS: [*Softly.*] There's been no decision made as to how much decision-making power the Planning Council should have in that kind of issue. Clearly, going in . . . it was agreed that employees should share in any increase in profits and productivity that come out of things we do. I think that's a different thing than the Planning Council having any final say on any general wage increase before the program is really active.

The understanding reached was that in the second year the council, or another joint committee, would be involved further after being trained in some aspects of wage and salary administration.

During the second year, the council voted early in its term to become involved in analyzing internal job classifications, comparing wage levels with outside surveys, reviewing benefit changes, and communicating such changes to the work force. It voted *not* to get involved in setting the percentage of increase or conducting external surveys. In fact little training was conducted; and participation was only effective on the questions of benefits (where management split) and job classifications, which latter (as it happened) were done by a council member who was a management trainee. When discussions of individual rate changes came up and council members began to question increases in certain areas, the director of employee relations suggested that these questions be taken up in the appropriate facility in a meeting with the plant management. Although no direct information on these meetings was obtainable, it is doubtful that one or two council members could have been successful in establishing a case that went against the wishes of supervision.[2]

Failure to establish a formal committee to ensure participation was the basic problem. Without such a mechanism, the normal routine was followed; and most critical decisions were made by Employee Relations in consultation with the management hierarchy. It is difficult to judge whether failure to take this rather obvious step was intentional or simply a case of neglect until it was too late. However, it is clear that workers lacked the power to force the issue. As one council member put it, "When push came to shove on that wage thing, we didn't have either."[3]

Subtle control   It is important to understand the finesse with which managers dominated these issues. With the one exception of the direct response to involvement in the first year's wage increase described above, there were no direct vetoes; nor was there any direct pressure on individuals. The arguments always suggested the complexity of the issues, relying on subtle threats only when necessary. Consider the following examples:

In talking about communication of council activities, after a heated grievance discussion, the manager of manufacturing engineering made the following suggestion and not specifically directed criticism: "You know, I think it would be a good idea to identify the names of speakers in the minutes; it might help to cut down on the pretty irresponsible statements coming out of here. You know, unless you believe what you say, don't say it." Again, following a complaint about the salaried increase for 1975, a manufacturing superintendent stated, "We've discussed this before, about the rate structure. This is the closest thing to a union I've seen if the QWL committee is going to go in and say, hey, we want more money for the folks out in the shop. Personally, I want no part of it. I've been into wages, and it takes a hell of a lot of work; and without us, all of us, putting in a hell of a lot of time, I don't think we're qualified to do it." In response to an employee suggestion that rate ranges could be improved because profits were up and SI's profit margin was higher than competitors', the head of manufacturing engineering initiated the following dialogue:

MANAGER OF MANUFACTURING ENGINEERING: It works for [president's name] just like for anybody else. There's just so many people available. It's a competitive market for presidents of companies. If it's necessary to raise a salary to attract someone to the job, then he is going to get a raise . . . and it's the same way with an assembler, an installer . . . it's what's the available market.

MARKETING CLERK: So you're saying that there are so many people available to fill the lower positions, and so as a result the people holding these positions [*voice rising*], doing an excellent job [*almost shouting*], are penalized for that very reason because they are easily replaced?

MANAGER OF MANUFACTURING ENGINEERING: The same way.

MARKETING CLERK: But God, you're losing time and money invested in your employees.

MANAGER OF MANUFACTURING ENGINEERING: Every employee has a right to go out and fight for a job.

[*An argument ensued, and the manager, somewhat unsuccessful in explaining the benefits of the labor market to the workers, took a more direct approach.*]

There's a company called the Champion Paper Company that's kind of like SI—excellent product, profit-making company—that took that philosophy, and they didn't set limits on the salaries of their people; so they were some of the highest-paid workers in the world. The company eventually went bankrupt and went into receivership; and when a new man came in to take over the company, he had to fire all those people because they couldn't make a profit, because of the competitive market. . . . This is a profit-making organization. There are limitations on what you can expend, or you price yourself right out of the market.

There was a long silence; then the director of employee relations made a more moderate speech supporting rate limits, and the subject was changed.

The answer to both the grievance and wage issues would be creation of permanent, formal committees with explicit powers to deal with the issues. Managers feared this; first because it would have the appearance of a union (and what is appearance one day may be reality the next); second, because without formal structures, without specifically defined responsibilities and authority, inevitably decisions would be made by those currently in control—in this case, the existing management. Serious worker participation was resisted by management on the wage issue because of its obvious importance in corporate profits; on the grievance issue, because it represented the essence of management control at the supervisory level.

In the vast majority of cases, participation in these issues on an ad hoc basis will eventually be subverted, forgotten, or shunted off to a group in which management domination is ensured.[4] Without the job security and advancement guarantees afforded by a union, even the most active, hostile workers will eventually give up; while more timid workers, protecting their futures with the company, will subside much earlier. One council member who was interviewed in depth described the phenomenon as more extensive: "You see, there's a little bit of fear out there; you know when a good issue is brought up and there's going to be good talk, nobody ever says anything. Any time an issue comes up that's important, it always gets buried." I asked him why he thought people were afraid to speak out, and he replied, "I don't know—job minded. They aren't thinking about why they're in the room there, but maybe they're thinking about their own job; maybe they are a little leery about it. If they say anything, they won't be able to advance."

It was not that these employees lacked the capability to argue such questions, or that they were persuaded to accept management's point of view; it was simply that they lacked the formal mandate and the organizational power of a union—power necessary to provide a degree of security and a more equitable basis on which to resolve these conflicting issues. Economic questions, grievances, and other traditional collective-bargaining items must be resolved through negotiation that takes place apart from a central joint decision-making structure. Although I agree with Blumberg that a joint worker-management policy-level committee can coexist with a strong union,[5] the union is absolutely essential. Without it, democracy at work will always be tilted against the worker, especially in those areas of greatest concern to the majority of employees.[6]

Dual hierarchies·

Joint committees, whether general policy-making councils or bodies designed to coordinate a narrow range of activities, form an addition to the existing day-to-day structure of authority and responsibility in the corporation. Unless these committees are formally constituted, with well-defined areas of responsibility and a clear demarcation of power, the resulting confusion and inevitable overlap between this structure and the existing management chain will create a tension that affects the operation of both structures. The Planning Council at SI, which was only informally constituted, suffered from just this sort of tension. Frustration occurred in both directions: the council lost influence over projects that at least some of the membership felt were rightfully theirs, and management reacted with hostility to what it felt was encroachment on its sphere of influence.

Council dependence on the existing structure   An excellent example of the Planning Council's reaction to its own loss of power is seen in the transcript from 4 February 1976 presented earlier. Here the employee council members reacted strongly to the formation of a management committee to coordinate the design of and move to the new facility. As stated, this issue was associated with the QWL program from its beginning; and it was high on the list of decisions in which workers and managers alike believed workers should be involved (fig. 1, p. 29). Thus, when a committee was organized independently by management (in this case, by the company president), the reaction was swift and vocal—and in this instance it was effective, in that the council became significantly involved in establishing procedures to ensure worker participation in facility questions.

The important point is not the incident itself but how the siutation arose. In this case, as in similar instances, the president did not deliberately set out to undercut the council's power. When it had been decided to make the move, and the lease was to be signed, time became an important factor. Since the jurisdictional boundaries of the council had not been firmly drawn, the president used the regular management chain, as a matter of routine convenience and out of a conviction that he was in the best position to select the mix of expertise required by the "coordinating task force." Here the problem was that the council had not been consulted about the creation of the committee and the assignment of responsibilities. It was a tactical error, in that such a solution would have gained council approval easily.

The council would have ratified proposals delegating and centralizing responsibility for the move to the new facilities because on several similar projects they did precisely this on their own accord. Responsibility for the creation of specific working alternatives, as well as implementation of final decisions, must be delegated to a relatively small group of functional experts (or individuals who become functional experts). A large, diversified committee cannot assume such burdens. The council itself reached this conclusion on many occasions. Although there were arguments about the details, there was little active or repressed resistance to the process. The council learned early that (1) it was too big to design concrete proposals adequately; (2) it lacked the required expertise on many subjects; and therefore (3) it had to rely on the existing day-to-day structure for a great deal of expertise and almost all implementation.

Possibly the best example of this process is the council's handling of the training program. Training in all of its various forms ranked high in the council's vote on priority problems. After several lengthy discussions that proved interesting but were not well focused and were certainly indecisive, several managers began complaining about their time away from their jobs and "lack of direction." In a meeting in July, after a particularly bitter complaint, one of the most outspoken workers suggested that a committee be formed to work on training in order to save the council's time. He also stressed the fact that the council could not deal with this issue because it lacked expertise.

> The idea I had also of the subcommittee is that they have the—I don't know if you want to call it the power or authority—I guess it would be correct to call it authority—to pull in people from the plant with the expertise. In other words, on this training program, get in people with knowledge about training programs as to where they can get information or ideas to come up with these programs.... There's a lot of information out there. There just doesn't seem to be any way for us in here to get the information, for me to make that good a judgment.

When the suggestion was made that, in conjunction with forming a committee, an employee survey be conducted to assess training needs from the workers' point of view, the council member who made the initial suggestion above emphasized the limitation on direct participation imposed by the assumption of expert knowledge: "I don't really know if what we're looking for is what people want. We're looking for ideas that'll *work*. You know, I mean there are certain things that are going to be acceptable, certain ways of training people. And I think if we could get the expertise, we could probably—I don't think we need, really, suggestions of what they'd like."

This worker felt that establishing a committee was enough of a democratic structure. However, two weeks later, when the question was raised again, the issue focused not even on a committee but on hiring a training specialist to take charge of the program. The decisive speech in favor of hiring a specialist was made by the director of employee relations. However, the following comment by a manager in marketing (together with the director of employee relations the most consistently democratic management member of the council) provides the inner logic which leads inevitably to delegation of responsibility for projects. "There certainly is a lot to be done . . . . The question is, how do we get it done? Who's going to administer it? We don't have the time or the expertise. We'd have to acquire it. We don't have the time for this. If we had an expert who has, rather, the time to learn about SI, that would require less time and help us get an effective program going." His emphasis was not on the lack of expertise among worker members of the council but on the insufficient time available for all members to acquire the necessary expertise. The basic limitation is that of time and structural impotence, not co-optation.

A training specialist was interviewed by the council and management and was hired within two months. The obvious question of the council's further role came up in November. The following exchange was decisive in cutting operational ties between the council and the training program:

MANAGER OF ADMINISTRATIVE SERVICES: One of the primary things on the supervisory survey [of attitudes toward the QWL program] was that there was a number of supervision levels who felt we lacked directivity and that we are paralleling other efforts and procedures and activities and committees that are already in existence. If we get involved, there is a degree of redundancy. I don't think we should get directly involved in these things.

TOOL AND DIE MAKER: I think how much we get involved in these things is partly up to the group itself. Now we've set up this training thing. If [trainer's name] wants some assistance from us, that should be up to him and his group.

COMPUTER PROGRAMMER: Really, all we should be getting is feedback from that person or group. I mean, we set it up for them to take care of, and all we need to know is how are things going. . . . If he needed any help on anything, he would come to us, but otherwise he'd just let us know what's happening.

The programmer's position was adopted; the training director was conscientious about keeping the council informed of his activities and plans, but he was left essentially on his own. The council had other things to occupy its time. Thus the pressure of time and the need for continuous expertise limited the power of this and other committees, much as a legislature is limited by the bureaucracy. The difference is that in this case the bureaucracy had little incentive to behave democratically.

The loss of oversight by joint policymaking committees can create several problems. In the first place, programs that begin with the interests of workers firmly in mind may, when refined and implemented, reflect more the needs of managers and responsible departments than those of the work force. In the case of training, the program was designed along relatively democratic lines, because of the residual influence of the council and the general philosophy which had surrounded its creation. However, this cannot usually be assumed to be the case.

Second, realization of the limits formed by the need to delegate large areas of responsibility to existing functional units within the organization had a curiously frustrating effect on the council itself. Its role was to decide, first, what projects and problems should be undertaken. Once a decision had been made to work in a certain area, the problem to be corrected or the intention of a new policy was discussed, roughing out alternatives at the same time in order to gain a grasp of direction and focus. Inevitably, however, the crucial acts of designing specific proposals, implementing decisions, and monitoring the results were accomplished outside the council, having been parceled out to the existing corporate departments. For action-oriented individuals, being limited to the discussion and planning process was frustrating in itself, because it did not lead to immediate action on problems. This was particularly true for leads, supervisors, and managers involved in production, whose experience was geared to relatively short-range problems and action-based solutions.[7] High initial expectations concerning the council's influence, as well as how much would be accomplished, aggravated this problem. In evaluating their participation, 73% of the council members and alternates said their initial expectations were only partly or not at all satisfied. When asked to explain why they felt that way, 60% replied that they had expected things to happen faster.

Frustration also grew out of the fact that only occasionally did members feel the satisfaction of observing and admiring a completed task, the visible symbol serving the important function of psychological closure. This added to the feeling that nothing significant was being accomplished. The tension and frustration in each successive council increased, as initial hopes were darkened by the realization that only so much could be done and that the council's influence was inevitably limited.[8]

Council intrusion on the existing structure   Paradoxically, because of the dual hierarchy created by the existence of the Planning Council, any action they took became a second source of tension. That is, by taking action on almost any question, the council entered the domain of some existing organizational unit and hence encroached on the authority of day-to-day management. The organizational form of modern corporations is carefully designed to envelop activities, organized by place or function, in a web of authority and responsibility. This familiar hierarchical form serves three purposes: the direction and coordination of activities; the assignment of responsibility; and the resolution of conflicts in the organization. The first and second functions are premised on the familiar ideas of unity of command and clearly defined accountability. However, clarity and symmetry of design are never achieved in practice. Conflicts arise when responsibilities are shared and activities are interdependent: difficulties arise between shifts, between the engineers who create products and those whose job it is to produce them efficiently, between production schedulers and plant managers, between employee relations and supervisors over defining guidelines for hiring and firing, etc. These conflicts are resolved by a wide range of consultations between the affected parties and their supervisors. In cases of unresolved disputes, the pyramidal form of the corporate hierarchy provides a common superior to adjudicate the conflict. As long as the structure and the individuals involved are regarded as legitimate, hierarchy plays a crucial role in resolving the inevitable frictions that result from overlapping assignment of responsiblity.

Introduction of a jointly constituted, company-wide council with potentially unlimited and (more important) unspecified powers upset all three functions of the existing authority structure, to varying degrees. Least affected was the directive function of the existing management chain, although the shop floor work projects set up by the Planning Council were very difficult when these lines of authority were blurred. What made accountability difficult was that the council accentuated the already overlapping pattern. Since its exact powers and duties were not formally specified, it often provoked an indignant reaction from managers when it made a decision that affected their departments. On the other hand, there were times when responsibility for a proposed action was not clearly specified, and implementation, monitoring, and follow-up on decisions were not properly carried out. In other words, either the decision would run in the face of existing assignments, or it would fall through because no one was compelled to assume responsibility for it.[9]

However, the council ran into its worst difficulty in the domain of conflict resolution. I have mentioned that, when individual grievances were brought to the council, managers tended to restrain the issues. Employees (mostly workers, but in several instances supervisors as well) perceived the council as an alternative source for resolving conflicts in which they were involved. The existing grievance mechanism was clearly inadequate. However, management council members, claiming quite honestly that they were expressing the feelings of the rest of management, vigorously resisted council involvement in these issues. As the following series of speeches indicates, this problem persisted over the two-year period, and management council members took a fairly unified stand. On 22 October 1975:

> MARKETING CLERK: [*Chairing and opening the meeting.*] Any interactions?
> VICE-PRESIDENT OF MANUFACTURING: Yes. I had a talk—it may be insignificant—it's from the manager types in manufacturing, who are not QWL members. Their concern is that the QWL Council is being used somewhat as a sounding board for complaints and things that could be taken care of on the floor. And that possibly some direction could be given in that area so that when things come up that's not necessarily a QWL project, the person can be referred back to the managers and supervisor that's involved. They think they're getting left out and haven't had the opportunity to, uh, find out and solve the problems if there are any.

On 14 April 1976, during the first meeting of the second council, a worker member conveyed a tooling problem that was brought to him by a supervisor.

> MANUFACTUIRNG SUPERINTENDENT: Tooling? Ah, is this the responsibility of QWL? Ah, is it tooling?
> FINANCIAL CLERK: I figure it would be from the point of view of work improvement.
> MANUFACTURING SUPERINTENDENT: When somebody approaches me and says can the QWL program do this, the first thing I ask is if they've asked their supervisor about it? Ah, we could get into, I think we discussed this last year, the thing can turn into a bitch board.
> MACHINE SHOP OPERATOR: I've clearly run into this, trying to use me as a defense lawyer against the supervisor, and I'm in no position to handle those problems. . . . We can't get involved in that.

However, council involvement continued; and seven months later (10 November 1976) the director of employee relations succinctly summarized the general problem in reporting to the council a discussion about QWL at a dinner meeting of supervisors. "Some reservations that we expressed here, by managers—that QWL operates in a way other than the way we get the rest of the work done. There's a QWL Planning Council, which doesn't always link back to supervisors. The whole planning and direction left the company management out. They heard about it later. Also some concern about the same relation with workers; this group can't adequately represent the workers.'' The tension created by managers feeling left out of decisions that they perceive as their responsibility is common to many projects. Yet in most cases it occurs in shop floor experiments, and the tension is created at lower levels of supervision. At SI, the intrusion of joint decision-making committees was felt at all levels, and management resistance spread to all levels as well.[10]

In considering the structural impotence of the joint committee system, one important question has not yet been adequately explored. What types of decision triggered management resistance? The limiting influences described above were most apparent in decisions which threatened critical organizational norms by proposing permanent, formal shifts of influence within the corporation. The pattern extended beyond a few traditional union issues, however. Little enthusiasm in the work force and open hostility among leads and supervisors were generated by the idea, suggested several times, that workers should be involved in selecting their leads and possibly their supervisors. Evaluation of supervisors by employees was discussed by the director of employee relations after it ranked high on the Planning Council priority list, but it never received serious consideration in the council. Private conversations with supervisors indicated that, if this proposal had ever been put into effect, it would have been met by open rebellion. All of these proposals challenged the basic norm that leaders should be chosen and rewarded by those above them in the hierarchy.

Thus the issues that led to limiting the power of joint decision-making committees were those which implied permanent changes in the structure of authority, confusion about the principle that subordinates are responsible to their superiors, and a serious adjustment of management's right to determine rewards. These are all critical norms for traditional economic enterprises. The existence of the Planning Council was itself a potential threat to these norms. What success it enjoyed was due to a sensitivity to these boundaries, to an implicit agreement that the council work to improve the organization but not challenge its basic tenets.

MISREPRESENTATION

The employee members of the Planning Council represented 70–150 workers each (an average of 120). In comparison with a U.S. congressman or even a state legislator, the worker representative would seem to have an easy job determining the interests and opinions of constituents. Theoretically, the inability of the politician to communicate adequately with his constituents could be corrected in a work place democracy. The level of information and the intensity of interest should be greater in the work place because of workers' experience with specific issues and the direct effects of decisions. Reducing the size of the polity and the scope of issues should enable a representative to carry out the will of his constitutents and allow the latter to judge his performance. Yet at SI representation remained a severe problem.

In the preceding chapter two theoretical forms of misrepresentation were defined, optation and isolation. For the most part, isolation was the problem at SI. Representatives took their jobs very seriously. Even when it was stressed that the council and committees could act without initiation or approval of the work force, members continued to try to determine the wishes of their constituents. The real problem was one of isolation; of establishing adequate communication between the representatives and their constituents. Adequate communication requires three things: (1) outgoing information about what a decision-making body is doing; (2) articulation of interests to the decision makers in the form of opinions on what has been done, what is being considered, or what should be done; and (3) aggregation of incoming communications in terms of the frequency and intensity of the articulated interests.

Communicating Results

The problem of outgoing communication was difficult for all the joint committees, but particularly acute for the Planning Council, in which many different types of issues were covered—some briefly, some in depth. An initial concern was the establishment of procedures for communicating with employees. After several long discussions, it was decided not to post full meeting minutes, which at times covered five or more single-spaced pages. Instead, the council decided to post shorter summaries of the meetings (in English and Spanish) and distribute minutes only to the president's staff, council members, and alternates. It was argued that people would be more likely to read a shorter notice and that some might get incorrect ideas and expectations about issues that had been introduced but were only under discussion or had been rejected. To give full rationalizations and arguments behind the disposition of each issue would be impossible if minutes were to be kept to a reasonable length. Full minutes were distributed to the president and his staff because the council felt it necessary to keep them informed. However, no other managers received full minutes because it was felt that this would constitute special treatment vis-à-vis the rest of the work force. Also, names were omitted from the minutes, in the hope that people would then speak more freely. The somewhat restrictive nature of this series of decisions was mitigated by making the tape recordings of the meetings available to anyone and by creating a communication subcommittee to work continuously on the problems. This committee later added a number of written forms: occasional handouts to all employees, a continuing column in the newspaper, announcement posters, and special summary postings. In addition, several mass meetings were held either by plant or individual work sections early in the program. Representatives also held informal sessions with their constituents during breaks and lunch hours.

None of these measures seemed to work very well, and communication was a source of constant discussion and frustration. The first signs appeared in May 1975, only two months after the first council was elected. This description by a representative from the main plant, where communication was believed to be best, was quickly endorsed by four or five others (21 May): "Myself, I've noticed it out there. They say, 'Hey, I thought this was going to involve all of us. You guys are setting up some kind of a deal and closed group we can't get into.' You know, one guy came up and said, 'All you guys are is another management group. You aren't involving us, you're setting down rules and we're going to have to live with them.'" On 14 April 1976, during the first meeting of the second council, this dialogue occurred:

> MACHINE SHOP WORKER: Well, that comes from people not knowing what QWL is really about.
> ELECTRONICS ASSEMBLER: Well, that was because we were kept in the dark. A lot of people didn't know all the things QWL had done. Many of them didn't even know training was a part of QWL.
> FURNITURE ASSEMBLER LEAD: Well, there are a lot of people who really aren't sure what QWL can do, anyway. They don't know what we can do.
> FINANCIAL CLERK: I think that's something we have to determine here among ourselves, anyway. What our purpose is. What we will try to accomplish.
> MANUFACTURING SUPERINTENDENT: I'm here the second time around, and I want to find out myself. I've been here eighteen months, and I still don't know.

The final three comments in this last exchange suggest that confusion over the council's purpose aggravated the problem of communication and inaction.

The second council's solution to the communication problem was to open up its reporting. Full minutes were posted; speakers were identified; and the distribution of minutes was increased to include more managers and supervisors. Representatives were encouraged to talk to the people in their facilities about the program on a more regular basis. This process was aided by an expansion of more visible QWL activities, such as voting by all employees on working hours and participation in the new facility design. Unfortunately, there was little evidence of success in keeping people informed. In July 1976 the director of employee relations reported on his discussions with office workers concerning their attitude toward the QWL program. As before, he described apathy and confusion. "There was a lot of expression about the move, and their chance to participate; but they didn't link that with QWL. A lot of things are going on like that. People don't make the links back to the program." Near the end of November 1976, the problem was as serious as ever. A machine shop worker commented, "They know there is something there, but they don't know what we do . . . they don't see anything happening to them." A QWL staff member replied, "The problem is they don't have anyone telling them what's going on." Nearly everyone disagreed about the basic causes, but no one denied the severity of the problem.[11]

As with many of the findings reported in this study, the problem of communication seems pervasive across a number of international experiments. Mansell reports that at Supreme Aluminium in Canada "communications between representatives and their constituents . . . was one of the least successful aspects" of the project. Kolaja reaches a similar conclusion in relation to the Yugoslav companies he studied. "There was considerable evidence to the effect that council members, on returning to their jobs after a meeting, did conspicuously little reporting of the council's activities, and that workers showed little interest in obtaining such information." Finally, the British study on joint consultation included an entire chapter entitled "Reporting Back." It began as follows: "Even in firms where joint consultation seemed to have developed well and to have achieved important results, it was not unusual for investigators to be informed by the management that the difficult problem of reporting back to the rank and file had not been solved, and that interest was much less keen and widespread than it might have been. This was often supported by the opinion of workers representatives."[12]

This very general problem of communicating results is only half of the difficulty in establishing and maintaining a meaningful link between a representative and the work force.

Interest Articulation and Aggregation

Communication becomes a problem because of the limits on more direct forms of participation such as mass meetings, petitions or surveys, and referenda. If there was any area where worker members of the Planning Council were persuaded to accept management views, it was on the great costs and dubious benefits of mass meetings. Early in both councils, members pushed for more direct forms of participation, to solicit both general input and attitudes on specific issues. However, after several disappointing experiments with mass participation, the majority accepted the counterarguments. In the first place, participation was very uneven, with the more extraverted employees exerting greater influence. Second, it was difficult to interpret input in terms of intensity or degree of consensus. Third and most troublesome, it was very difficult to respond to the large numbers of suggestions and problems raised at these meetings. Expectations were raised, but the follow-up procedures were slow. The costs involved in mass meetings were always clear. Benefits could be challenged as vague, but dollar costs and production loss figures were accepted as concrete reality.

The single instance in which these objections did not prevail was participation in the design of the new facility. In a council session in April 1976, the head of manufacturing engineering opened a discussion about involving plant workers in the design with a pessimistic but not entirely inaccurate speech. "It's logistically impossible to get everyone involved in the layout. The different areas are related, and people don't see this. We need a plan by the engineers, then get feedback from leadmen and supervisors. After that we'll post the layout and ask people for their suggestions. If they have a suggestion, they can go to their supervisor." The council voted instead to include both a mass meeting with the whole plant to discuss the overall layout and meetings with each section to discuss details.

Similarly, the council rejected the use of petitions. The transcript from June 1975 (pp. 65–66) brings out some of the problems. Several people questioned the validity of informally drawn petitions or opinion surveys. However, the most telling argument was offered by a furniture finisher concerning the petition on the four-day work week: "There is no way we can satisfy each little community in each plant, you know; everyone has specific things that are bothering him. . . . We are trying to take this is an orderly way. If we get off the track, we'll never solve anyone's problem."

Later in the year, the subject of petitions came up again in a slightly different form. A new council member decided to pass out to the people on his shift a questionnaire relating to what the council should be doing and to some proposals currently being discussed. His supervisor concurred in his idea; but his superintendent, a council member, said it would have to be discussed in the council. The discussion (19 November 1975) was extremely bitter but clearly demonstrated the concern about getting too much participation. The shop worker had just been criticized for his proposed survey:

SHOP WORKER: Personally, I think that, uh, QWL is wasting time. You don't want to invite written suggestions, so how can you find out from people? And then you're only talking to people interested in QWL, and you're only talking to a minority of people; what is the purpose of QWL? Isn't it to invite suggestions from employees?

TECHNICAL WRITER: No.

SHOP WORKER: No? How can you improve the quality of working life without getting suggestions from the people? Do you think you know everything?

TECHNICAL WRITER: Can I answer that? Wait a minute! Can I answer that?

SHOP WORKER: You answered a lot of things last week that didn't make sense either.

TECHNICAL WRITER: [*Angrily.*] I can remember a few comments you made last week that didn't make sense either, if you want to get into that. If you can't understand that, number one, if people submit a suggestion and if it isn't followed through, they are going to lose hope.

SHOP WORKER: [*Speaking at the same time.*] If you can't explain to them, then you're not doing your job.

TECHNICAL WRITER: If you get a stack of suggestions, and all the people see no progress made—and you asked how this thing operates, it's not an easy thing.

SHOP WORKER: So, in effect, you're only taking suggestions from the people who are interested in seeking you out, rather than going looking for suggestions; you're waiting for someone to come to you.

TECHNICAL WRITER: Right, that's correct.

MARKETING MANAGER: Well, it's perfectly fair. You know we have found—I know, I myself, we had very noble ideas when we started this thing about specific things we wanted to accomplish; and we drew up a list, nominated a list of twenty-two topics and then voted on priorities; and we aren't halfway through the list yet. And some things have gotten accomplished and finished, and many are in progress, and many haven't been touched yet. It's beyond our scope to conceive of taking on another whole shopping list of things which we can't really consider because of the logistics of it, the practicality of it. And the more things we take on, like if we go out and solicit all things they'd like to have done, many of which are possible and a great many of which are not; in any case, whether they're valid or not, we won't get to them for a long time, and they're going to be more dissatisfied thinking that if we solicited them, we're going to do something about them.

In the end, the principal mode of input was the list of verbal interactions between employees and council members considered at the beginning of each meeting. This solution had two drawbacks: (1) it allowed managers to restrain important issues; and (2) the council interaction section of meetings took a great deal of time and thus created a feeling of inactivity and frustration. In the first case some individuals, usually supervisory members, took advantage of the inherent problems of aggregating interests and continually interrogated workers as to how many people were involved in a specific suggestion or proposal. This became nearly the standard response of two or three management members to everything that resembled a personal problem, but the technique was also used to constrain other important issues. For example, the following discussion took place on 30 July 1975. It was initiated by a woman Q/A who was respected by the group for her unquestioned honesty and sincerity.

TOOL AND DIE MAKER: [*Chairing.*] O.K., should we go down to interactions? Any interactions with employees? Yes?

Q/A: Oh, O.K., I got a [garbled] from the machine shop. They want to know QWL's opinion, or if QWL will help them. They want a union!

[*A pregnant pause, then low, nervous laughter getting louder, then a whistle, then chatter all over the room.*]

MANUFACTURING SUPERINTENDENT: I just want to clarify, is it one individual or is it the machine shop?

Q/A: It's a segment of the machine shop.

MANUFACTURING SUPERINTENDENT: Because I know one individual.

TOOL AND DIE MAKER: Did they give any reasons for wanting the union?

Q/A: Not necessarily more money; it's just they just want someone to fight for them.

In this particular case, the attempt to cut off discussion of the issue on the grounds that no more than a few individuals were concerned was unsuccessful, because of the unique nature of the issue in a nonunion plant.[13] On a number of other occasions, making issues appear to be the concern of only a small minority was a successful tactic for limiting debate.

As the program continued, the council interaction section of meetings was considered by some a waste of time. At one point in November 1975, the vice-president of manufacturing, reacting to the discussion of a council interaction, blurted out angrily, "We're not obligated to stay here until 4:30 P.M. We don't have to make idle conversation." Several weeks later, the head of manufacturing engineering reiterated the theme, stating that he did not think anything positive was coming out of these sessions and suggesting that the meetings be open-ended to grind out one priority subject, getting rid of "the fillers." In response to this pressure and to the general feeling that precious time was being wasted, the council unanimously agreed to limit its interaction to a specified time period. This rule was adopted by the second council as well. Predictably, communications dropped off appreciably.

These communication problems may have been exaggerated by the nature of the individuals involved and mistakes made in the program (such as restricting postings and circulation of minutes), but the underlying problem is significant. Individual work areas have specialized problems, and on plant-wide issues there is a diversity of opinion which is difficult to tap. It is very likely that the maximum size for effective representation is closer to the size of a work section (ten to fifteen people) than a whole plant. The problem, then, is how to hold a meaningful dialogue with seventy-five individuals. As one bright young woman responded in an interview, "To make this thing really work, you need factories of fifteen people." She laughed, but if the goal of joint decision-making bodies is to use representatives as a funnel connecting the masses with the decision-making process, her conjecture becomes deadly serious. If, however, this form of decision-making structure is viewed in a more Platonic fashion, emphasizing its company-wide base and its leadership function, it could be much more successful. The experience at SI demonstrates the difficulty in establishing that form of leadership. The work force and the council members viewed geographically elected individuals as representatives—as conduits through which they might seek solutions to problems unresolved by the normal hierarchy. Furthermore, and most important, when these conduits were restricted, people tended to lose interest and become apathetic about any system of representation.

Apathy

The problem of representation was further complicated by the fact that interest in the QWL program declined markedly over time. This seemed to apply equally to workers and managers. In mid-session of the first council (22 October 1975), a report on attitudes toward the QWL program showed lack of knowledge and only casual concern on the part of supervisors and mid-level managers. The reports from the supervisory council members who interviewed their peers were consistent on this point:

> ADMINISTRATIVE SERVICES MANAGER: In general their reaction was, "Oh, yes, QWL? They've been going for a while now, what are they doing?
>
> MANUFACTURING SUPERINTENDENT: A very blasé attitude about the whole thing. "Yeah, it's great; don't bother me with it."
>
> Q/A SUPERVISOR: Yes, I think my group had almost the same feeling. The general feeling about QWL was quite passive. . . . They didn't know much about it and didn't show much interest in the activities that are being taken.

There was little evidence that the attitudes of workers were different. We can see their lack of interest and the demoralizing effects it produced, and gain an understanding of the factors that created this chain of apathy, from the following discussion (3 March 1976). It is impossible to convey adequately the oscillation between depression and frustrated anger in the voices.

> MILL OPERATOR: The people at the furniture factory aren't informed; they don't know what we do here; they don't know what's been accomplished, and a lot of people have become completely disinterested in it. Right now, during the election time, there's nobody really getting interested like last year.
>
> TOOL AND DIE MAKER: One thing that bothers me, though, is everyone is saying why don't you tell us, why didn't you [angrily] . . . why the hell don't they come in and ask? [Pause.] If they've got any interest in this program, why are they sitting on their cans? Why don't they come in and ask? Why should it be up to the representatives to go out and talk personally to five or six hundred people? You know, you just can't do it, there just aren't enough hours in the day. And if the people don't have that much interest, you know, how are you going to do it?

TECHNICAL WRITER: First of all, it's rough, and I remember this from the very beginning of the program. It was rough for people to understand that what we wanted to do was going to be foreign. In most companies people go to work, they do their work, and they go home; big deal. They're only there for one purpose, and that's to earn their pay, and then you go home. . . . There's got to be some method of closing that gap. . . . Sure, it would be a lot better if the employees actually did take an interest and come up to the representatives, but how do you get them interested?

TOOL AND DIE MAKER: The thing that bothers me is that we've come out with articles in the newspaper, handouts, stuff on the bulletin board, and nobody even bothers to read it. I know people that look at the newspaper, get to QWL, "Forget that," and on they go, so. . . .

TECHNICAL WRITER: [*Plaintively.*] But why?

TOOL AND DIE MAKER: I think if they had any interest they'd want to read it.

MARKETING CLERK: People don't believe in the program. I've gone up to the people and talked to them, but they don't believe in it. . . . I don't know what to do, either. They say that supervisors aren't behind it, managers aren't behind it, that it's just a cover.

MACHINE SHOP LEAD: That's true, you know. A lot of the supervisors will mention the fact that QWL is a waste of time and money. Somebody will ask about a problem they have, and I'll volunteer to do something; and the supervisor will say, "What are you going to do about it?" That's the attitude you get from supervisors. They feel QWL's an obstacle; it's in their way, and it's not helping any.

FURNITURE ASSEMBLER: People just don't believe, they don't have the faith. I think people have the wrong expectations. In the case of a grievance or some kind of bitch, they would expect me to go over a supervisor's head to prove my effectiveness. And if I can't do that, what the hell good am I? Which is wrong, but I think it's partly true.

Interest in participation revived somewhat over the summer of 1976, when employees were involved in the design of the new facility and in referenda on working hours and holidays, but the change-over-time statistics on belief in participation showed that overall means were very similar to those in the first survey. Additionally, as the mill operator in the transcript above anticipated, interest in the second council elections was greatly reduced. In comparison with the first council elections, when some slates contained 25 nominees and 101 in all ran for election, only 32 people ran in the second election for all 8 employee positions.[14] Finally, many studies, including those of Great Britain, Yugoslavia, Norway, Canada, and Germany, report similar problems of apathy.[15] Thus it is important to understand the underlying factors and the dynamics by which apathy can spread. The insightful observations of the council members quoted above provide an excellent starting point.

In order, the suppositions are that apathy is (1) a function of the program's failure to sustain and communicate its activities (mill operator);

(2) rooted in the people themselves (tool and die maker); (3) a result of the uniqueness of the program (technical writer); (4) a result of management indifference (marketing clerk, machine shop lead); (5) a result of misplaced expectations as to the function of representatives (furniture assembler). As earlier data have indicated, there is fairly convincing evidence for each claim. What is less obvious is the vicious circle which reinforces the lack of interest in joint decision making on the part of the work force.

The initial problem was what the technical writer referred to as the "foreign" nature of the program. Lack of experience with or conceptualization of an alternative form of authority created confusion about what workers' participation would mean and led to unrealistic expectations about what the representatives would be able to do and about the program in general. This initial confusion was partially responsible for the only moderate personal interest taken in participation. It could have been overcome through action—clarifying roles, powers, and purposes as decision-making mechanisms were established and began to have an impact on company policies and procedures. However, a number of factors tended to constrain and blur activities, and the required conceptual development never crystallized. On one hand, it was difficult to communicate what the council was doing; on the other, it was difficult to get the work force directly involved or to assess their feelings as to the direction the program should take. Additionally, once the council began to take action, it found itself either facing an angry hierarchy if it tried to accomplish changes itself, or in the position of delegating responsibilities so that as a body it gained little legitimacy. In either event, members became individually frustrated and depressed. All these factors combined to forestall decisive actions that would have served to meet or clarify expectations. This failure compounded the initial indifference, apathy, and confusion; and pressure mounted to change or abandon the attempt.

Several factors at SI aggravated this cycle unnecessarily. Clearly the presence of a union not only would have helped to overcome the potential for management coercion. It also would have provided a formalized grievance mechanism which would have relieved the representatives of an impossible task, eliminated some of the problems of a dual hierarchy, and saved the policymaking council both time and psychic energy. In addition, the council should have been more formally constituted, with specific powers and areas of responsibility clearly defined. Direct actions would have then had more refined aims, met less resistance, and provided a focal point at which communication to and from the work force could be directed. Direct participation could have been further improved if referenda had been used to a greater extent to supplement occasional mass meetings.

Still, the level of interest in participation and desire for involvement on the part of employees remains problematic. In the absence of an ideology to legitimize the idea of participation and energize the work force, workers will undoubtedly look on joint worker-manager committees as another type of managing group. They may view this form of management as somewhat more benevolent and possibly more accessible than others; however, since decisions made in general will not immediately alter the major portion of their everyday working life, it will be difficult to sustain their interest. In the original surveys, although there certainly were individual disagreements and complaints about specific supervisors, there was little evidence of any rebellion against the *structure* of management authority. As long as the problems of representation persist, the appearance will simply be the substitution of one form of control for another. Satisfaction with job and company will still depend primarily on the individual's job, his evaluation of working conditions, wages and co-workers, his relationship with his immediate supervisor, and his desires and expectations for the future. As long as joint decision making is perceived as an addition to the corporate hierarchy, leaving day-to-day management and job structure relatively unchanged, it is difficult to envision active interest on the part of most workers.

CONCLUSION

The weakness of joint decision making, as it has been outlined, is not co-optation per se. The major idea of the last chapter—that workers have the potential to be effective, reasoned decision makers not easily dominated by managers—was reinforced by many of the transcripts included in this chapter. On the other hand, this individual capability may not be enough to realize the objectives claimed for industrial democracy. The real problems are the structural impotence arising from the juxtaposition of democratic and hierarchical systems of authority and the misrepresentation caused by the isolation of representatives. The result is an illusion of democracy. This illusion is not without its benefits. It allows for initiation and innovation within the organization, through the identification of problems that in other circumstances would go unnoticed. It also provides a degree of mutual understanding between workers and managers. However, the illusory nature of joint decision making cannot engage or sustain participation of a large segment of the work force; and it cannot greatly affect the routine structure of authority and responsibility that dictates the behavior, opportunity, and ultimate satisfaction of employees.

Thus attempts to build a democratic structure over and around a traditional hierarchical system can be only partially successful under the best circumstances. The solution seems obvious: democratize the existing structure, decentralize joint decision making to individual plant and shift locations and extend participation and self-control to individual work groups. However, if the experience at SI is any indication, this strategy is not easily accomplished.

7. Shop Floor
Democracy

The idea that workers should control the organization and work processes in which they are engaged is not, as some tend to believe, an original concept growing out of the human relations school of management. Such a notion was at the very heart of the English concept of guild socialism[1] and early American efforts at both agricultural and producer cooperatives. In recent years most experimentation with democratizing work at the shop floor level has occurred in the United States, Scandinavia, England, and Israel. The basis of research in most cases has been one or more experimental projects in small portions of a company. The designs vary from job enrichment—in which the intent is usually to redesign individual jobs to extend the scope of activity, increase feedback and learning, and possibly give the employee more control over factors affecting the job—to autonomous work groups, where the emphasis is on equal participation, teamwork, group incentives, and job rotation. At SI the latter approach was more appropriate, because the existing organizational structure in factory areas was roughly analogous to six- to fifteen-member teams with leads in charge.

Discussion of "work projects" began in the first meeting of the Planning Council. In the beginning, the general attitude in the council was extremely cooperative, enthusiastic, and optimistic. Everyone admitted that the projects were intended as a learning experience, but the evidence from a number of extensive reports on work humanization[2] had acquainted many people with the basic design features and assured them that success was very likely. Additionally, the first wave of interviews had indicated relatively high belief in participation on shop floor issues. Although there was less support for participation in interpersonal group decisions (hiring, firing, promotions, and job assignments), this was a minor concern. As the experimental projects progressed, enthusiasm waned; and by the time they were finally terminated, council members had come to realize that introducing worker control at the shop floor level was not as simple as it had been assumed to be.

PROJECT ORIGINS

After several months of intermittent discussion, both within the Planning Council and in committees in each plant, the design of an ideal autonomous work team was introduced by the manager of manufacturing engineering. In a speech to the Planning Council, on 25 June 1975, which he later repeated in meetings with the actual work teams, he defined its structure as follows:

> A group within an assembly area... could specify themselves how parts could come to them; they would determine exactly how material would be supplied to them. They would have the authority to accept or not accept defective parts. And if the parts came to them per print and the engineering drawings were wrong, they would have the authority and responsibility to see that the prints were changed. Their only requirement is to send on parts to the next station based on the next station's requirements. They would hire and fire people by majority vote. Order their own materials. Make group decisions on who would do what for a set period of time. Recommend and cost justify their own tools needed for the job. Determine their own sequence of operations and set their own time schedules.

A lively discussion followed, with only the rework lead arguing against the concept. He felt that workers "would not want the responsibility to hire or fire" and that a number of workers were incapable of self-direction and needed "someone to tell them what to do a lot of the time." Everyone else in the room supported the concept presented as the ultimate guideline for autonomous teams. The strategy agreed upon was to begin with a small number of projects that, if successful, could be used as models for conversion throughout the company.

The initial discussions within the facility committees (see p. 18) created by the council to locate and recommend specific work sections to serve as projects, were not so enthusiastic. In all five groups, there was serious questioning of the practicality and, in many cases, the need for such projects. In the two white-collar groups, the managers involved felt it was "meant for the factory" and not needed in the office areas. As a result, the only office area selected was the Employee Relations Department, in which the director began a project more or less on his own in July 1975. The council did formally approve the project, however. For the most part, supervisors in the plants believed there was a need for some effort at work improvement; but although they were not averse to work teams, a number of managers were clearly bothered by the idea of their operating without a lead.

The most difficult problem in the plants was to locate an area that fulfilled most of the criteria that had been established by the Planning Council. These criteria were posed as a series of questions framing the proposals submitted by the facility committees to the council:

1. How many people are involved? (Six to twelve was the ideal range.)
2. Is there "room for change in the structure of work"?
3. Is there a chance for individual learning?

4. Are there potential rate problems if job rotation is instituted?
5. What are the costs involved?
6. What are the risks of failure?
7. What is the attitude of the people and lead person in the area?
8. Will it be difficult to make the project voluntary?
9. What are the chances of expanding the project at a later date?
10. How much learning is transferable to other areas?

The process of selecting four areas took from May to October 1975 and included at some point a discussion of nearly every section in each plant. On a number of occasions, projects seemed very close to being organized when changes in demand or product design made the project less attractive. As proposals were finally adopted, discussions spread to include all supervisors, leads, and workers who were potentially involved. The reaction of supervisors was mixed. Most were understandably skeptical, because the ideas involved in autonomous work teams so radically altered normal procedure. However, in most cases the "action orientation" of production managers, the spirit so important in the Planning Council, produced a sincere willingness to experiment, to give the new approach a try.

The plant manager at the main plant provided a perfect example of this attitude. His eighteen years in the plant, starting as a shop worker, had produced some deeply ingrained ideas. He felt that decision making without a leader would be hard and that discipline might be a problem. He also doubted that participation in decision making and increased autonomy would lead to changes in motivation. He felt that "motivations are inherent, more or less; you can tell in several weeks if a man's going to be a good worker. It's very hard to change most people that much." He voiced these feelings from the time of my first conversation with him in December 1974, but there was no arrogance in the man, and his concern for the workers under him was genuine. As a result, his mind was open; and he was even excited about seeing if the experiments could work. Like many production managers, he enjoyed solving problems; and he was willing to go against his strongest instincts to find a solution. The truest and most strenuous test of the autonomous-team concept took place in his plant on what was called the L606 line. In the end, he supported the project completely; and in the face of severe production and economic pressures, he fought to keep it going, well beyond the point when almost everyone else involved had given up.

The reaction in another plant was much more negative. The furniture factory's entire management chain viewed the concepts with extreme skepticism. In two long meetings in September 1975, they projected every potential difficulty with autonomous work groups. "Everyone will want rate increases if you rotate jobs." "People won't be able to work together and get along." "You'll destroy the authority of the supervisor." "Who will maintain discipline?'' Nevertheless, following the cues of the plant manager (who feared embarrassment in the Planning Council, where his boss was a member), they rejected suggestions that in fact it might be better to forgo experiments in their facility, and all agreed they wanted to be included. However, reflecting a basic reluctance and suspicion, these managers made sure the projects were in "safe" areas (well-organized, simple job structures) and insisted that the leads remain in charge of day-to-day activities, at least in the beginning. It is interesting to note that, once the projects began, the immediate supervisors tended to reverse course completely and support the projects very well; they actually became spokesmen for participation, several times taking themselves out of decisions because they thought the process would be more democratic without their participation.

The reaction of leads throughout the company was predictably cool. The implication of experiments using work groups without leads was clear; they were assured that no one was to be demoted, but they never really believed it. Many argued that a lead was necessary, and several predicted that one would eventually be selected by the people themselves. In two meetings, a concern was raised that without lead positions it would be almost impossible to advance to supervisory positions from the shop floor. "When you don't have a lead, people that want to advance, to get ahead, how will they do that? What'll happen in a group is that they'll compete to look good and become leaders. It's the only way, but it'll happen. It's the only way for all of us. Remember I told you that."

The initial reaction of the workers varied from project to project. In the Employee Relations Department, meetings began very informally, so the reaction was favorable. Two of the shop projects were in sections building new products, and volunteers were sought among workers with the required skills. One of these projects was in electronic assembly, making a complex amplifier; and the other was in mechanical assembly, making a loudspeaker component (L606). They were to be set up without leads, operating as autonomously as they desired and as was practical to maintain production. The work areas required ten and eight people, respectively.

When the amplifier project was presented to the electronic assemblers (twenty-two women), their reception was very enthusiastic. The head of manufacturing engineering repeated his Planning Council speech; and it was supported by the vice-president of manufacturing, the facility manager, the industrial engineer, and the Planning Council member for the facility. The meeting was very lively. The ideas generated a great deal of excitement; and by noon the next day, seventeen people had volunteered. This reception was in part also due to the fact that the department itself had been having a very difficult time over the previous two years, and the workers were as eager as management to try something new. Unfortunately, enthusiasm did not last very long. In the two months required to set up the assembly area, nine volunteers withdrew their names. Various reasons were given, but the fact was that the department had been organized informally for years around several strong opposing personalities; and when one of these women left the project, a number of her friends also went back to the department. As finally constituted, eight people began working as a team on 5 November 1975.

The L606 project, also set up to operate autonomously, without a lead, was not so well received. Since it was in the main plant, which was also the oldest, many of the workers had been in their sections for years and were reluctant to get involved in a new product and an uncertain working environment. Adding to the difficulty was a woman who had been involved in assembling the prototypes of the L606. She was to remain with the group as a trainer. She had the long-standing reputation of being hard driving and short tempered. Several years before, when she was being considered for a lead position, a dozen workers had complained to the plant manager, who later cancelled her promotion. In the end, four women volunteered, and four new employees were asked if they would like to join the group.[3]

The other two projects were on the first and second shifts in the lacquer-finish section of the furniture factory. They were established lines, with leadmen who had been in the areas for several years. The initial meeting with the first shift (composed of twelve men) in late October 1975 went well, after a slow start. The leadman and the supervisor explained the basic idea of the meetings as a vehicle for making group decisions and discussing problems. The group immediately agreed to the project and spent the rest of the meeting discussing substantive issues. The second shift (composed of ten men) knew about the proposed project before the first meeting. At this meeting, they insisted that they would only participate if they were guaranteed that their leadman, who obviously was well respected, would not lose his position or status. When told that the Planning Council and the work project committee in their facility had agreed to that arrangement already, they were more than willing to cooperate.

Thus, after six months of planning, proposing, and persuading, five work projects were finally established. These projects formed an interesting pattern of experimental variation. One was in an office area, and four were in the factories. Two were set up around new products, one extremely complex (6208 amplifier), and one thought to be quite simple (L606). These same two were meant to be autonomous, operating without a lead, while the lacquer-finish areas were meant to be semi-autonomous teams, with their leads to handle day-to-day decision making. The latter set-up also provided an opportunity to deal with intershift conflicts, a perennial problem in most manufacturing plants.

PROJECT HISTORIES

The development of the projects was not planned in advance; the groups were given maximum latitude to decide organizational and procedural questions. What all five groups had in common was that meetings were to be held regularly, with all team members participating on an equal basis. I attended all the meetings in manufacturing, in much the same capacity as in the Planning Council and other committees. In addition, I worked in each area for approximately one week as the experiments began.[4]

Employee Relations

The experiment in Employee Relations was the first to begin and the only project still continuing as of this writing. The department was located in the main facility, and its size varied from eight to thirteen members over these years. The department head was the director of employee relations, although day-to-day activities were directed by a supervisor. The expressed purpose of the project was to improve the services of the department, the individual structure of jobs, and the interpersonal relations within the group. These goals were to be achieved by open participation, discussion, and decision making in departmental meetings. No formal provisions were made to alter the authority structure in the section. However, a number of issues discussed would normally have been decided by the supervisor and/or director. For example, before a new person entered the department, the job was formally outlined in the meeting. On most occasions, the department members also had an opportunity to interview applicants. In one dramatic incident, the director raised the question of how a salary increase that had been granted should be distributed among members of the department. He said he was willing to go along with whatever method the group wanted. Their decision was to leave it to the judgment of the director and the supervisor, requiring only that both had to evaluate each employee independently.[5] The group also made numerous decisions on procedures, writing an elaborate manual in the process. They established cross-training goals and schedules and set up an (unsuccessful) experiment in job enlargement in which members of the department would become one-person departments in the outlying plants (hiring, wage and salary, insurance, credit union, etc.).[6]

The potential for meaningful participation was present. However, as evidenced by interviews with some of the project members, this potential was only partially fulfilled. Participation in meetings and desire to attend them in the first place were highly skewed. Three or four of the higher-ranking department members did almost all the talking, while another three or four, usually the senior clerks, rarely said anything. Many times, at critical points, the supervisor and manager would end up deciding the issue or (more often) deciding to treat the issue outside the meeting. The lack of formal structure and voting mechanisms made this way out very easy. Finally, it was difficult to ascertain any real changes in the day-to-day workings of the department. The supervisor involved had great difficulty delegating authority and continually monitored the work of his subordinates. There was little evidence that his style changed over the first year of the project. The junior people were most affected by the actions of the supervisor and thus were even less likely to participate in the meetings. Without changing the day-to-day style of supervision, the effectiveness of the department meetings was limited.

Lacquer-Finish Projects

One of the semi-autonomous work projects in the lacquer-finish area suffered from a similar constraint. On the day shift, the leadman and supervisor were both fairly rigid in their supervisory style; and this made it difficult to extend participation beyond the meetings. The night shift supervisor, on the other hand, delegated complete responsibility for running the section to the leadman. The leadman followed the same principle. He would begin the shift with a short meeting, discussing schedules and assigning jobs, which he regularly rotated. From then on, he would fill in where needed, training workers on newer jobs or "touching up" finished cabinets. The problem of job rotation best exemplified the differences in the organization of the two shifts. The jobs in the department consisted of sanding and puttying assembled cabinets, then spraying them with several coats of paint and lacquer, while continuing to sand between each coat. The main operation was done on an oval roller conveyor ("the racetrack") with a spray booth at one end. Besides the five to eight men who worked at the racetrack, three men on each shift were in charge of finishing a very expensive cabinet with a high-gloss white finish. The latter job was highly skilled and coveted by most of the finishers. The next preferred job was painter at the racetrack. Not only was this job cleaner and less tiring than sanding and puttying, but it also led to a higher wage classification and offered the opportunity to learn a new skill.

On the day shift, men were permanently assigned to these prime jobs. The rationalization was that the best painters had to work these areas and that it was essential to reserve positions that could be given as a reward for hard work in the more menial, entry-level jobs. In discussions of this arrangement, the workers split along self-interest lines—painters arguing against rotation and the rest for it. Rotation in one form or another was suggested four or five times in day-shift meetings. Some modest proposals were agreed to, but they were never implemented consistently on the floor, where the lead and supervisor were unquestionably in control. On the night shift, rotation was the established pattern *before* the project began. Discussions in the meetings only worked out formal schedules and agreed lengths of apprenticeship. Differences between the two shifts in productivity were negligible. The morale on the night shift was noticeably better. During the nine months of the experiment, only one person left the night shift; eight left the day shift.

The presence of the leads and supervisors also affected the tone of the meetings. To begin with, excluding the issue of job rotation and some very beneficial discussions of outside educational opportunities, the topics of conversation almost always concerned either minor design features of the work area, tools and equipment, or relations between the shifts. There simply was little substance for discussion beyond these areas. As one of the workers on the night shift said in an early meeting, "You putty, you sand, you paint—you putty, you sand, you paint. What else is there to say?" In a very important sense, he was right. While the jobs required skill and some learning, they were, like most factory work, routine to the point where decisions, participation, or even discussions were minimal. In the autonomous work groups, there was always too much to discuss. In groups where a lead or supervisor had the responsibility for job assignments, coordination, and discipline, participation was somewhat superficial, with meetings serving at times only as a way to get off the line. This was particularly true for the day shift, where the potential scope of decision making was even less and the presence of an unsympathetic lead and supervisor made open discussion difficult.

Participation and enthusiasm in the meetings varied with the respective styles of supervision. Discussions were taken more seriously on the night shift, and participation was much more evenly spread. For the first half of the project, everyone in the group was interested. On the day shift, one-third of the people said very little, and about half the group never really showed much interest in the discussions. For both shifts, participation declined over time. The major problems of equipment and the relationship between shifts were brought up early, and the solutions that came up within the group seemed practical and were agreed to on both shifts. However, as time went by either the problems were resolved or implementation was blocked or delayed, sometimes by manufacturing engineering, sometimes by the plant superintendents or managers. As with the Planning Council, implementation required the services of the existing support functions and management. In this facility, the idea of participation was viewed as "socialism" and responded to mostly with lip service.

Delays in responding to some of the physical requirements (more air drops, larger paint cans, etc.)—some unavoidable, some the result of vetoes—began to wear on the groups. Also, problems between shifts were not solved so easily as was first thought, in that the "understandings" agreed upon were not always followed in practice. The meetings became redundant discussions of an ever dwindling number of minor problems and annoyances. Enthusiasm began to decline after four or five months. After my departure in June 1976, there was only one last meeting of the groups. The Planning Council declared the lacquer-finish experiments over in August.

To some extent, these experiments could be called successful. Near the end, the style of supervision began to change, particularly on the day shift. Productivity was also increased (clearly due in part to equipment changes suggested by the workers). However, the combination of a limited range of decisions, designated group leaders, and at best a reluctant acceptance of these projects by the facility management made it impossible to sustain any formal mode of group decision making.

L606 and 6208 Projects

The histories of the fully autonomous work teams were substantially different from the projects in Employee Relations and the lacquer-finish departments. In general they were much more difficult and, by some measures, less successful. Because they provided a more extreme test of the principles of autonomous work teams, they tended to bring out both the best and the worst in the people and the concepts. In contrast to the lacquer-finishing areas, one of the complicating features of these projects from the very beginning was the technical difficulty of the product designs and manufacturing processes. In selecting the 6208 and L606 for experimental projects, it was argued that new products would allow for new beginnings. The resistance inherent in changing established work procedures and existing structures of expertise and authority would not be a problem. Indeed, the development of these procedures and whatever system of coordination or authority was required would be partly the responsibility of the work group itself. Unlike the lacquer-finish area, in these groups the potential scope of decision was extremely broad. The arguments were attractive; the only miscalculation was that the usual start-up problems in manufacturing a new product were significantly prolonged, not being fully resolved until months after the experiments were officially concluded.

The 6208 amplifier was the most complex product the company made. Designed for professional use in recording studios and concerts, it consisted of more than 4,000 individual parts and carried a price tag of approximately $1,500 per unit. The company's record in electronics assembly was abysmal. It was a very small portion of the business (employing a total of about forty workers) and the only unprofitable sector. Before the new 6208 line, assembly had taken place on individual benches. There was no systematic product flow. Quality-assurance procedures were subject to negotiation, not well documented, and a long-standing source of irritation. The system was equally frustrating to the workers and the supervisors and managers involved. The one possible advantage was that most of the workers had at least three years' seniority, and many had eight to ten years. The drawback here was that factions had formed and, at least in the opinion of the department supervisor, "bad work habits had developed as a result of the years of disorganization."

The L606, on the other hand, was thought to be almost the exact technical opposite of the 6208. It consisted of only four parts (several requiring minimum subassembly), and the company had twenty sucessful years of experience in manufacturing high-frequency loudspeakers. Additionally, the workers eventually involved in the work team were a mix of new hires and experienced workers with long seniority. Still, in spite of all the apparent differences at the start, the L606 project turned out to have a great deal in common with the 6208.

The initial discussions in each group were enthusiastic, open, and seemingly productive. Unlike the lacquer-finish projects, participation remained at a very high level until close to the end of the experiments. However, the content and tone of the meetings shifted dramatically. The initial discussions dealt primarily with the physical layout, equipment needs, work procedures, job design, and job assignments and rotation. Assembly steps were listed and discussed, and job training matrices were created.[7] After some argument, training and rotation schedules were established. Several weeks into the operation, discussions began to focus more on operation deficiencies: material problems, interaction with quality-assurance personnel, adequate time standards, and maintaining records. With some variance, the quality of participation was excellent. The workers knew the jobs and the product as well as anyone and, in most cases, had as much knowledge and information as their supervisors. The difficulties that arose did not stem from a lack of technical capability or desire to succeed.

Because of high reject rates and material problems, production fell behind schedule in both sections. As this happened, the discussions in each group turned more to disciplinary problems, with supervisors and several workers in each group "suggesting" that some people were taking advantage of operating without a lead. Workers initiated discussions of disciplinary problems, questioning the degree of individual effort being put forth. In each group, this resulted in a climactic and highly emotional meeting to work through the differences. Although these meetings appeared to have therapeutic effects and temporarily soothed hurt feelings, the cleavages that had formed in the groups around these and similar issues never completely closed. The pressure of falling behind in production fueled tensions and magnified interpersonal problems. On the 6208 line, this led to two members quitting the team; on the L606, several women talked about quitting, and one eventually moved to an adjacent line.

My efforts to defuse the conflicts in these groups extended well beyond the meetings themselves. I met at various times with individuals, pairs of antagonists, and separately with opposing cliques. Some progress was made, but in the end it was not enough. It is surely possible that a highly skilled psychologist might have been more successful. However, it is quite apparent that, if this type of intergroup conflict were the norm and autonomous work groups were to be extended throughout a corporation, teams of psychologists and a great deal of time away from production would be required. Theoreticians and advocates of this form of industrial democracy must realize that the potential for interpersonal conflict within groups is a serious matter that may require costly solutions.

The ambiguous role of the supervisor and the relationship between work teams and support groups (manufacturing engineering, material control, production control, and quality assurance) were other sources of stress. Several factors caused supervisors and support personnel to avoid involvement with the groups, leaving them to a great extent to their own devices. First, everyone was aware that a basic premise for the experiments was self-management. Supervisors, engineers, and quality experts, being in positions of authority, were concerned that they might exert undue influence. Since their appropriate roles were never specified, the easiest way to ensure self-management was to back away from the projects completely. The magnitude of this problem was expressed by the head of manufacturing engineering in a Planning Council meeting in January 1976:

> To some degree, that's happened in all the projects, because the supervisor doesn't really know what his role is. Even my ME's [manufacturing engineers] are having trouble relating to this group [6208]. They are afraid to say anything, afraid to do anything that is going to upset them.... They're afraid they're going to do something wrong that's going to screw up the whole works. I think the supervisor is reticent about helping them. Ah, everybody is a little. [*Pause*.] I'm reacting myself, you know, because I like to kid a lot. I'm almost afraid to kid with those people, because they are already in an upset condition; and I might really trigger some animosity.

In addition to fears of upsetting the experiment by imposing too much external authority, there was in all the projects some overt resentment of the basic concept of workers' participation and the involvement of the Planning Council and QWL staff (primarily myself) in shop floor operations. Although there had been some resistance by middle-level management to Planning Council involvement in company-wide issues, that aspect of the program had been inconsequential to first-line supervisors and technicians, who had little influence in those decisions anyway. However, when the program moved to the shop floor, disaffection spread to the lower levels of supervision. As the projects progressed, the tempo of complaints charging the council with usurping the authority of regular management increased. On one occasion, my participation was also questioned. There was some basis to this objection, in that for a short period of time I was very much involved in the day-to-day operations of the L606 line. But there was also little doubt that, for many supervisors and support people, neglect of the projects was both the path of least resistance and the one most likely to ensure failure of the experiments and end incursion into their domain.

Finally, the least dramatic but probably most important explanation for the hands-off approach was that supervisors and technicians simply had no experience interacting with an entire group of people rather than their leader. The normal pattern of communication was always through the lead, who served as a channel for orders, complaints, and suggestions. Once that channel had been closed off, interactions became confused. When a manufacturing engineer had a suggestion for a new assembly fixture, he either had to call a group meeting or tell one person on the line and rely on that person to convey the message accurately. If a supervisor was concerned that a worker was taking too many breaks, leaving the work area too often, etc., he had to tell the person directly rather than pass the warning through the lead, who could discuss the situation with the employee more informally. The quality assurance inspectors, instead of reporting reject rates to a lead, as was normal, usually just posted the reports, with no guarantee that they would be looked at. The result of all this was a significant drop in communications and increasing isolation.

The tendency for external sources of support to isolate the work teams was understood to be a problem very early in the experiments. Despite this, a suitable compromise was never reached for the autonomous work teams. Only with the establishment of a lead on the L606 line and the suspension of the 6208 project did external support become effective. Although it was apparent that planning and training of supervisors and support personnel was inadequate, one questions whether anything short of massive retraining and reorganization would have eliminated the problem. Even if adequate communication with the group could be maintained, supervisors experienced in directing, overseeing, and monitoring operations would approach participation with some hesitation. Technical specialists, trained to provide solutions to specified problems, are not experienced in the negotiation and explanation workers demand. Theoretically, these roles can be modified to accommodate autonomous work groups; however, the experience at SI suggests that, except in the case of one or two rare individuals, this task may require substantial time and investment.[8]

The problems created by the absence of a leader to coordinate activities, centralize record keeping, and serve as a point of contact with other departments became apparent to each group within the first two months. The answer in each case was to assign these responsibilities on a rotating basis to volunteers in the group. However, after short trial periods with rotating leadership, pressures forced the reestablishment of permanent leads. Pressure to meet production schedules steadily increased. In the case of the L606, an entire speaker system depended on the production of this high-frequency component. Backlog orders reached $500,000. On the 6208, production failure forced marketing to retract an intensive sales campaign. In both groups, workers began to get nervous and irritable. In the beginning, they had joked about getting ulcers; after several months, it was no longer clear what was a joke and what was not.

The work also became frustrating. The workers were expending a great deal of effort, but in each project reject rates prevented significant production increases. Also the promise of job rotation had failed. The lines could only afford to cross-train one or two people at a time. They had miscalculated the time required to train people and the lost production inevitable in the training process. These conditions in turn increased the level of interpersonal conflict and placed anyone in a temporary lead role in a vulnerable position. While perceived as being responsible for the group, she lacked the full authority of a legitimate lead. This was particularly apparent on questions of discipline.

Both projects effectively ended following a severe conflict within the group. On the 6208, one woman provided the spark for what appeared to be a permanent breach of cooperation by saying to the group that some members were taking it easy and not really trying. Since sales had dropped off because of early field failures (of units made before the team began to function), management suggested suspending the project for several weeks. The project members approved; however, the suspension dragged on for several months, and management finally appointed a lead in the area.

The L606 line, which for a time seemed on the verge of success, also ended up with a lead, albeit one of the group's own choosing. After six months, conflict within the group led to the expansion of the temporary coordinator's role beyond record keeping, ordering materials, etc. It was agreed that the person in that position (which was being rotated) should be "listened to like a lead." After two weeks and several incidents in which workers refused to follow instructions of the coordinator, the woman in charge withdrew from the position, and several other volunteers withdrew their names from the rotation. In a group meeting called to discuss the situation, one of the younger team members said she thought the group needed a permanent lead with the same power as on other lines. Everyone agreed immediately, including the supervisor, who was visibly relieved. The woman who had remained in charge of training in the group had developed into an excellent leader and had won the respect of everyone in the group, and she was elected unanimously. No one else was interested in the job.[9]

At this point, it was clear that the project would change with a lead, but it was not assumed that the project was at an end. Most people felt a lead would stabilize the group, and that is precisely what happened. However, what was not expected was that stability would also mean the end of any interest in participation. In the two meetings following the lead's election, participation was almost nonexistent—even less than in the lacquer-finish projects. The lively, emotional meetings of a month before became dry, technical discussions, with an embarrassing silence from some of the previously most active members. The lead did most of the talking. On 17 May 1976, one of the group asked if they should continue as a work project. I outlined a possible structure differentiating "tactical" (day-to-day) decisions, to be made by the lead, from longer-range "strategic" decisions, to be made by the group as a whole. There was no reaction to the proposal. When asked if they wanted to have any further say in decisions on the line, everyone again remained silent. The silence was finally broken by a woman who had been extremely active in early meetings but who had been very upset by conflict within the group. She was quite concise: "We need a lead, and we elected Lydia. Let her do it." Several women verbally supported her statement, and all nodded approval. Nine months after it began, the experiment was over.

THE PROBLEM OF AUTHORITY

In one way or another, all the manufacturing work projects quietly evaporated. They all began, like the Planning Council, in a burst of enthusiasm and hope; but in the end they lacked the proper mixture of stability and necessity that would have ensured their permanence. The central problems were a need for leadership and authority, and the effect authority had on the desire, utility, and character of participation. These questions were raised in one of the most emotional Planning Council sessions that took place in the first two years of the program. The transcript is presented at length to display the feelings and internal struggles of people grappling with the problem of authority. The meeting took place on 21 January 1976, just as the work teams were beginning to have serious trouble. The discussion was started by the woman Q/A who had so abruptly announced the request for a union (see p. 103).

> Q/A: Looking at the 6208 work project, basically its a no-lead structure in order to give the individual more incentives. What I want to say is that it is a waste of time logically and theoretically. A manufacturing structure is involved around order and authority. And, ah, even the world we live in, it's based on order, authority, and organization. And I think after a closer look at the project, it's not really what we're looking for. I was wondering if QWL couldn't restructure the project; define an ideal lead, and train a person to be that ideal lead. The more I think about it, the structure of manufacturing is authority and supervision; and without it, it would be chaos.

Tool and Die Maker: I don't agree. I've seen the L606 go from six people to fourteen, and it's not chaos.

Q/A: I don't [*pause*] it's feasible for a small group, yes; but it's not something that can expand and help the company, company-wide. If you had that whole structure throughout the whole company, there would be chaos.

Manager of Manufacturing Engineering: I'd like to add some inputs, because I've talked with the girls out there. They're really down. One of the group is quitting. They are dissatisfied, because they don't feel they've been getting the things to do the job properly. That's partly our fault. I think we've gone through a bit of a learning process in that we've kind of turned them over on their own. A brand new product, a different concept of working, and it's floundering. I think, given enough time, we could make it successful, even without authority. There's some natural leadership coming out of this.

Q/A: Still, the main thing I want to emphasize is that areas cannot exist without the chain of command, without the system, the organization; and something like that is not organized.

Manager of Manufacturing Engineering: O.K., you're right.

Q/A: Like you said, a leader is coming out of this; but then you go to a lead again. It's going away from the original idea.

· ·

Manufacturing Superintendent: You know, I'd like to inject something here. You know we've discussed the problems with the hand tools, getting the benches fixed the way they wanted, and so on. . . . With all the frustrations they've suffered as far as hand tools and benches not being right, I haven't had anyone come up to me and say, "I don't want any part of that program because I don't have a screwdriver or I don't have the right height bench." But I *have* had people come up and say, "I can't work with those people any more—I want out!" I think the major problem is that they can't get along with each other.

Manager of Manufacturing Engineering: I have some other comments, and we might as well bring it out in the open. I've had some feedback, and there's beginning to be a little resentment towards you [*points at Witte*] on the supervisors' and support groups' part. They kind of feel you're usurping their authority, because you're getting intimately involved in production methods, production flows, layouts, and so forth, and no longer acting as an objective observer.

Witte: You're talking about the L606? Certainly not anywhere else. Because I really haven't been involved in the 6208 to any extent. That may be part of the problem.

Manager of Manufacturing Engineering: I don't know.

· ·

Manufacturing Superintendent: Well, in one of the meetings, the supervisor didn't know what to do. He's still responsible to make projection schedule. I'm not coming down on anybody but [6208 supervisor's name] when the schedule is not met. This morning in that brief meeting we had—this morning he made the comment [*voice rising*], "If it's O.K. I will do this." And I thought to myself, "What the hell are you asking if it's O.K.? You're responsible for that area; and as production supervisor, unless it's something that's some god-awful move, he doesn't have to check to see if it's O.K. to move an individual from here to here. Because if that's the case, we just might as well say you're not a supervisor."

Q/A SUPERVISOR: [The problem is] guidance, leadership, people, I mean . . . you know. I know for sure I want to have a boss, and I want to be guided. You let ten people out there on a complex thing like that without any guidance, and no one really knows who to go to to ask and. . . .

MANAGER OF MANUFACTURING ENGINEERING: [*Cutting in.*] I've got to support what John Witte said at this point; because, you know, authority is the way we're used to working.

Q/A: The whole world's built on it.

MANAGER OF MANUFACTURING ENGINEERING: Exactly, but the world is changing. [*Pause.*] We've got an awful lot of dissatisfied young people in this world right now who refuse to join society, because they don't like the way it's structured. [*Pause.*] They don't like the way it's happening. [*Pause.*] They don't like authority.

Q/A: Yes, but actually you can't jump in there and say this is the way we're going to do it, and do it this way, you. . . .

MANAGER OF MANUFACTURING ENGINEERING: [*Cutting in.*] That's the whole objective of this program. We don't know what's a better way, because we'd like those young kids out there to get in amongst us. And maybe there's a better way of doing work, and maybe it's without authority.

Q/A: I'm not saying there's not a better way; you should be looking for a better way; but if you try to do everything all at once, you're going to have to change the whole entire structure to build it up and create a new structure. You just can't rip a hole in the middle and expect it to work.

This final statement adequately portrays the thesis of this book which will be argued in the final chapter. The general discussion adequately frames the problem of shop floor democracy: authority serves the functions of coordination and communication and provides a mechanism to at least suppress, if not resolve, conflicts. And, unquestionably, "authority is the way we're used to working." In the semi-autonomous experiments there was a reluctance on the part of workers and supervisors alike to remove existing forms of authority. The autonomous groups followed consistent patterns of restoring authority that had undoubtedly been too abruptly removed. To understand the conditions leading to this end is to understand the dilemma facing shop floor democracy. By understanding that dilemma, we can critically evaluate recommendations for the future.

8. The Dilemma of Self-Managing Work Groups

The dilemma facing self-managing work groups involves the design of work and the requirements and effects of leadership within groups. The dilemma can be put in the form of a theoretical paradox consisting of the following propositions:

1. The more simplified the work environment, the less likely the possibility of meaningful worker participation.
2. However, as the work environment becomes more complex, the greater the need for coordination and the greater the potential for conflict within the group.
3. The need for coordination and the management of interpersonal conflict creates pressure to select a leader with singular responsibility for the group.
4. Once a leader is established, there is a strong tendency either to defer to his authority and judgment, thus limiting active participation, or to give the opinion of the leader unequal weight, thus endangering the legitimacy of the participatory process.

Each of these propositions will be considered in turn.

ENVIRONMENTAL COMPLEXITY AND MEANINGFUL PARTICIPATION

Five job-design variables distinguish complex and simple work environments:

1. *Job scope*—measured as the cycle time of a job and/or the number of different operations performed by an individual worker;
2. *Interdependence*—the degree of mutual dependence of jobs within a work section;
3. *Choice*—the opportunity the job affords an individual or group to make decisions, solve problems, or otherwise engage the mind;
4. *Variance*—the opportunity to vary either job procedures or the functions assigned to specific individuals;
5. *Work and social interaction*—the opportunity for workers to work together, share jobs, or simply communicate with others on the job.

A simple work environment is one in which job cycles are highly repetitive, there is little interdependence between jobs, not much thinking is required, little variance is possible, and individuals are isolated from their co-workers. These factors can vary independently, and there is a progression from simple to complex work environments in any organization.

The work projects in the lacquer-finish areas, which were more complex in terms of the working environment than some other areas at SI, demonstrated limitations of a team concept and worker participation in a relatively simplified work environment. In these particular experiments the presence of leadmen was a confounding influence, but there was no denying the dramatic decline in participation over the life of the projects.

These experiments suggest that, unless the work group is given broad latitude to reorganize the jobs within a section (complicating an otherwise simple environment), discussions relating to the work itself will be inherently shallow and unproductive. What does "teamwork" mean in a production section where individual jobs are fully independent of each other? What point is there in rotating between two jobs with a combined cycle time of sixty seconds? How does one inject learning and imagination in a job that has been deliberately designed to consist of placing a component in a cabinet and affixing four screws? Group discussions and the concept of a team will gravitate away from the work itself toward outside education, training, and very probably schemes to receive bonus pay or time off in exchange for more production.[1]

The answer to this problem seems as obvious as the dilemma itself: design more complex work environments. The difficulty is that this would require a massive effort in most modern corporations where the impact of highly refined scientific management techniques has been widespread and is probably expanding. At SI a careful inventory of the social and technical characteristics of various jobs was not taken, but statistics on training requirements for jobs gave some indication of the distribution in job complexity. Findings based on interviews with all leads and supervisors in the company showed that a worker could become "proficient" at 27% of the jobs in less than one day and 51% in less than one week. Only 21% of the jobs required more than a month of training. The conclusion reached was that most areas would have required significant job redesign to make participatory teams feasible. It was this situation which was primarily responsible for the delay in identifying potential experimental sites in the company.

Although more complex work environments may appear to humanists as a logical and inevitable end for modern organizations,[2] there is little evidence of any such trend. The mainly academic proponents of sociotechnical systems design, or even simple job enrichment, have not as yet had much of an impact.[3] Their efforts are praiseworthy, but it cannot be denied that existing forces in most contemporary organizations point in the opposite direction. The reflex response of industrial engineers and managers is toward further division of labor, more mechanized assembly lines, increased isolation, and decisionless jobs. The arguments they give are not based on experimentation or testing but on common sense and experience. Their rationales for a simplified work environment can be listed thus:

Reduced job scope	Less training time
	Reduced error
	Greater speed
	Lower base wage
More mechanization	Forced work rates
	Even product flow
Increased isolation	Working instead of talking
Decisionless jobs	Decision making takes time
	Decisions are subject to error and introduce variance

These arguments are based on efficiency. Accepting the efficiency criteria, those arguing for greater complexity must employ a more complicated chain of assumptions than the very direct logic contained in the list above. No one can argue that decision making does not take time; rather, the humanist must argue that mindless jobs reduce satisfaction and morale and have a negative impact on productivity. The same is true for arguments against increased division of labor and mechanization. In my experience, managers, and particularly industrial engineers, are suspicious of the more complex arguments.

An obvious alternative is to ignore the theoretical arguments and demonstrate empirically the greater efficiency of complex work environments. Unfortunately, humanists have not been able to do this.[4] Furthermore, with the force of experience and accepted practice clearly on the other side, future evidence will have to be convincing indeed.

Another possibility is to consider criteria other than efficiency in evaluating work designs. Job satisfaction, learning, and personal development could be considered end values, regardless of the further link to productivity. Although the link between satisfaction and productivity has not been verified, the empirical evidence on the correlation between satisfaction and more complex work environments is quite persuasive.[5] However, a shift of emphasis away from efficiency would require a significant normative commitment. Opponents would immediately argue that, if relative productivity were to decline, this would mean less profit, lower wages, and a lower standard of living for employees. These tradeoffs are rarely considered by the more humanistic management theorists, for they assume that more humanistic work will inevitably increase productivity. At present, although it is interesting to speculate about the individual's willingness to trade material well-being for more intrinsically satisfying work, there are few incentives in our system for managers to consider seriously criteria other than efficiency.[6]

At SI these issues were discussed continually, but most production plans and designs were still drafted in accordance with traditional assumptions. In the absence of countervailing expertise, the previous training and experience of the manufacturing engineers and plant managers prevailed, and new designs were usually in the direction of more simplified work environments. Without a significant normative conversion or substantial evidence establishing the profitability of more complex work environments, the visible logic of the assembly line will almost inevitably win out in American corporations. If it does, the prospects for meaningful self-managing work teams are very limited. To superimpose participatory work teams on such highly simplified work will have at best a short-term impact.

COMPLEXITY, COORDINATION, AND CONFLICT

That a fairly complex work environment is required for successful autonomous work groups has been observed by a number of organizational theorists.[7] However, most of these same authors, in their support of this new work form, fail to emphasize that with complexity comes an increasing need for coordination and conflict resolution within the group. In most economic enterprises, the natural response to problems of coordination and conflict is to appoint a leader who assumes responsibility for the group.

Coordination

The relationship between complexity and coordination is fairly obvious. As the interactions among people, materials, and machines become more complex, a number of complications force centralized coordination upon the group. The ordering, inspecting, and staging of materials is more complicated and may well require the mutual efforts of several people. Similarly, as work stations become more dependent on one another and materials and machinery become more technically sensitive, the potential for critical production bottlenecks increases. Also, the more complex the environment, the more important and the greater the frequency of contact with support groups. Finally, the simple act of reporting results can become a complex procedure including units in process, subassemblies completed, etc. The simplest method to ensure material availability, oversee production, interact with support groups, and report results is to assign individuals continuous responsibility for these tasks. At SI, for both the 6208 and the L606 projects, the need for this form of centralized responsibility was apparent early in the projects and was supported by all the workers.

Conflict

The proposition that conflict increases with complexity and that its resolution requires centralized authority is more controversial. The first part of the argument requires only brief comment. A complex environment increases the frequency of interaction and interdependence. Thus the probability of a conflict situation developing is increased, especially when there is production pressure. When a subsection of workers must depend on another group in the team for the successful completion of their jobs, any latent hostility between the groups will surface if there is a failure to perform the required work satisfactorily.

But need this form of conflict result in centralized authority? To understand the pressures that tend to lead to that end, we need to explore the character and behavioral effects of responsibility in a traditional organization, and specifically the tensions created when a system of *shared responsibility* is introduced. Since this problem extends beyond autonomous work teams and is critical for more generalized conceptions of organizational democracy, it will be considered in some detail.

Social scientists attempting to understand organizational behavior consistently focus their attention on authority or power as the crucial variable in understanding behavior. This concentration on authority tends to overshadow a more observable phenomenon—the assignment of responsibility. In a hierarchical corporate organization, the assignment of responsibility has three critical characteristics: it is specific; it is unitary; and it is psychologically indivisible. Responsibility is *specific* in that it is concise, clear, and quite often specified in quantitative terms. A sales representative is assigned a particular territory, possibly with his salary pegged to a dollar quota. An engineer is given the job of designing a new product, within a specified cost range, by a set date. A superintendent is responsible for a weekly production of 2,000 speakers, a supervisor for 500 of these, and his lead for 500 subassemblies. *Unitary* responsibility means that assignments are made on the basis of a single individual or, at best, several individuals. This responsibility is *indivisible* in the sense that, while tasks will almost always need to be subdivided further and responsibility delegated to subordinates, the individual assigned the original task alone will be held accountable by his superior for the larger task.

This system of responsibility results in a psychological tension that extends and increases as one moves up the corporate hierarchy. The tension arises from two conditions. First, at all but the lowest levels within an organization, an individual's responsibility for a task extends beyond his own ability to accomplish that task. Completion thus requires delegation. This leads to the second condition, namely, the dependence of superiors on the successful performance of subordinates. The theoretical answer to this problem is to assign authority commensurate with responsibility. The tension exists because, in the vast majority of cases, this proves impossible—there is an inevitable gap between authority and responsibility. The first condition seems obvious; the second requires explanation.

In the vast literature on authority, two methods of defining authority seem to prevail. The first and older stresses political rule making and the formal assignment of power.[8] This definition emphasizes legal authority conferred in a nation-state by constitutions, laws, and executive orders. In an organization, this form of authority resides in policy and procedure manuals, by-laws, rules of incorporation, and similar official documents. The second way of thinking about authority is in what Simon called "purely objective and behavioristic terms."[9] A number of definitions in this vein have been offered, but it seems most useful in understanding superior-subordinate relationships to define the authority of person A over person B as the ability of person A to induce the willing compliance of person B in carrying out an instruction, even if person B may disagree with the specific instruction. This definition provides for varying degrees of authority based on two factors: inducements available to person A and the legitimacy of A in B's eyes. Notice also that formal authority, based on rule making, falls within the domain of this definition, rules serving as a means of inducing compliance and conferring legitimacy.

According to a number of scholars, a superior faced with achieving a specific task that requires the cooperative efforts of a number of subordinates will rarely have formal authority commensurate with the task.[10] Formal authority is usually limited to a specified group and is granted in general language. To accomplish the task in many instances will require the efforts of those beyond the control of the superior, be it someone in another department outside his chain of command or perhaps someone (a supplier, for example) outside the organization itself. Even within one's specified domain of authority, it is impossible to maintain direct control in most instances. Formal authority, written in general terms to cover a range of applications, is necessarily vague and therefore open to misunderstanding and argument when applied to a specific case. Even if this were not so, the use of sanctions and rewards to induce compliance takes a great deal of time and will probably require information not readily available to a superior directing a large number of people. A plant manager with 300 people under him will have great difficulty determining which employees deserve recognition and which deserve reprimand. Finally, since authority must be accepted by subordinates, the formally conferred sanctions available to managers will be used sparingly in practice. Although inducing fear (as one supervisor put it, "making them know I mean business") can produce short-run results, over time superiors must induce voluntary compliance in their subordinates.

As a result of the vague and limited nature of authority, stress is created within the organization. To relieve the psychological tension created by the gap between authority and responsibility, a manager will employ the same strategy used by his superior: assign specific tasks to subordinates and make it clear they will be held individually responsible for their completion. In this way he establishes a clear point of accountability and a centralized source of information. His problem is reduced from motivating and monitoring perhaps 200 workers to working with a handful of supervisors. His responsibility has not disappeared, and his authority still does not extend to all the factors that will directly affect his success or failure; but the problem is now bounded and focused. This same process occurs throughout a corporation and, more than anything else, defines the structure and character of a hierarchical organization.

Autonomous work teams are premised on a different concept: responsibility shared equally by a group of individuals. Although this shared responsibility is intended to increase the feeling of group solidarity and consideration of the needs of the group as a whole, it also results in spreading the anxiety inherent in leadership roles to all members of the group. In fact the tension will be greater because the emphasis on equality reduces the authority of any individual, and so the differential between perceived responsibility and authority is greater than would be felt by a lead. In addition, if we assume that leads are selected in part because they desire responsibility and are better able to adjust to the pressure, random assignment to autonomous teams will put under stress a number of people who wish to avoid such situations, are not used to them, and may not be able to handle them.

In a complex work environment, the possibility of this form of tension is increased. Even in the most well coordinated systems, production is more likely to vary in complex groups, and with this variance comes a degree of pressure and tension—tension felt not by a lead but by all members of the group. This anxiety increases the susceptibility of the group to internal division and conflict and produces counterpressure to establish centralized authority.

The effect of shared responsibility on the supervisor of autonomous work groups is just as important. A lead provides a specific reference—a specific point of information and accountability. This contact is missing in an autonomous work team. The supervisor has lost one of the basic mechanisms for relieving the tension created by the imbalance between authority and responsibility; he has lost the right to promote and motivate a worker to aid him in accomplishing the tasks he has been assigned. He has lost a very important element of control over his working environment. The effects on the supervisor were clearly expressed in the Planning Council by the superintendent in charge of the 6208 line, who admitted in the lengthy transcript previously discussed that he came down only on his supervisors when the schedule was not met. There is an angry tone to the speech:

> We can talk frustrations and the whole shot, but again being here as a representative for supervision, I don't know that there are too many volunteers who would want to be in charge of those groups as supervisors. Getting back again as a rep from supervision, I don't know how

much consideration is being given to the guy who's in the middle of this mess. We're talking about all of the people that don't have the hand tools. What about the guy in the middle?

The average supervisor will naturally favor a permanent lead of his choice whom he can motivate to take responsibility for the tasks required of the group. If the tension inherent in complex work environments creates conflict within the group, this conflict and the need for coordination will lead workers to a similar conclusion, although perhaps with a leader of their own choice. The remaining question is what effect a formal leader has on participation and joint decision making.

Participation and Leadership

In the experimental projects at SI, there was no doubt that both the distribution and effectiveness of participation were skewed by the presence of a leader in the group. This was clear in the lacquer-finish areas and the Employee Relations project, and conspicuously apparent when the L606 line selected a lead. Is this result a general phenomenon, or was the reduced level of enthusiasm and participation a function of the particular combination of personalities and circumstances in these projects? Several strands of evidence suggest that formal leadership in a group will have a similar effect in most work sections, particularly in the more complex environments that hold the greatest potential for meaningful participation.

A good portion of that evidence relates to the workers' beliefs in participation. Although they clearly expressed the strongest desire to participate in areas that most directly affected their work, their overall interest in participation was moderate at best, particularly when potential costs were weighed in terms of trade-offs in time and money. Additionally, support for participation was much less in those critical areas that suggested the possibility of interpersonal conflict and the application of sanctions by the group. The inference is that at least initially there would be little interest in transferring power from the lead and supervisor over decisions concerning hiring, firing, promotions, and job assignments. From the reasons given for not wanting to participate, it can be concluded that workers consider these decisions to be the proper function of more experienced leads and supervisors, and that many workers view these decisions as an unpleasant responsibility. I believe that deferral to a lead or supervisor in these areas would be automatic unless introduced for discussion by an outside participant like myself. If the issues were discussed at all, I can conceive of only rare occasions when the opinion of the lead would not be extremely influential.[11]

Another piece of evidence is the general acceptance of authority that most workers exhibit on the job. The conception of a job as a contract that includes an agreement to follow the dictates of the existing structure of authority makes it much more difficult to encourage wider influence in

work groups and makes deferral to a lead all the more likely. Undoubtedly, the style of the lead and his legitimacy in the eyes of the workers will
have a bearing on the effectiveness of participation. In the case of a lead
whose authority is based primarily on the power of his position, such as in
the day shift lacquer-finishing project, participation will be diminished,
and the opinions of the lead will tend to dominate because of apathy and
fear. When the lead is strongly supported by his workers, we can expect a
more nearly equal level of participation, although the judgments of the
lead may carry even more weight than in the prior case.

Finally, because the lead is in a better position to accumulate information about the work process, materials, and product quality, unless a
special effort is made to share this information, the lead will speak in the
group with an authority based on superior knowledge and expertise. This
advantage will increase as the work environment becomes more complex,
unless jobs are so integrated that information about the understanding of
the entire work process is a necessity for everyone. However, since the
knowledge required in most departments is quite specialized and narrow,
it can be mastered by most workers in relatively short periods of time.
Thus, just as workers on joint decision-making committees were almost
equal to managers when problems were narrowly defined, workers considering shop floor problems could obtain the required information in
most cases. The trouble at SI was that some workers clearly had little
interest in acquiring this sort of knowledge. The old refrain, "He's the
lead; it's his job," was heard on many occasions.[12]

It is possible that the influence of an officially sanctioned authority
figure in a group could be neutralized by a very effective outside mod-
erator. Proponents of autonomous work teams stress that everyone must
participate on an equal footing. The argument here is that this will not be
the normal pattern in groups with formally designated leaders. I personally question whether it is possible, in the short run, to change this situation, even with the aid of a highly trained specialist. However, even if it
were possible, it would surely take a great deal of time; thus extension
throughout a company would require a very significant investment that, to
my knowledge, no large corporation has been willing to undertake.

The dilemma posed here is not meant as an unresolvable paradox. It is
meant, however, as a warning to future practitioners that the conversion
from a traditional shop floor organization to a more participatory structure
may be much more difficult than theories of self-management might lead
one to suspect. More specifically, one of the currently popular axioms of
many work-improvement programs, that changes must come naturally
from within the group itself and not be imposed by managers or specialists
in organizational design, is clearly ill-founded, at least in the initial stages
of a work project. There must be planning in the design of the work
process, the structure of the jobs, and the ways in which workers will be
trained in job skills and group dynamics. The role of the supervisor and

lead (if necessary) must be clearly stated initially. If permanent authority is to be removed, it must be done gradually.

To some, these suggestions may sound like dictatorial social engineering. This may be so, but anything short of this amount of planning in the initial stages of a project will lead to certain failure. As both the Q/A and the manager in charge of manufacturing engineering so dramatically put it, "Authority is the way we're used to working." Stating a few abstract principles and cutting workers loose to recreate their own environment is analogous to giving a person a dictionary of a foreign language and telling him to write a book. Once a group is formed and functioning in a relatively stable manner, conditions can be modified by the group; however, everyone involved will be better served by an explicit statement of initial conditions. The conversion from a strict hierarchy to a shop floor democracy requires authoritative planning.

In the months following the termination of the work projects in August 1976, the Planning Council conducted a study of the projects to determine modifications in future experiments. The opinions I have expressed above became part of that study, but the same recommendations were made independently by the workers in the projects and by the leads and managers involved.

My recommendations also contained two further suggestions, neither of which was greeted with much enthusiasm. The first was for a wage and incentive system based on the output of the work group; and the other was the simple, yet feared, practice of electing leads and possibly supervisors. If this analysis of the forces at work in a complex work process is correct, both suggestions are practical correctives. If complete autonomy in work groups is impractical and a leader is required, a compromise solution makes that leader at least in part responsible to his followers. Additionally, increased autonomy for workers brings with it increased responsibility for fulfilling organizational goals. Workers will and should expect to be rewarded for accepting this responsibility. A wage incentive, based on meeting group standards, is a convenient and logical method of accomplishing this goal. A further benefit of this form of wage system would be underscoring the conception of equality within the group and promoting the integration required for the successful functioning of a work team.

These suggestions may seem superfluous in view of the problems encountered in the shop floor experiments at SI. While the fate of the experiments and the dilemma that has been discussed suggest the difficulty of self-managing work groups, the change-over-time statistics are much more encouraging. For although the work groups proved impossible to sustain in the form originally envisioned, and the costs in terms of human and organizational turmoil were evident, the change-over-time results imply that even small increments of autonomy at the shop floor level have significant consequences.

9. The Effects of Participation

Measuring and analyzing changes over time in a natural experiment is extremely difficult. In the present study, two problems extend beyond the usual limitations of unprogrammed, nonrandom experiments. The first is the limited time span of the study. For changes in alienation in work, job satisfaction, and belief in participation, the period of change was on the average only sixteen months. Changes in productivity and related measures ranged from twelve to twenty-four months. It is reasonable to argue that this is simply not enough time for significant changes to occur. Another problem common to all the measures considered here is the lack of an adequate control group in another company. For this reason, there is no real way to estimate Hawthorne effects.

Therefore the following results must be considered tentative. Within the class of evidence with which they may be compared, however, they rank quite well. In the first place, the generalizability of controlled, programmed experiments on questions of democratic leadership and employee participation is questionable. For example, one simply must wonder if the famous Lewin leadership studies on small groups of preadolescent boys have any relevance for factory life. Second, there are very few real-world projects that consider different forms of participation at the same time. There are even fewer that offer objective measures of change, particularly within the framework of a "before-after" design.

CHANGES IN PERCEIVED PARTICIPATION

A great deal has been said about the extent and quality of participation at SI. The interviews conducted at the beginning of the QWL program and again some sixteen months later afford a more objective measure of the changes in participation as perceived by the employees. The primary measure, introduced as "present participation on the job," is an index based on responses to the question, "How much say do you have in the following decisions?" The decisions, listed in table 3 (p. 28), provide a conservative measure of participation, because the QWL program established worker participation in several areas that were not measured on the first wave of interviews (planning the new facility, working hours). If these and other issues had been included, undoubtedly the changes would have been more dramatic. The questions, responses, and means for the included items are presented in appendix C, table C-2.

The changes in perceived participation are presented in figure 3 in the form of "box plots," developed by Tukey.[1] A box plot is a simplified and compact version of a frequency distribution—in this case, the distribution of change scores between the first and second interviews. The scores

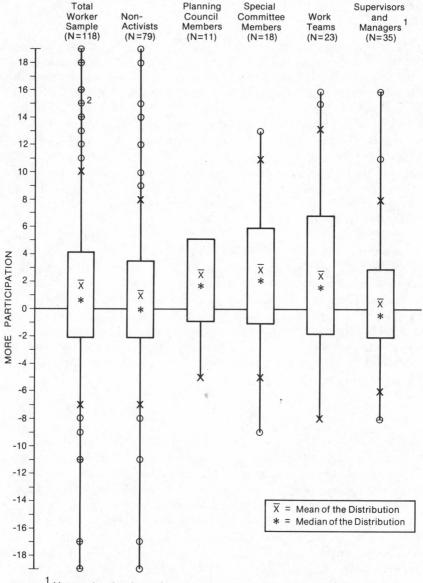

[1] Measured as the change in management's perception of worker participation.

Figure 3. Box Plots of Changes in Present Participation on the Job

represented are the second-wave score on the participation index minus the first-wave score. The box in these diagrams encloses all the scores from the first to the third quartile, or the middle 50% of the distribution. The location of the box relative to the scale of change scores on the left indicates the magnitude of change, while the length of the box represents the dispersion of the middle half of the cases. The length of the box is called the "interquartile distance." The X's on the lines extending from the box mark the scores less than or equal to one interquartile distance from the twenty-fifth and seventy-fifth percentiles, respectively (the ends of the box). The empty and crossed circles denote individual cases that can be considered outliers in the distribution. The crossed circle is used to distinguish more extreme scores that are 1.5 interquartile distances beyond the box. The symbols $\overline{X}$ and * denote, respectively, the mean and median of the distribution. Thus, in one illustration, we can represent the center point of the distribution, the spread of the majority of scores, and the number and magnitude of extreme scores.

The change scores are broken down into six categories, including the total sample of workers, supervisors, and managers, and four categories of participation. The final sample is less than the first wave because of employee turnover.[2] While the layout of the diagram seems to invite comparisons between categories, this is not intended and may lead to erroneous conclusions. If this were a controlled experiment, it would be considered a nonequivalent group design. Since it has been established here that, at least for joint policymaking councils, there are systematic differences between activists and nonactivists (thus violating an assumption of random selection), any comparison between "treatment groups" must be assumed to be confounded with these differences.[3]

Table 17 gives more precise information about the means and standard deviations at both points. "Estimated true scores," which have been computed to compensate for regression to the mean effects, are included. In this method, which assumes that the variable and its error term are normally distributed at both points, the true score is estimated from observed values by means of an ordinary multiple regression equation.[4] The estimated scores are calculated across the whole sample with a constant term adjusted so that the sample mean of the estimated scores is the same as that of the observed scores. The effect of this procedure is to draw extreme scores toward the mean.

Considering the total sample first, both the difference of means and the location of the box in figure 3 indicate some perceived increase in participation, but less than one might have hoped. The mean gain was only 1.59 points, compared with a maximum potential gain of 21 points (if everyone had felt they had "a lot of say" on all issues on the second wave). The median shows even less change, because of the influence of a large number of extreme cases in the positive direction. However, as table 17

TABLE 17
Statistics on Perceived Participation

	Total Worker Sample (N = 118)	Nonactivists (N = 79)	Planning Council Members (N = 11)	Special-Committee Members (N = 18)	Work Teams (N = 23)	Supervisors and Managers (N = 35)
Observed scores:						
Mean Wave 1	14.77	14.32	17.64	18.83	14.00	17.51
Mean Wave 2	16.36	15.22	19.45	21.72	17.83	18.90
S.D. Wave 1	4.77	4.52	5.18	4.67	4.71	4.80
S.D. Wave 2	6.15	5.98	3.80	5.29	6.79	4.81
t value	2.78*	1.25	1.76†	2.29‡	3.11*	1.71†
Estimated true scores:						
Mean Wave 1	14.77	14.34	17.10	18.15	14.33	17.51
Mean Wave 2	16.36	15.37	19.18	21.17	17.52	18.90
S.D. Wave 1	3.69	3.45	3.99	3.59	3.74	3.85
S.D. Wave 2	5.30	5.12	3.51	4.60	5.88	3.87
t value	3.90*	1.99‡	3.10*	3.35*	3.51*	2.99*

NOTE: A higher number indicates *more* participation.

†$p \le .10$, two-tailed.

‡$p \le .05$, two-tailed.

*$p \le .01$, two-tailed.

indicates, assuming a null hypothesis of zero change, perceived participation increased significantly if one considers either observed or estimated true scores.

The changes for the subgroupings are somewhat more encouraging. Each of the three modes of participation produced greater perceived participation, but the special-purpose committee members and work teams experienced more change in the nine decision areas measured by the index. Since the decisions included are closely connected with individual jobs and less with policy issues, we would expect the work teams to report greater gains. As stated, for all groups this is a conservative measure of actual participation, since it does not include questions about the design of the new facility, wages, working hours, or other policy-level decisions. A separate question which read, "Do you feel you ever get consulted about company-wide policies?" showed some increases for the total population (9.7% said yes on wave 1, 17.8% on wave 2); and, as expected, dramatic increases of 50% and 28% were seen for council members and participants on special committees.

The distribution of change scores is also important. For the whole sample, there is a higher proportion of the outliers in figure 3 in the positive direction (increased participation). Also, the positive changes are disproportionately activists, while the negative changes are mostly nonactivists. The records kept on the workers in the sample showed that of the five extreme negative changes, four were the result of job changes or changes in supervision; of the nine positive changes, only one could possibly be the result of a change in job.

The statistics in table 17 show that, for all but the Planning Council members, these changes had the effect of increasing the variance in participation levels both across the whole population and within the subgroups. A comparison of the means reveals that, not only was participation spread more widely, but the initial difference in participation between activists and nonactivists became even more extreme.[5] Although this was precisely what was intended, it underscores the difficulty of directly involving large numbers of workers in decision making. The sharp increases in perceived participation of the work teams and the negligible increases for the nonactivists (who are in the majority) make it apparent that, if participation is to be significantly increased across an entire corporation, a representative structure can have only a minimal effect; and increased autonomy at the shop floor level is essential.

In summary, dramatic increases in participation are difficult to achieve, especially for the mass of workers. However, the participatory mechanisms established at SI were successful at increasing participation for the activists in the program. The remaining questions to be addressed here are the effects of the participatory programs on measures of productivity and cost, alienation in work, and the belief in increased worker participation.

However, before these more quantitative measures are considered, a brief review of some of the unmeasured benefits is in order.

BENEFICIAL OUTCOMES

One of the officially stated purposes of the QWL program was "to improve the quality of working life at Sound, Inc." A number of specific programs and projects were established that were of benefit to the employees. The training program provided not only job training but also career counseling, lead training, management training, and pre-supervisory training for workers. In another aspect of the program, which was very popular, free language training (English and Spanish) was provided on company time. An orientation program for both new and older employees was begun. Job classifications were rewritten and adjusted to reflect more accurately the wishes of both supervisors and employees. A job-posting procedure was established. The layout and many additional features of the new facility (including air conditioning) were significantly affected by worker participation. Working hours were set by plant-wide votes. Wages and benefits remained high; and on the most recent review, the Planning Council successfully blocked a management proposal to base increases on performance evaluation (see chap. 6, n. 2). In addition to these major accomplishments, literally hundreds of "hygiene" problems—lights, music on the public address system, safety containers for acetone—were handled through the program.

Beyond these physical and material changes, there was noticeable improvement in the style of management and in communication within the company. The development of a Likert pin system of management was in itself a major accomplishment. The trend toward a more participative system was evident in several other forms as well. For example, leads (and sometimes work groups) were increasingly involved in interviewing job applicants and recommending advancements and wage increases. Also, with the subcouncils that began in each facility in the third year of the program, performance-review procedures were being rewritten, and employee evaluations of supervisors were being discussed.

Finally, although communication of QWL activities was a serious problem for representatives on the various committees, there is no doubt that communication between employees and management improved. For upper-level managers, the council and other committees provided one of their only communication channels with the general work force. Just by listening to council tapes, they could get a sense of general feeling and information on specific problems. To a degree, the same applied to middle-level managers and supervisors, although the later establishment of subcouncils in each facility was the important step in improving communications at that level. As the vice-president of manufacturing said, just before I left, "People seem to be talking more; they may be shouting, but they're talking."

PRODUCTIVITY AND RELATED MEASURES

In many experiments in organizational change, productivity is the critical variable. The absence of discussions of productivity in relation to the experiments at SI may be of concern to some. Productivity became a serious consideration in the two autonomous work groups, but it was rarely discussed in relation to other aspects of the program. The reason was essentially that top management had adopted the premise that, although profitability was the essential organizational objective, the purpose of the QWL program was to improve the working life of the employees through participation in decision making. This did not mean that management would not take action if productivity declined dramatically. As the president of the company stated in a memorandum to the entire work force introducing the QWL program in March 1975, "SI is part of a public company. That is, we're owned by stockholders and are answerable for our actions to them. Seen in those terms, we have a primary obligation to maintain ourselves as a profitable business enterprise. Only in this way can we continue to provide the employment opportunities that form the basis for everything else we may want to do."

Since productivity was not the central concern of the various experiments in worker participation, it was difficult to assess the effects of participation on productivity and related measures such as turnover, absenteeism, scrap rates, and reject rates. In general, the statistics were available. The problem was linking changes in productivity and organizational changes. This problem is shared by many other experiments; published accounts of other projects suggest that the link between increased employee participation and increased productivity is not firmly established. Even without considering the real possibility that reports which are published are likely to be biased in favor of increased productivity, the results that have been publicly reported are still mixed. Experiments like those at Harwood Mills or Harwood-Weldon report increased productivity and profits; others, like the Prudential experiments or the experience at Non-linear Systems, provide contradictory results.[6] Also, in nearly all cases, it is very difficult to determine whether the results actually reflected the effects of increased participation. Many projects, such as those in Norway or at Bolivar, confound participation with changes in monetary or leisure time incentives.[7] In others, such as those at Harwood-Weldon, it is very difficult to disentangle the effects of participation from reorganization, improved equipment, production design changes, etc.[8] Unfortunately, through distortion and selective use of positive evidence, influential books based on reviews of these projects suggest that higher productivity is no longer a hypothetical result of participatory management but, rather, an established fact.[9]

Company-wide Trends

The results at SI add to the evidence supporting the positive effects of participation on economic indicators. However, many of the qualifications that should be attached to other experiments apply to SI as well. During the two-year period of the project, from all indications available to me, growth in sales and profits increased substantially.[10] The relationship between these increases and worker participation is impossible to establish.

Company-wide trends in labor productivity were also encouraging, but only slightly less ambiguous in their connection to employee participation. As can be seen in figure 4, productivity was at a low point following layoffs in December 1974 and January 1975. It increased for the first three-quarters of the program before declining slightly in the last quarter for which statistics were available.[11] However, the pattern during the experimental period may be little more than a return to normal following a period of discouragement and slowdown by workers afraid of further layoffs. Also, although the productivity figures have been computed in terms of real dollars, it was not possible to allow for changes in capital investment or indirect labor costs, which we must therefore assume to be constant over the three-year period. Given these qualifications, the most conservative conclusion is that the costs of the program in terms of direct expenditures, lost labor hours, organizational changes, etc., did not re-

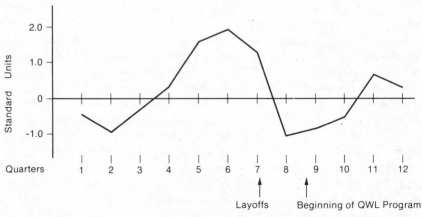

*Measured as dollar output in terms of real dollars per direct labor hour. The plotted points are z-scores across the twelve quarters. Positive points represent higher productivity.

Figure 4. Company-wide Labor Productivity, 1973–76

strain profitability or productivity. Furthermore, it is certainly possible that the QWL program contributed to these increases.

Trends in scrap and reject rates, impossible to represent graphically in comparative form because they varied widely by product, appeared to be relatively unaffected over the two-year period in question. The overall scrap rate increased, but it had been rising steadily for five years, primarily because of the increasing complexity of the products (closer tolerances, more complex assemblies, etc.) and the rapid growth of the company. The trends in reject rates for the various product lines also remained stable, and no amount of analysis could decipher any radical changes that could be associated in any way with increased participation.

Turnover rates for the company fluctuated more dramatically. In the first year of the program, turnover dropped from 55% to 28%. Without question, part of this decline was because layoffs had increased average seniority and because there was a generally tight labor market. In 1976, as the company returned to full capacity and unemployment in Los Angeles declined, turnover went back up to 42.9%. Again, as with the results for productivity, there is no indication of a detrimental effect, and there is some reason for optimism.

Work Teams

In early discussions of work projects in each facility, the ability to measure the economic impacts of the experiments was an important consideration. However, as the problems with selecting suitable locations multiplied, this criterion became secondary. In each project, specific problems made the calculation of "hard" productivity measures somewhat suspect. For the Employee Relations Department, measurement of "productivity" was meaningless. In the lacquer-finish areas, where pre-experimental trends were available, estimates (e.g.) of completed cabinets per man-hour were subject to a number of variations. Volumes required would fluctuate; as they did, workers were shifted to other finishing areas, quite often without accurate accounting. Variations in the quality of wood or the quality of assembly also produced fluctuations. The 6208 and L606 projects were new lines, so historical figures were not available. Also, the trends during the experiment were affected by unmeasured increases and changes in equipment, materials, etc. Thus the computation of productivity was subject to a great deal of variance, and it was very difficult to determine if the errors in measurement biased changes over time.

Of the statistics available, the most reliable were for the lacquer-finish areas. In these areas, manufacturing engineering could calculate efficiency ratings based on worker-recorded hours spent on specific tasks. Since this system was less than six months old when the projects began, it was not extremely accurate. However, if we assume that errors randomize over the lives of the projects, over the eight months of the project the results show an increase in efficiency of 7% for the day shift and 13% for the night shift. When I left in June 1976, the plant manager said that he supposed it might be difficult to convince a cynic of a substantial increase, but it was clear the productivity had not declined.

On the 6208 line, measures are really meaningless because the project lasted only three months. Also, the production process was completely disorganized in the beginning, and there were extreme inaccuracies in recording labor hours.

On the L606 line, my personal records demonstrate that, although the number of man-hours per unit decreased slightly over the six-month period, total acceptable units and therefore total dollar output per man-hour fluctuated greatly from week to week. This variation was due to experimentation with methods and materials and to differences in the quality of materials supplied by contractors. Monthly productivity started quite high, then fell drastically in the second month. The final four months were relatively stable around the mean of the first two.

Given the limitations of measurement, the available evidence indicates a slight increase in productivity for the work teams. Perhaps the best indicator is that only in rare instances were the enthusiasm and effort expended by the participants questioned by either supervisors or support personnel. To the extent that productivity is a function of how hard people work and how seriously they take their jobs, the work projects can be considered a success.

PARTICIPATION AND ALIENATION

Alienation from work was considered as an independent variable in my analysis of belief in participation and activism in chapters 3 and 4. It was first shown that alienated workers were more likely to believe in increased participation. However, when controlling for other variables, there was no evidence that those most alienated would become actively involved if given the opportunity. In this section, the effects of various forms of participation on worker alienation will be considered. In other words, alienation will now be treated as a dependent variable.

As explained in chapter 3, alienation from work was measured as four separate dimensions that could be combined as a single overall measure. A first test of the relationships between alienation and participation (the one used almost exclusively in the existing literature) was comparison of initial levels of alienation with how much say people had on their jobs when the program began. For the first wave of interviews, the correlation between the "present participation on the job" index and the overall alienation scale was $-.25$, meaning that greater participation was associated with lower levels of alienation. The effect remained statistically significant after controlling for background variables (age, education, sex, race), societal alienation (measured by the Srole scale), attitudes toward supervision, and the level and attributes of the individual's job, using multiple regression techniques. Since many of these variables were correlated with participation on the job, the fact that the relationship between participation and alienation was still significant at the .01 level suggests that this is not an artificial effect—that, regardless of one's personal circumstances or situation within a company, employees with greater influence over their jobs are less alienated.

Knowledge that under ordinary circumstances participation on the job is related to lower levels of alienation encourages actions to increase worker participation. Unfortunately, increasing participation does not by itself guarantee a reduction in alienation. Even in the ideal corporate democracy, a great many forces would be at work that could nullify the potential effects of participation. Worker participation at SI was far from ideal, and so were the hoped-for reductions in alienation and dissatisfaction on the job.

The box plots of change scores in the composite alienation index are depicted in figure 5. For the overall sample, there was virtually no change in either the mean or median. The middle 50% of the distribution reported changes no greater than four points in either direction on a scale with a potential range of fifty-five points. Although disappointing, the result was somewhat understandable for nonactivists. What was unexpected was the change for activists. For those individuals involved in joint decision making, especially members of special committees, alienation apparently increased. This effect was offset by the reduced alienation of the twenty-three individuals involved in the work teams. For a null hypothesis of zero change, the results for special committees and the work teams are significant at the .05 level. There is little deviation in any of these findings when estimated true scores are used instead of the observed change scores.

The apparent increase in alienation for those participating in joint decision-making committees can be explained by analyzing the changes in the separate dimensions that make up the overall index. For both Planning Council and special-committee members, the increase in the composite index was primarily due to a perceived decrease in the individual's control over rewards associated with doing one's job (see app. C, table C-7). This result makes some sense, given the characteristics of activists. They were young and ambitious and in relatively high-level jobs at the beginning of the program. For the new, ambitious employee, opportunities seem numerous, and advancement comes early. However, he soon reaches a point in the hierarchy where further upward movement becomes difficult, and advances in wages marginally decrease. This occurs just below the level of supervisor for most employees. When this happens, a sense of powerlessness sets in. No longer does the employee see his efforts

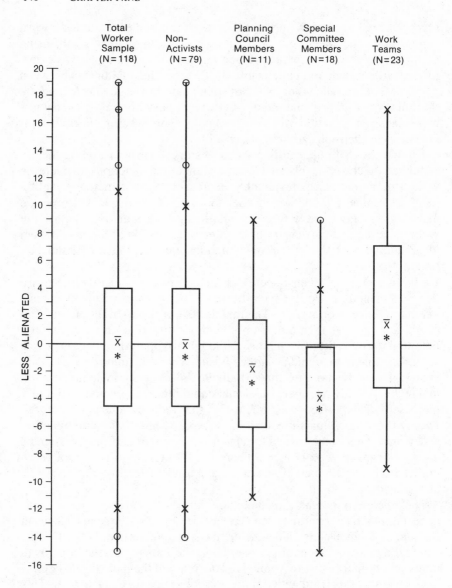

Figure 5. Box Plots of Changes in Alienation from Work

matched by what he considers just rewards. This cycle, an assured consequence of hierarchical organization, produces what was earlier called
frustrated ambition. These frustrated individuals become effective spokesmen of worker interests in joint decision-making councils, but that
participation is apparently insufficient as a remedy for their underlying
sense of powerlessness.[12]

It is very unlikely that even the most ideal form of worker participation will reduce the overall level of powerlessness in an organization as long as the traditional status hierarchy is maintained. Losers will always outnumber winners, and workers quickly become aware of the long odds against advancement.[13] The young and ambitious rarely accept their lot with equanimity. For the organization, this increase in alienation is partially counteracted by the influx of new, hopeful employees, as well as by a gradual lowering of expectations for older employees. However, increasing education with a commensurate rise in expectations, as well as the continuing emphasis in American society on competitive individualism, feeds this sense of powerlessness. This suggests an escalation of the problem over the coming decades.

If democratizing the work place provides any answers for worker alienation, the experiments at SI clearly favor worker participation at the operational level. Participation on joint decision-making committees did nothing to reduce alienation and may even have increased it, but participation on work teams had the reverse effect. The decrease in alienation, significant for both raw scores and estimated true scores, is apparent in figure 5. Of the four dimensions of alienation studied, the largest improvements were in measures of normlessness and self-estrangement. Unlike those involved at the policy level, who felt that they had less control over the rewards and sanctions that affected their jobs, those participating at the shop floor level felt that there was no appreciable change in the powerlessness dimension.

These findings are all the more remarkable given the disappointing developments of the work teams. When the second wave of interviews were conducted, all but the 6208 experiment were still under way, although plagued with troubles. Even with these problems, satisfaction with many aspects of their jobs and working environment had improved. The direction for future research is clear. If the problem of worker alienation is to be taken seriously, research in the design and organization of work itself provides the greatest potential for its resolution.

In summary, there is evidence supporting the correlation between participation in decisions that affect one's job and lower levels of alienation. Creating mechanisms that sufficiently increase participation relevant to the worker's life on the job is another question altogether. Representative policymaking within a factory seems to have no more influence on work alienation than representative systems in a democracy on political alienation. If any answer is appropriate, decentralization of representative systems is essential; and, most important, meaningful participation must be made available at the shop floor level. In making this recommendation, the obstacles should not be understated; for increasing shop floor democracy requires significant changes in the structure of most jobs and a serious effort to reshape accepted ideas of leadership and responsibility. To accomplish this requires a moving force, a concentrated pressure from some point in the system supporting a philosophy of industrial democracy. Without such a normative base, industrial democracy will be nothing more than an unending series of experiments initiated and enacted by the eccentric few.

CHANGES IN BELIEF IN PARTICIPATION

At many points in this book, the importance of beliefs supporting worker participation has been stressed. I have stated that workers and managers intially favored a moderate increase over the current levels of employee participation. This somewhat conservative attitude was explained by the workers' willing acceptance of management authority and prerogatives in many areas and by their total lack of experience with the idea of a democratic organization. Because of the latter factor I argued that initial beliefs could be discounted to a certain degree, and that more accurate beliefs would emerge once workers began to exercise more influence in the enterprise. In this light, the lack of changes in beliefs in participation depicted in figure 6 are all the more disappointing.

Figure 6 graphically portrays the change scores on the seventeen-item belief-in-participation scale described earlier (see app. C, table C-1). As is immediately apparent, there was almost no change in the average or median support for participation in the total sample of workers. The range of changes also reflects the consistency from one interview to the other. The box which represents the middle 50% of the distribution shows that half the change scores were between +4 and −5, for a scale with a potential range of 51. Extreme scores are divided fairly evenly between positive and negative changes.

Not shown in the diagram is the consistency in individual items. If these items are ranked by individual means, as depicted in figure 1 (p. 29), the Spearman rank order correlation between wave 1 and wave 2 is .963. Interestingly enough, the only significant increases were for participation in the selection of leads and supervisors. Managers' responses went in the opposite direction on these issues. Thus the difference between workers and managers in attitudes concerning the selection of direct supervision, significant on the initial interviews, became even more extreme. However, workers still wanted only between "a little say" and "some say" on these issues.

With the notable exception of Planning Council members, there was also very little change for activists. The medians for special-committee members and work teams are very close to zero. The increase in the average for those work-team members interviewed twice is due primarily to an increase of twenty-eight points by one woman on the L606 line.

The apparent loss of normative commitment by council members, albeit

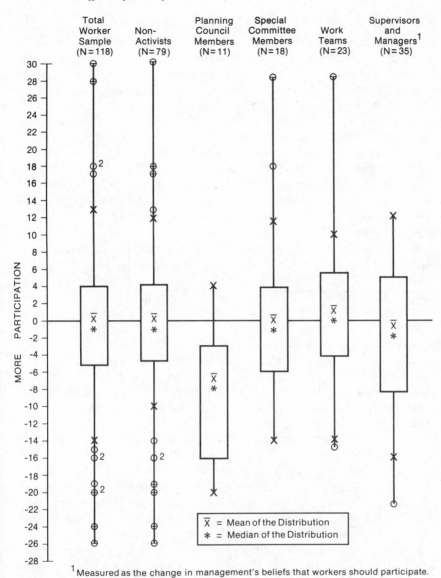

Figure 6. Box Plots of Changes in Belief in Workers' Participation

disappointing, may be exaggerated somewhat. Part of this decline (statistically significant at the .05 level) is an accurate expression of the disenchantment felt by some council members at the apparent apathy of their fellow workers, but regression to the mean also explains some of the change. On the first wave of interviews, council members averaged over six points higher on this scale than the rest of the sample. On the second wave, that six-point spread had disappeared. Correcting for regression effects reduces this difference to 4.3, still significant but not quite so dramatic. The small number of interviews makes any generalization very difficult. However, at the very least it can be said that there is no evidence that long, intense experience with joint decision making increases the participants' belief in the appropriateness of worker participation.

The change in management attitudes is more than merely statistically significant. Although in absolute terms the change is minor (but significant at the .05 level), it demonstrates some of the hostility and disappointment managers and supervisors felt toward the program. Comments from managers elicited in response to questions about the program fell disproportionately into complaints of "too much talking, too little action" and expressions of concern that participation would erode the authority of the supervisor.

The consistency in attitudes between waves 1 and 2 is also reflected in answers to the participation trade-off questions (see pp. 33–34). On wave 1 only 48% of the workers interviewed said that, in a choice between otherwise identical jobs, the prospect of participating in decisions would be important enough to lead to a choice of the participatory job. On wave 2 the percentage was 50. In addition, in a random sample of sixty workers drawn in January 1978 by my successor at SI, the comparable figure had dropped to 46%. Furthermore, for those who would take the more participatory job, in both of the last two surveys there was no appreciable change from the figures reported in chapter 3 in those willing to trade participation for less pay or additional hours (see p. 34, table 5). Thus over three years there was no evidence of increased interest in participation measured either by the decision-making index or by considering the tradeoffs of participation.

A drive for more worker participation simply did not occur among workers, and there is some evidence of a reactionary effect among supervisors. In a larger political system, this unfortunate level of support can be tolerated. This is not the case for industrial democracy at the plant level. In direct forms of decision making, particularly in work groups, participation must be active in order to maintain interest and prevent more aggressive workers from assuming positions of authority. Similarly, representation in the close environment of a factory is very personal, as witnessed by the frustration of Planning Council members when faced with the apathy of their co-workers.

Belief in participation is also essential because a serious attempt at democratizing an organization requires dramatic changes in the theory and practice of organizational behavior. If what we think of as democracy is no more than a consultative and humanistic approach to management, that is one thing; but if what we mean by democracy is a system based on a fundamental principle of equality within the organization, we are faced with a radical conversion of thought and structure. That conversion will not be brought about by the idealism of a few top-level managers, workers, or union leaders. Without the commitment of middle-level managers, supervisors, and a majority of the work force, attempts to democratize a corporation will be lost amid the frenetic, day-to-day activity directed toward achieving accepted corporate purposes.

10. Democracy and
Meritocracy in Work

In this book I have described the complexity of the issues surrounding industrial democracy. Taking an optimistic overview, significant participation is still going on, three years after SI began its program. There are special-purpose committees, a company-wide worker-management council, and subcouncils at each plant location. Profitability has varied but has not been adversely affected by the program. Even though the parent company was recently purchased by a huge conglomerate and the top managers who served as the catalysts for the experiments are no longer involved, there is no evidence that the program will decline in importance.

On the other hand, a closer look at the history of the various participatory experiments suggests a number of constraints that limit the possibility of meaningful industrial democracy. Joint labor-management committees were plagued by problems of communication and apathy, by resistance to establishing formal committees on wages and grievances, and by the impotence and tension that resulted from a dual hierarchy.

An obvious answer is to democratize the day-to-day operations of the corporation, but attempts to accomplish this on the shop floor level at SI were fraught with difficulties. Reduced levels of alienation for those involved in these experiments indicates the utility of further research, but fully autonomous work groups are certainly not so obvious or simple a solution as some proponents envision.

An appropriate characterization of the QWL program at SI is that it was most successful in areas marginal to the existing operational core of the corporation, composed of standard procedures and an established pattern of authority and responsibility. Attempts to penetrate that system were not strongly supported by most employees and were met with active resistance from leads, supervisors, and managers. In order to understand the exact nature and magnitude of this constraint on organizational democracy, we should look in detail at the conflict between the meritocratic norms which define a traditional corporation and those norms on which a more democratic structure would be based.

THEORETICAL ISSUES REEXAMINED

The theoretical issues discussed in chapter 1 were of two kinds: general problems of direct democracy and issues associated with specific modes of participation. Here I will concentrate on the four general criteria considered critical for the realization of industrial democracy: belief in participation; physical requirements of time, space, and communication; worker competence; and realization of satisfactory outcomes in terms of reduced alienation and increased productivity.

Our most optimistic conclusion concerns worker competence. Both quantitative and subjective analyses of tape recordings of joint worker-management meetings demonstrate that workers were very nearly as effective as managers in these meetings. The only significant difficulties were that managers had access to more information and general knowledge concerning business activities and that efforts to establish effective mechanisms to handle grievances and resolve wage and benefit issues were successfully resisted. For the Planning Council, there was evidence that over both of the first two years, the information advantage of managers diminished. Further use of special-purpose committees, with a narrow range of responsibilities, and longer tenures for worker members might well eliminate this problem altogether.

The conflicts over grievances and wages can only be solved by the creation of formal, legal procedures. Although the Planning Council did have some effect on these problems and the humanistic bent of the top-level managers prompted decisions that were quite fair, management still resisted the creation of formal mechanisms for worker involvement in these decisions. If there were changes in management personnel, decisions on these and other important issues could easily cease to reflect the interests of workers. It is difficult to conceive of a lasting program in industrial democracy that does not provide a formal system of rights and procedures to protect employees on these vital issues. Given the resistance of American managers to such legal formality, this implies a union.

Although the experience at SI demonstrates the potential of workers or their chosen representatives to participate in critical decisions, this conclusion does not necessarily carry over to the most common form of industrial democracy around the world, employee representation on corporate boards. Especially in large companies, which employ the great majority of people in America, it is very doubtful that an employee, who spends most of his time in a factory or office job, could effectively compete with professional managers who, with their staffs, invest a great deal of time in the top-level decisions that require board approval. The only answer that seems viable is for professional union leaders, backed by staffs of their own, to present the employee side of issues. This solution is certainly plausible; however, it would exaggerate the problems of representation and communication to the point where any pretense of direct democracy would be illusory. This form of representation is really nothing more than an extension of pluralism; however, it can still be commended on the grounds that it would increase the inclusiveness of the system.[1]

American union leaders, if they were so inclined, could easily assume these roles. Given that, for this study and other sample populations, public opinion seems to support the idea of employee representatives on corporate boards, it should not be dismissed so easily as many top labor leaders and executives would have it. This innovation would not provide the type of direct participation that has been the focus of this book, but it is a progressive idea that surely deserves serious consideration in this country.

The SI experiments were not so successful in terms of the other three theoretical issues. Constraints of time and the ability to communicate adequately among the members of the organization both created difficulties. The limitations were somewhat more subtle than the hypothetical problems of holding mass meetings that have been used by a number of prominent theorists to dissuade overzealous proponents of direct democracy. Time, however, was an important influence at both levels of worker participation. For plant-wide decisions, the need for a representative structure was apparent from the beginning, although the size of the representative unit was debated. However, as illustrated by the Planning Council's loss of control over program implementation, the time required to gain specialized knowledge of substantive issues required the delegation of authority from democratically structured committees to the normal organizational hierarchy. Much as Congress faces complicated policy issues by writing broadly worded legislation and delegating massive authority to specialized agencies, policy committees within a corporation can only provide direction to and some monitoring of the functional departments that will actually determine and carry out policies. Time condemns the generalist to a subordinate role.

At the shop floor level, the inability of work teams to maintain continuous coordination, monitoring, and reporting through group decision making led quickly to the assignment of these tasks to specific individuals. This consequence was due partly to the lost production time resulting from group meetings and partly to the psychological security derived from established routines and assigned responsibility. Thus, even in the smallest and most basic organizational unit, the efficient use of time serves to limit the individual's control when group activity is required.

Communication was also a problem at SI, particularly for the Planning Council and special-purpose committees but also for the plant-level subcouncils that came into existence in the third year of the program. The physical side of the communication problem is more amenable to solution than are the psychological problems stemming from employee apathy. More complete meeting minutes, regularly scheduled reports by representatives, occasional mass meetings, imaginative use of media, and more frequent referenda within the plants are possible solutions to the physical problems of communication. Making people want to listen and to take interest is another question altogether. Nothing is more discouraging to an employee representative than to work extremely hard, possibly jeopardizing his future with the company, only to be confronted with constituents who do not know what is happening and do not care. One council member bitterly replied, when explaining why he was not running for a second term, "They deserve every kick in the ass they get."

The effects of the innovations at SI on productivity were mixed, and generalizations are somewhat dubious because of the short time period involved and (for several variables) the difficulty in making causal inferences. However, for those concerned with the bottom line, the results are promising: by conservative estimate, profitability and productivity were not adversely affected; in fact, using available measures, productivity increased over the first two years of the program. How much of this increase can be attributed to worker participation is only speculative, however.

Changes in job satisfaction and alienation were dependent on the mode of participation. Although the numbers of subjects were quite small, workers who participated in joint decision making were actually slightly more alienated in the second wave of interviews. The shop floor experiments seemed to have a positive effect nevertheless, reducing levels of worker alienation for most of those involved. Surely, considering the changes recorded at SI, the promises offered by industrial democracy are realistic possibilities. The changes cannot be expected to be dramatic in the short run, but healthy corporations will not be ruined by the infusion of democratic practices.[2]

The major disappointment of the SI experiments was failure to build a normative foundation for worker participation. At first the idea of workers participating in decisions affecting their working lives was new and somewhat confusing. It is difficult to claim this condition as a rationale for the moderate interest in participation expressed after many months of participation and discussion of democratic concepts. The majority of responses in the second wave were dishearteningly similar, as were the rationalizations given for limiting participation. Their ideal distribution of power still greatly favored the rights of management. For many of those who participated in the most exciting aspects of the program, initial enthusiasm about participation subsided. For managers and supervisors, there was a significant retraction of an earlier commitment to worker participation.

Without a positive, active commitment to worker participation, it is extremely doubtful that any movement toward industrial democracy can materialize in the United States. In those isolated companies where serious projects are begun, usually at the insistence of an unusually liberal top management, democratic mechanisms will be very difficult to sustain. Industrial democracy requires active participation; apathy and overt resistance have direct consequences that are not easily ignored.

It remains to discuss the apparent reluctance of workers and managers to embrace democratic principles as a central form of organizational design. I will argue that meaningful democracy in an organization is not a minor adjustment of style and priority but requires a truly radical shift away from traditional norms of corporate organization. Furthermore, this contradiction exists not only for behavioral rules but also for underlying assumptions concerning the purpose of the organization and the nature of human motivation. The contradiction is rooted in the fact that the traditional corporation is based on meritocratic principles that exploit human differences, while the democratic enterprise is premised, at least in part, on political and substantive equality.

MERITOCRATIC AND DEMOCRATIC MODELS OF ORGANIZATION
Underlying Assumptions

The basic assumptions of meritocratic organizations are reasonably simple and concise and are deeply ingrained in the American corporate ideology. These assumptions, from which more concrete principles of organizational behavior are derived, concern the purpose of the organization, the structure of modern productive activity, and the nature of human motivation in work.

The concept of organizational purpose is one of the most confusing and debated topics in the literature on organizations. Beginning with the discovery by Elton Mayo and his colleagues of the importance of group dynamics and informal group norms, and continuing with the emphasis by Simon, March, Cyert, and James Thompson on the multiple objectives sought by various participants in the economic enterprise, there has been a consistent retreat from the earlier assumption that the sole purpose of the corporation is securing profits.[3] These theories not only challenge the economists's assumption that corporate decision makers act to maximize profits but also argue that behavior throughout the organization is the result of a complex web of competing goals.

In one sense, these theories are obviously valid. That decision makers cannot adequately accumulate or process the information required to maximize profits under conditions of uncertainty is commonsensical and readily apparent from observation. This fact should not be misinterpreted, however: securing profits may still be by far the most important factor considered in corporate decisions. Similarly, either theoretical consideration of what the goals of various participants might be or observation of organizational activities can be expected to uncover activities divorced from the exclusive pursuit of profits. The important question is not the existence of these diverse goals but how important they are in relation to the goal of securing corporate profit.

The problem is how to determine the goals of a complex organization. If the intention is to understand the "real" or "operative" goals of the organization,[4] as opposed to either formally stated or theoretically derived objectives, analysis must center on activities within the organization. This is easy to say but very difficult to accomplish. One solution has been to ask managers and workers either their own personal goals or the goals of others in the organization.[5] The obvious difficulty in this approach is that what an individual may think or desire may not coincide with his actual behavior. Thus the manager who says one of his goals is to provide the public with quality products may in practice consistently succumb to production pressures, disregarding quality considerations in order to meet a specific quota. An alternative to this approach is to observe actual decision-making sessions, concentrating on the criteria that are used to evaluate proposals. At levels within the organization where "decisions" really become a matter of routine administration, activities can be analyzed by observing the factors that seem to be most obviously determining behavior. Relying on these two devices, I would argue that the profit motive as a guide to decision making and routine operations looms large in relation to other possible goals.

Consider first the decision-making function in the corporation. As already stated, it is very difficult to argue that executives act according to a profit-maximizing principle. However, in observing and discussing many decisions at SI, I found that economic factors consistently provided a yardstick against which nearly every decision was measured. For most decisions, the discussion was in terms not of final profit but, rather, of cost, effects on capacity, productivity, margins, sales, or the like. However, to argue that, because choices are made on the basis of their effect on these intermediate measures, profit is not the overriding factor is to misunderstand the close relationship here between means and ends. Cost reduction is not an end in itself; it makes sense only in relation to profit. The same is true of increasing productivity and establishing sales goals. The relatively direct effect on profits when these goals are changed should be emphasized.

Some theorists have argued that corporate goals like growth, stability, diversity, or market share are not only independent goals of the corporation but also goals that can run counter to profits.[6] Both claims are true in certain instances, but again this is a matter of frequency and relative importance and in many instances may be merely the result of differences in time perspective. A goal of capturing a certain percentage of a product market may require extensive advertising, resulting in a short-run decline in profits. However, in all but the most deviant cases, such decisions are based on an assumption of eventual profits that will more than offset an initial loss. Similarly, although the rapid expansion of conglomerates in the 1960s may have suggested to some that growth and diversity in assets were goals independent of profits, the rapid decline or bankruptcy of some of these companies has led to more conservative acquisition policies. It is simply difficult to imagine these decisions being made very often without major consideration of effects on profit. In terms of Simon's conceptualization of decision making as means-ends chains, the end of realizing profits is overwhelmingly important, and the chains establishing intermediate goals are short, linked to profit by one or two steps at most.

At the operational level, two assumptions—that employees have individual goals inconsistent with the profit objective and that group influences may further divert behavior—appeal to common sense and have been verified by numerous empirical studies. But again we must ask how important these factors are in explaining corporate activity. The potential for this deviation from the corporate goal is well understood by managers and engineers. The response is to enmesh the organization in elaborate monitoring mechanisms that ensure behavioral conformity. Timetables are established for the completion of projects; production scheduling becomes an elaborate art; sales quotas and commission schemes guide the behavior of marketing specialists; bonus systems, geared to specific profit targets, direct the ambitions of managers; records are established and individuals are held accountable for scrap rates, reject rates, budget overruns, labor productivity, and inventory control.

The pulse of the corporation varies as behavior deviates from the norms established by these devices. Certainly these schedules, quotas, and rates may be the subject of negotiation and at times even cause rebellion, but behavior is nevertheless controlled by these numbers. And the numbers are directly related to profitability. To suggest that corporate decisions and behavior are the result of a diverse range of equally influential goals is to misunderstand the driving force, to concentrate on marginal factors while ignoring the central purpose of economic enterprises.

A second basic assumption of traditional theories of organization is the hierarchical structure of authority. The rationalizations for this form of control are common in the literature on organizations and need not be reviewed in detail.[7] This literature dwells on the effects of task specialization and the need for coordination, unity of command, conflict resolution, and regularized patterns of communication as essential to the efficient operation of complex organizations. To this I would add the argument concerning the nature of responsibility and the system of accountability that develops as responsibility is delegated. Because of the overwhelming emphasis on economic factors in corporations, task assignments are very specific, and accountability is aided by reference to quantitative measures of performance. Thus the superior faced with delegating responsibility will attempt to make precise assignments and will resist interference with his prerogative to select and reward those subordinates to whom responsibility is given. This results not only in a pyramidal structure of authority but a structure in which crucial decisions about assignment of responsibility and rewards for performance flow from the top to the bottom.

The establishment of a hierarchy of offices is a natural outcome, given a relatively large, complex organization geared to achieving a concrete, measurable goal. It is an assumption accepted by nearly all organizations and organizational theorists. What is arguable is the proper nature of that hierarchy. Who selects individuals to fill hierarchical positions? What are the grounds on which such selections are made? According to what principles are rewards distributed? What style of supervision is employed? To a large extent, these important characteristics of hierarchy depend on assumptions concerning the characteristics and motivations of individuals. For the traditional corporation, these assumptions lead to a structure that can be summarized by the word *meritocracy*.

Ironically, assumptions concerning man's nature in traditionally managed enterprises have been most prominently displayed by critics of traditional organization theory, such as Douglas McGregor. His assumptions are admittedly posed in extreme form, but they are nevertheless wholly misleading on a crucial point. The primary assumptions of a meritocratic organization are not, as McGregor claimed, that workers inherently dislike work, are unambitious, reject responsibility, and are motivated only by threats of punishment and a sense of security.[8] On the contrary, the basic assumption is that workers *vary* in ambitions, drives, and abilities. A meritocratic organization is designed to promote and reward those individuals whose characteristics and performance are compatible with the organization's goal. A great deal of time is spent in meritocratic organizations trying to sort out individual variances, matching talents and abilities with job requirements.

Several important assumptions concerning motivation distinguish meritocratic organizations from more ideal democratic forms, but they have little to do with the assumptions discussed by most humanists. The first is that motivation relates primarily to the individual; thus incentives should be administered on a person-by-person basis. Despite the volumes of studies on group dynamics, there are very few examples in American organizations, public or private, where significant rewards are granted on a group basis. This is particularly true for critical decisions on promotions and wage increases.

A second set of assumptions is that rewards are to be granted in relation to individual performance and that the rewards will consist of a combination of material and status incentives. Although this does not preclude motivation based on organizational identity or group norms, the relevance of such incentives is secondary in meritocratic organizations. I do not suggest that the incentive system is based on crass materialism. Status incentives may well consist of rewards that work through an increase in the individual's self-esteem, perhaps a prominently displayed advancement in the hierarchy, a luxurious office, or a more intrinsically interesting job. Thus the assumption is that individuals vary in their ability and efforts to contribute to the organization's goal and that reward should therefore be varied individually in relation to these contributions. To some these may seem to be very tame assumptions. Their relevance is apparent when compared with assumptions underlying a democratic organization.

Clearly specifying the basic assumptions of a democratic theory of organization is difficult because of the lack of real-world examples from which a model could be fashioned. The problem is immediately apparent when we consider assumptions concerning organizational purpose. Bennis and Slater, arguing with some literary license about why organizations of the future will be increasingly democratic, emphasize the purposeless nature of democracy: "These new professional men are remarkably compatible with our conception of a democratic system. For, like these new men, democracy seeks no new stability, no end point, it is purposeless, save that it purports to ensure perpetual transition, constant alteration, ceaseless instability."[9] In one important respect, this concept of democracy is compatible with much of contemporary democratic theory. From pluralist theories one can argue that democracy is only a mechanism for resolving conflicts arising from the individual purposes of its citizens. Thus, at least theoretically, democracy is not meant to achieve a specific substantive end.[10]

It is frivolous to suggest that industrial democracy operate from this extreme assumption. Unless we wish to restrict ourselves to a very small class of noncompetitive, nonprofit cooperatives and religious or ideological communes, we must assume that a democratically organized economic enterprise will have to achieve a specific productive goal, exactly like its meritocratic counterpart. The difference is that in the democratic organization there are competing goals which must be achieved as well. Of these, a sense of equality among members of the organization is most important. Again, we need not exaggerate this assumption to the point where we forsake all authority and hierarchy, for achieving productive goals will require coordination and direction of activity. It does of course mean that the structure of that hierarchy (who assumes authoritative roles and how they are rewarded) must take into consideration the norm of equality, both in the political sense (equal rights and participation in decision making) and, to a degree, in the distribution of rewards.

In conjunction with this premise of equality, assumptions concerning the nature and motivation of employees differ significantly from those in a meritocracy. While the meritocratic system emphasizes variance among people and thus concentrates on motivating the individual in a competitive environment, democratic theories tend to assume greater similarity in abilities and willingness to act responsibly, emphasizing communal rewards and a cooperative environment. It is not necessary to assume equality in terms of material and status rewards, but pressures for a more equal distribution will be much stronger than in the meritocratic model. Additionally, a democratic model would place greater emphasis on organizational belonging. While the meritocratic organization stresses individual competitiveness, the democratic organization must stress the cooperative and communal instincts of man.[11] The conflict in these underlying assumptions carries over to more concrete principles of organization.

Organizational Norms

The underlying assumptions discussed above lead to contrasting sets of organizational norms at a less abstract level. When the democratic principles of organization are discussed with workers and managers, "the nature of man" rarely enters into the conversation. The norms described in table 18 are much closer to the rationalizations that are used in such discussions. Norms at this level vividly demonstrate the radical departure of industrial democracy from traditional, meritocratic forms of organization.

The norms of table 18 serve as answers to questions essential to a description of any organizational structure. The first describes the overall shape of the organization. The prescriptions are somewhat vague because of the wide range of alternatives in each system. Democratic enterprises would not lack a hierarchy completely, but the stress on equality would suggest a reduced hierarchy in terms of both power differentials between steps in the hierarchy and the number of levels in the system.[12]

The general role structure may not be so important as the question of selecting leaders. Deciding who should occupy positions of authority is obviously a critical question and a major source of contradiction between the two models. Kibbutz plants and, to a limited extent, Yugoslav corporations have adopted the rotation or election of management as a central feature of their systems. This is the logical compromise between requirements for coordination, centralized reporting, and direction and the principle of political equality. The principle that leaders should be selected by those led is at some point a central aspect of all democratic theory. Given the current level of theory, the use of the word *democracy* surely implies this norm to some degree.

However, notice that, with the selection of leaders from below, norms defining responsibility within the organization are also affected. Election of leaders implies that workers share responsibility for both their actions and the actions of the leader. Whereas in the meritocratic organization the

TABLE 18
Democratic and Meritocratic Organizational Norms

Democratic Organization	Norm	Meritocratic Organization
Less pyramidal Reduced levels of hierarchy	Role structure	Pyramidal Large number of hierarchical levels
From below Possible rotation	Selection of leaders	From above Permanent
Toward equality	Rewards	Consciously inegalitarian
Assignment: shared, delegated Leader's responsibility: 　To subordinates 　To organization goals 　To superior	Responsibility	Assignment: individual, retained by superior Leader's responsibility: 　To organizational goals 　To superior 　To subordinates
Degree: less direct supervision Based on persuasion, competence, role Style: democratic, compromise, negotiation	Authority/supervision	Degree: variable Based on role, competence Style: variable

superior is held responsible for those under him, in a democratic organization the work group itself, by virtue of the fact that it picked its own leader, shares this burden. This also affects the responsibility of the leader, who, unlike his counterpart in a traditional organization, will be responsible first to those who selected him, then to organizational goals, and last to the wishes of his superior.

The distinction in principles of reward can be derived directly from differences in underlying assumptions concerning equality. However, apart from an independent principle dictating that rewards should be relatively equally distributed, a more equal distribution of responsibility would also lead to this end. If we assume successful performance, workers would argue that greater responsibility should lead to greater rewards, and equal responsibility to equal rewards. Thus a strong interlocking relationship appears, linking the election of leaders, shared responsibility, and equal rewards. This interrelationship is important, because experimentation with changes in one of these norms can be expected to involve the others quickly. For example, if jobs of varying responsibility are to be rotated among the group, attempts to maintain pay differentials will be opposed. Managers will quickly point out that the solution favored by workers in this situation will be to "equalize up" to the highest wage in the group.

The final norms described in table 18 have to do with the degree, the source of legitimacy, and the style of supervision in the two forms of organization. We can be more specific in describing the norms in a democratic organization than in a meritocratic one, because meritocratic organizations do not rule out democratic management styles. The difference is that, in a meritocratic system, the degree of supervision and the style employed will depend more than in a democratic organization on personal whim and the effectiveness on the performance of subordinates. In a democratic system, autocratic behavior by leaders would be affected first by the fact that leaders are selected by those led and second by the underlying emphasis on equality.

The conclusion from comparing these two models is not surprising: a democratic system of organization implies a radical change from a traditional meritocratic system. But notice also that the most dramatic differences are not in the structure of roles within the organization or in the way authority is carried out but, rather, in those norms which are most directly related to the meritocratic incentives that form the essence of management control. Differing assumptions about the reward structure, the assignment of responsibility, and the selection of leaders distinguish a democratic form of organization. Without their inclusion, schemes of industrial democracy are defined apart from an assumption of political equality and become merely exercises in organizational decentralization and humanistic management. Beneficial as both may be, they do not provide the critical elements that theoretically differentiate democratic from authoritarian political systems. The task remains to speculate as to the balance of support for these alternative principles. Regrettably, it must be argued that the scales are tipped heavily in favor of meritocracy.

The Tendency toward Meritocracy

The emphasis on meritocracy in American culture is historically based and extremely pervasive. The loss of the work ethic, always assumed to be in a state of decline, seems to be more strongly lamented by each succeeding generation of parents as they appraise the efforts and attitudes of their offspring. Unions, currently representing only one worker in five, are charged both in the public and private sector with assault on the "merit principle." Legislative and court actions conspicuously favor equality of opportunity rather than equality in the absolute distribution of income or power. Our schools are designed in "tracks," with continuation based on grade performance and examination. Indeed, one of the most romantic theories of American democracy emphasizes not political equality but the rugged individualism made possible by an expanding frontier.[13] The potential list of examples is virtually endless.

In relation to work, the comparative study of five nations by Tannenbaum and his colleagues provides the best evidence to date on the importance of meritocracy in American corporations. While ranking United

States companies very high on a number of humanistic dimensions, the researchers describe a sharp contrast with the democracy of the kibbutz factories. In summarizing these findings, they emphasize the normative differences in terms very similar to those I have employed earlier.

> While the two models, exemplified by the kibbutz plants on the one hand and by American on the other, share some common values, they are sharply divided on a central value that is the basis for many differences between them—equality. Democracy and justice in the kibbutz conception hinge on equality of power and reward, and unlike the American system, the material rewards provided a member need not correspond to his ability or contribution. . . . American plants could, in principle, be organized and evaluated on the basis of these criteria, but they are not, and very few persons in industry (including workers) argue that they should be. Achievement rather than equality is the prepotent value here, and the organizing and functioning of American plants are expressions of this central value. The difference in values between the two systems is illustrated by the strong aspiration to move up the hierarchy expressed by members of American plants, and the very little desire on the part of the kibbutz members to "advance" in this way. In a society designed to function on the basis of individual achievement, as American society is, aspiration to advance is functional because individual advancement is a source of motivation, and competition for leadership is presumably a way of assuring that the most highly qualified persons move into positions of responsibility.[14]

Although the evidence from SI suggests some possible future weaknesses in this meritocratic edifice (particularly frustrated ambition), in general it supports the contentions of Tannenbaum and his co-workers. The adverse reactions of those in power (from leads on up) to the idea that leads, supervisors, and managers be selected by their subordinates have been described. The change-over-time results concerning the belief that workers should participate in the selection process produced a significant decrease in support by supervisors and managers. However, there was a noticeable, though not significant, increase in workers' belief that they should participate in the selection of leads and supervisors.

Interview evidence was not directly available on attitudes toward equalizing rewards. Still, worker participation in setting management salaries drew the least support of any item in both waves of interviews for both workers and managers. On the second wave, 106 out of 153 believed there should be no involvement whatsoever. Perhaps more important were Planning Council and later plant subcouncil discussions of wages. In July 1977, when the Planning Council successfully restrained management efforts to base the annual wage increase totally on performance, their argument was not that performance was an inappropriate criterion for wage differentiation—there was unanimous agreement on that point—but that the transition should be less abrupt and that current methods of

evaluating performance were wholly inadequate. Workers clearly supported a wage increase for themselves and lower-level supervision, but
they also felt that increases should be distributed in relation to their
responsibilities and contribution. More than two years before the council
session described above, the rework lead who so strongly challenged
managers and co-workers exemplified this attitude in a rare (for him)
gesture toward supervision in the midst of a discussion in the first council
of the impending wage increase: "The same thing goes for supervisors and
superintendents. The amount of money they get paid isn't enough with all
the pressures they handle, especially those with 100 people under them.
You know they're supposed to be responsible for getting the product out
the door, and they aren't getting paid for it. Even if there are reasons for
it." As of this writing, two of the plant subcouncils are working on systems for fairly instituting merit differentials.

Finally, I would emphasize the argument of chapter 8 concerning the
importance to the management hierarchy of maintaining unitary responsibility and thus centralizing accountability. Several studies have described
the problem of responsibility in democratically managed corporations.
Adizes, in his excellent and sympathetic study of Yugoslav factories,
pointed to the disjointed sense of responsibility and accountability
as a major weakness in that system.[15] Tannenbaum also points to the
differential between the amount of responsibility and influence of leaders
as a problem in the kibbutz system.[16] American advocates of participative
management rarely support the selection of leaders by subordinates, with
its implied inversion of responsibility. This conservatism is due in part to
an acceptance of the meritocratic norms of responsibility. Likert, in the
most persuasive chapter of his seminal work, *New Patterns in Management,* concludes as follows: "If the costs are likely to be excessive, the
superior may feel that he has no choice but to do what his own experience
indicates is best. But whatever course of action is taken, he is responsible
and must accept full responsibility for what occurs."[17]

American belief in meritocracy is strong. It affects our lives continuously and extends especially to the organization of our work places.
The moderate belief in and desire for participation may be more a reflec-
tion of these norms than an expression of apathy. However that may be, if
the preceding analysis is correct, industrial democracy, based on
meaningful worker participation and a serious consideration of equality, is
not a prospect for the United States in the near future. But what of the
long run: what of the prospects for future generations?

FUTURE CONSIDERATIONS

It is quite apparent that theories of political democracy are not easily
adaptable to the economic enterprise. At a very critical, pragmatic level,

principles derived from democratic theory and those in current practice in corporations are diametrically opposed. At a more abstract level, this conflict can be understood in theory in relation to two critical issues—sovereignty and purpose. By examining these issues, factors that will determine the future of industrial democracy will become apparent.

The theory of political democracy (applied to a nation-state) is consistent on a general ideal principle of sovereignty: those being ruled should have the ultimate say in acts of governance. There are endless debates over both the proper governing mechanisms (structure of influence, "directness of participation," appropriate constitutional design, etc.) and how closely real institutions do or can approach the ideal. Few would disagree that a democratic polity must be based on such a principle.

Sovereignty in a capitalist economic enterprise is obviously at odds with this ideal. Employees, those controlled most directly by corporate decisions, are not accepted as sovereign in any sense. The legal and rhetorical sovereigns are the owners of the capital of the corporation. Since the work of Berle and Means, the inability of owners to control management directly has become an accepted fact.[18] However, this does not affect the idealized legitimacy of owner sovereignty. This lingering notion of sovereignty weakens the more general conclusion that has been reached by some of the best theorists of industrial democracy—that control, not ownership, is all important.

I would argue that this idealized conception of sovereignty, which managers emphasize as justification for their actions, serves an important role in guiding managerial behavior. In the first place, there are instances in which managers are held directly accountable to ownership groups for their performance. This will be increasingly more likely as institutional investors acquire control over larger blocks of stock. However, more important, managers are socialized into actions which they *believe* would fulfill the requirements of owners if they were to be held accountable. To take a recent example, in the 1978 round of the New York City financial crisis, the chairmen of the leading New York banks all went to the microphone in the Senate Banking Committee chambers and argued that their responsibility to their shareholders prevented them from underwriting rescue operations to any greater extent. Their arguments sounded particularly hollow to suspicious liberals, and it is extremely doubtful that shareholder revolts would have resulted from, say, doubling the banks' contribution. But the decision made business sense, given the speculative nature of the bonds and accepted theories of portfolio diversification. It is unlikely that economically minded shareholders would argue with their decision. I might add that the argument of responsibility to shareholders was accepted by the great majority of senators.

The importance of all this is that, if we accept the political notion of sovereignty as a basis for a democratic ideal, industrial democracy requires an alteration of the current single-minded emphasis on owner sovereignty in the corporation. This entails either an acceptance of the idea that employees have an independent claim at least to share that sovereignty, or a merging of workers with owners through employee ownership. Juroslav Vanek and others, attempting to mitigate fears of socialism, have repeatedly argued that ownership is not a critical aspect, that control is what counts.[19] But without radical acceptance of the legitimacy of employee sovereignty, control and ownership are linked. Managers will consistently operate in accordance with the expectations of owners. If this leads to policies counter to the interests or freedom of employees, we can expect little else. The question of ownership is central to the possibility of realizing organizational democracy in the future.

The second basic incongruity that develops when traditional democratic theory is applied to organizations is the problem of purpose. Earlier I argued that in relative perspective economic enterprises operate under the influence of a very narrow range of goals that are highly visible, quantifiable, and will be understood by members of the organization. Present theories of democracy simply do not allow for such a possibility. In classic and contemporary theories alike, democracy is seen as a procedure, or a mechanism, for ensuring a legitimate resolution of diverse individual purposes. When speaking of the purpose or role of government, other than protecting the polity from outside interference, the most common refrains are upholding civil liberties and maintaining economic and social stability.

Even if these "purposes" were completely accepted (which they are not), they are of a different nature from the purpose of most organizations, particularly the corporation. For organizations, purpose is the accomplishment of a specific end through a chain of activity; purpose in democratic theory concentrates not on the ends but, rather, on the nature of activity and particularly on the relationships between the parties engaged in the multiple social and economic activities of a society. The distinction leads to a hard fact: in modern organizations the relationships between members and the character of human interaction are only tangentially important as they relate to the end for which the organization originates. Democratic practices may apply in certain circumstances, but democratic theory does not provide an *independent* rationalization for these actions.

From this analysis, two conclusions can be drawn regarding the future of industrial democracy. First, democratic theories being applied to organizations must be developed in full recognition of the importance of reaching a positive end. This might entail resurrecting long-forgotten theories of functional representation,[20] creating limited and conditional forms of participation based on technical qualifications, or a host of other devices. Not realizing the inadequacy of current theory, many experiments fail through reflex application of familiar democratic mechanisms. If industrial democracy is to succeed, a different and more powerful theory is required.

The second conclusion relates to the other end of the problem. Theories of democracy must be altered to consider the accomplishment of a specified end, but future prospects also depend on weakening the profit norm. This change must go beyond the plaintive cry by human relations advocates that humanism and democracy are "good business." The belief must be encouraged that the nature of activities and human interactions in the work place are an independent consideration, a value to be considered completely apart from profitability. To my mind the chances that such a conversion will take hold rapidly are very slight.

However, it is important to consider briefly two concepts that are potential sources of such change. The first is the sense of community that in many ways takes a more natural form in the work place than within the geographical boundaries of people's homes. In most instances, our lives away from work are relatively independent of those who live near us. Social lives vary greatly, but most still revolve around family or close friends—some probably associated with work. We cherish our individual rights and control over our homes. But most important, it is only on rare occasions that neighbors, residents of a city or town, are forced by common purpose to integrate their actions and will. This is not the case for modern productive enterprises.

In a corporation, particularly one that requires complex work environments, the efforts of the individual are naturally and continuously integrated with those of his fellow workers. In contrast to the academic world, where for the most part one's work is one's own, this integration and the resultant productive, social, and economic sense of community binding participants together are very strong. At SI my wife and I observed and shared the rituals of retirement ceremonies, awards, management pep talks, and massive Christmas parties. But we also celebrated the births of children and the marriages of sons and daughters; we attended parties where managers and workers drank, sang, and argued without consciousness of rank or position; we witnessed the fear of workers and the anguish of managers when layoffs were required; and we joined hundreds of employees in burying an all too young manager whose entire working life had been spent with the company.

These are things that communities do. Postponing a discussion of this sense of community until this late point may be interpreted by some as inappropriate. But a meaningful realization of community is an idea for the future. The necessity of continuous interaction and integrated efforts provides the stimulus and lays the foundation for a sense of community within the work place. But the emphasis on meritocratic individualism and administrative processes and programmed work procedures geared to the accomplishment of a clear objective relegate this sense of community to a secondary role, one greatly overshadowed by the day-to-day management of the firm. The sense of community, established in the work place, is exercised primarily outside of it. In discussions of teamwork, identification with organizational goals, and the sense of family that existed in this corporation perhaps more than others, managers and long-time employees did most of the talking.

The second consideration for the future is more difficult to discuss. It has to do with the concept and sheer power of what I have described as frustrated ambition. I have argued that those individuals whose expectations concerning advancement did not match their organizational ambitions played a decisive role in maintaining equilibrium and upholding worker interests in joint decision making. Given the marked increase in education in the last thirty years, especially at the college level, and assuming a proportionate increase in expectations, it can be predicted that frustrated ambition will create stress in hierarchical organizations in the future. The question is whether this unique twist of the meritocratic system will force a move toward more democratic institutions.

The answer must be conjecture. It depends on how this energy, ability, and talent will be used. It is surely possible that, for those employees who remain in the company, either their expectations will fall as time progresses and a sense of psychological security sets in, or their ambitions will be satisfied by suitable promotion. For those who rise to leadership positions, the question of their adherence to the democratic norms which they hold, relative to most members of the work force, remains. They may proceed to fulfill the hopes for an enlightened management extending throughout the organization, or they may retreat to the more comfortable posture of protecting their privileged status, nourishing a self-esteem based on that status and relative position.

On the other hand, frustrated ambition may be vented in a demand for more meaningful jobs and a continued desire for increased autonomy. Achievement may be seen not as advancement decided from above but as acceptance and recognition by fellow employees. This could foreshadow a break in the meritocratic system, fostering both an increased sense of community and an ideology supporting organizational democracy.

It it somewhat more likely, however, that this would arise in nonproduction jobs, where there is already greater autonomy and insistence on participation and where jobs can be most easily changed to provide intrinsic satisfactions. If this were to be the case, those factory workers whose ambitions are blocked would attempt to move to white-collar jobs (which they were at SI), leaving the factory workers with less effective leaders. Democracy may well begin in the offices, with the consequent effect of an even greater difference in white-collar prerogatives than currently exists.

The future of industrial democracy awaits the resolution of these issues.

A more appropriate theory of democracy, addressing the paradox of promoting equality and achieving a clearly specified goal, must be developed. The natural basis of community must be realized, studied, and promoted; and the problem of rising expectations must be resolved.

At present, however, against these possiblities and conjectures stands the inertia of the existing structure. It is a massive structure of administration, with a history, practice, and ideology built around principles adverse to the development of democratic organizations. The ideology of individualism and inequality and the overwhelming pressure to accomplish a single purpose shape the organization according to meritocratic principles. As beliefs that support this system persist, feelings of community and a sense of equality will be secondary, and industrial democracy will remain an academic exercise, a dream.

Appendix A. Sample Characteristics

	Company Statistics[a]	Wave 1		Wave 2	
		Workers	Managers[b]	Workers	Managers[b]
Mean education	11.0	11.4	14.6	11.2	14.6
Mean age	32.4	31.6	37.7	33.2	39.1
% Female	49.1	44.1	2.9	47.9	2.9
% Spanish surname	45.0	45.8	11.8	45.5	14.3
% Black	5.0	4.2	2.9	3.3	2.9
% Hourly wages	92.0	90.3	0	90.1	0
N		145	35	118	35

[a]As of 1 January 1975, for nonsupervisory personnel only.

[b]Includes all levels of supervision and management.

Appendix B. Chronology of Events

1974

October   Planning meeting for the QWL program at SI is held in Washington, D.C., attended by the president of SI, the director of employee relations, John Witte, and a group of consultants experienced in work humanization.

Management steering committee is created.

December 3–10   Witte visits SI, files a preliminary report, and agrees to work with the company for at least a year.

1975

January   Witte arrives in Los Angeles.

Steering committee works on a plan to create a large representative body, with a representative from each of fifty work sections.

Administrative assistant is selected to work with Witte. Procedures for program documentation are established.

Meetings are held with supervisors to discuss the best ways to begin the program and increase worker participation.

February   Steering committee proposal is changed to an executive worker-management Planning Council, to be composed of eight workers and five managers.

Worker groups are established in each facility to design the nomination and election procedures for representatives to the Planning Council.

March 10   Initial memorandum explains the QWL program and the upcoming elections to the work force.

March 12–14   One- to two-hour meetings are held with all employees to discuss the program.

March 19–20   Planning Council elections take place.

April 2	First Planning Council meeting is attended by both members and alternates.
April–May	Planning Council works on defining its role and operating procedures, establishes task forces in each facility to discuss shop floor experiments, and establishes a priority for major projects it will consider.
May–June	Initial meetings of work-project task forces are held in each facility. Proposals are brought to the Planning Council.
July	Employee relations experimental project begins.
September	Final meetings of the work-project task forces take place, as do meetings with employees in the electronics department about the 6208 autonomous work team.
	Communications, noise-reduction, and employee-suggestion special-purpose committees are established.
October	Experimental projects on both shifts in the lacquer-finish area and on the L606 line begin.
	Special-purpose committees on training are established.
November	Operations on the 6208 work project begin.
December–January 1976	Planning Council continues on its working agenda and discusses the progress of work projects and plans for the new facility.
	Orientations special-purpose committee and newspaper editorial board are established.

1976

February	6208 work project is suspended.
March 17	Second Planning Council elections are held.
April	Crisis occurs on the L606 line, ending in the election of a lead.
May	L606 votes to cease operating as an experimental project.
	Department and section meetings begin to work on the layout of areas in the new facility.
June 13	Witte leaves SI.
July	Replacement is hired for Witte.

	Employees vote on working-hour changes.
	Planning Council reviews wage and salary increase.
August	Lacquer-finish projects are terminated by the Planning Council. Interviews are conducted with project participants for all projects.
December	Subcouncils are established in each facility. Elections are held in some facilities.

RESEARCH ACTIVITIES

1974

December	Observations log is begun.

1975

February	Interview format is designed and pretested with the help of a group of employees.
Feburary–March	Random sample of the company is drawn and first-wave interviews conducted.
April	Content analysis of Planning Council tapes begins. Interviews are conducted with newly elected Planning Council members and alternates.
July–September	Work-project members who were not in the original sample are interviewed.
August	Interviews are held with all leads and supervisors regarding training and opportunities at SI.

1976

April	In-depth interviews are conducted with retiring Planning Council members.
June	Second-wave interviews are conducted.

Appendix C. Scale Items, Frequencies, Means, and Scale Properties

TABLE C-1
Belief in Participation

How Much Say Should You Have in These Areas?	Wave	(1) None (%)	(2) A Little (%)	(3) Some (%)	(4) A Lot (%)	Mean
1. When the work day	1	25.0	9.3	42.1	23.6	2.64
begins and ends	2	28.2	18.8	31.6	21.4	2.46
2. Selection of leads	1	27.4	11.5	29.2	31.9	2.65
	2	17.7	18.8	30.2	33.3	2.79
3. Selection of supervisors	1	40.8	15.4	23.9	19.7	2.23
	2	29.6	20.0	30.4	20.0	2.41
4. Which workers join your	1	45.7	14.3	20.7	19.3	2.14
work group (section)	2	33.3	22.2	26.5	17.9	2.29
5. Who should be fired if they	1	61.1	12.5	19.4	6.9	1.72
do a bad job or don't	2	59.1	17.4	17.4	6.1	1.70
come to work						
6. Who gets promoted	1	51.1	12.8	27.7	8.5	1.94
	2	45.7	17.2	27.6	8.6	2.02
7. Hiring or promotions	1	64.7	14.0	16.2	5.1	1.62
to upper-level management	2	54.5	18.8	21.4	5.4	1.78
positions like plant manager						
or department head						
8. How much work people	1	25.2	18.0	36.7	20.1	2.52
should do in a day	2	31.4	20.3	29.7	18.6	2.36
9. The level of quality	1	19.1	9.9	36.2	34.7	2.87
of the work	2	12.8	15.4	30.8	41.0	3.00
10. The way the work is						
done—methods and	1	9.7	7.6	34.0	48.6	3.21
procedures	2	9.3	11.9	39.8	39.0	3.09
11. How fast the work should	1	11.4	15.0	34.3	39.3	3.01
be done—the work rate	2	12.8	21.4	37.6	28.2	2.81
12. Who should do what	1	39.6	12.9	28.8	18.7	2.27
job in your group or	2	27.1	20.3	34.7	17.8	2.43
section						
13. Handling complaints	1	15.0	16.4	35.7	32.9	2.86
or grievances	2	20.7	19.8	37.1	21.6	2.62
14. Pay scales or wages	1	18.4	12.1	41.8	27.7	2.79
	2	22.2	16.2	41.9	19.7	2.59

TABLE C-1 (*continued*)

How Much Say Should You Have in These Areas?	Wave	(1) None (%)	(2) A Little (%)	(3) Some (%)	(4) A Lot (%)	Mean
15. Management salaries	1	78.5	4.6	10.8	6.1	1.44
	2	63.6	17.3	9.1	8.2	1.67
16. The way the company spends its money, how it invests its profits	1	50.0	17.1	22.1	10.7	1.93
	2	43.6	20.0	28.2	8.2	2.01
17. Helping to plan the new plants SI is going to move into	1	14.7	12.6	32.2	40.5	3.00
	2	18.3	13.0	41.7	27.0	2.77

SCALE STATISTICS:
  Wave 1: Mean = 38.70; S.D. = 10.00; Cronbach A = .87; N = 127.
  Wave 2: Mean = 39.85; S.D. = 10.60; Cronbach A = .88; N = 94.

TABLE C-2
Actual Participation

How Much Say Do You Have in These Areas?	Wave	(1) None (%)	(2) A Little (%)	(3) Some (%)	(4) A Lot (%)	Mean
1. Which workers join your work group	1	78.2	9.1	11.3	1.4	1.36
	2	73.7	8.5	14.4	3.4	1.47
2. Who should be fired	1	88.8	6.3	3.5	1.4	1.17
	2	78.8	11.9	7.6	1.7	1.32
3. Who gets promoted	1	87.6	8.3	2.7	1.4	1.18
	2	82.2	7.6	7.6	2.5	1.31
4. How much work is done in a day	1	61.8	18.7	9.7	9.7	1.64
	2	58.1	15.4	13.7	12.8	1.81
5. How fast the work is done—the work rates	1	44.7	17.0	24.8	13.5	2.07
	2	47.0	18.8	18.8	15.4	2.03
6. The quality or accuracy of the work	1	44.4	16.1	21.1	18.3	2.13
	2	39.3	18.8	20.5	21.4	2.24
7. The way work is done— methods and procedures	1	29.7	26.2	29.0	15.1	2.30
	2	29.7	21.2	27.1	22.0	2.41
8. Who should do what job in your group or section	1	59.6	18.4	14.9	7.1	1.69
	2	51.7	21.6	13.8	12.9	1.88
9. Handling complaints or grievances	1	57.3	23.0	14.7	4.9	1.67
	2	50.8	18.6	22.0	8.5	1.88

SCALE STATISTICS:
    Wave 1: Mean = 14.90; S.D. = 4.80; Cronbach A = .77; N = 127.
    Wave 2: Mean = 16.03; S.D. = 5.90; Cronbach A = .85; N = 95.

TABLE C-3
Job Attributes

	Wave	(1) Very True (%)	(2) Some-what True (%)	(3) Not Very True (%)	(4) Not True at All (%)	Mean
1. I receive enough help	1	21.2	53.1	18.6	7.1	2.12
and equipment to get	2	23.4	59.8	11.2	5.6	2.00
the job done						
2. I have enough time to	1	36.0	50.9	11.4	1.8	1.79
get the job done	2	32.7	53.3	12.1	1.9	1.84
3. The work is enjoyable	1	34.5	47.8	10.6	7.1	1.91
	2	25.2	55.1	15.9	3.7	1.99
4. The equipment I work	1	11.4	14.0	24.6	50.0	1.87
with could be a lot better	2	48.6	30.5	11.4	9.5	1.82

NOTE: Items reversed for scaling.

SCALE STATISTICS:
Wave 1: Mean = 10.0; S.D. = 1.86; Cronbach A = .58; N = 113.
Wave 2: Mean = 11.0; S.D. = 2.05; Cronbach A = .51; N = 105.

TABLE C-4
Self-Estrangement in Work

Goal Satisfaction	Wave	(1) Not at All (%)	(2) Partly (%)	(3) Fully (%)	Mean
1. Being able to *buy* the things	1	16.5	69.0	14.5	1.98
I want	2	15.3	58.5	26.3	2.11
2. The opportunity to *learn* new things	1	29.7	42.1	28.3	2.00
and develop my abilities	2	26.3	49.2	24.6	1.98
3. *Getting ahead* or having a	1	53.2	34.0	12.8	1.60
special position	2	41.5	35.6	22.9	1.81
4. The chance to use my *imagination*	1	44.1	39.3	16.5	1.72
to create new things	2	38.1	37.3	24.6	1.86
5. The feeling that I'm *doing what*	1	2.1	21.5	76.4	2.74
is expected of me	2	3.4	29.7	66.9	2.64
6. The chance to *cooperate* with	1	13.8	35.2	51.0	2.37
other people toward a common goal	2	7.6	41.5	50.8	2.43
7. Keeping myself *active*	1	5.5	22.7	71.7	2.66
	2	.8	29.7	69.5	2.69
8. The *freedom* to decide when I do	1	33.1	29.0	37.9	2.05
what on my job and how I do it	2	22.2	41.9	35.9	2.14

NOTE: Items reversed for scaling.

SCALE STATISTICS:
Wave 1:   Mean = 17.10;   S.D. = 2.90;
Cronbach A = .64; N = 145.
Wave 2:   Mean = 17.62;   S.D. = 3.12;
Cronbach A = .72; N = 117.

TABLE C-5
Job Normlessness

	Wave	(1) Very True (%)	(2) Some- what True (%)	(3) Not Very True (%)	(4) Not True at All (%)	Mean
1. Sometimes one person tells me one thing, while another person tells me something else	1	31.0	31.0	19.5	18.6	2.26
	2	29.0	33.6	20.6	16.8	2.23
2. The company has a lot of rules, but I don't really pay much attention to them	1	8.0	25.0	33.9	33.0	2.92
	2	2.8	22.4	40.2	34.6	3.05
3. Often I don't know what I should be doing on my job	1	.9	7.9	30.7	60.5	3.51
	2	2.9	4.8	29.5	62.9	3.52
4. One of the problems at SI is that too many people don't follow company rules	1	24.3	37.4	30.8	7.5	2.22
	2	26.0	39.4	28.8	5.8	2.14

NOTE: Items reversed for scaling.

SCALE STATISTICS:
Wave 1: Mean = 10.90; S.D. = 2.30; Cronbach A = .49; N = 113.
Wave 2: Mean = 10.94; S.D. = 1.93; Cronbach A = .23; N = 104.

TABLE C-6
Job Isolation

	Wave	(1) Very True (%)	(2) Some- what True (%)	(3) Not Very True (%)	(4) Not True at All (%)	Mean
1. My job gives me a feeling	1	23.2	45.5	16.1	15.2	2.23
of working on a team	2	22.4	43.9	21.5	12.1	2.21
2. My job is important to a						
lot of other people in	1	49.6	39.8	8.0	2.7	1.64
the company	2	50.5	31.1	12.6	5.8	1.74
3. I feel lonely when	1	3.5	9.6	28.1	58.8	3.43
I'm working	2	0.0	14.3	32.4	53.3	3.41

NOTE: Item 3 reversed for scaling.   SCALE STATISTICS:
Wave   1:   Mean = 9.50;   S.D. = 1.90;
Cronbach A = .61; N = 113.
Wave 2:   Mean = 9.46;   S.D. = 1.86;
Cronbach A = .55; N = 103.

TABLE C-7
Job Powerlessness—Rewards

Rewards for Doing Your Job Very Well	Wave	(1) Extremely Likely (%)	(2) Quite Likely (%)	(3) Somwhat Likely (%)	(4) Not Very Likely (%)	Mean
1. You will be offered	1	9.1	27.5	25.3	38.0	2.93
a better job at SI	2	8.5	16.9	37.3	37.3	3.03
2. You will get a	1	19.3	21.4	18.6	40.6	2.81
bonus or pay raise	2	9.3	27.1	21.2	42.4	2.97
3. You will increase	1	31.3	38.2	15.3	15.3	2.15
your job security	2	23.9	36.8	24.8	14.5	2.30

NOTE: Items reversed for scaling.   SCALE STATISTICS:
Wave   1:   Mean = 7.10;   S.D. = 2.40;
Cronbach A = .59; N = 143.
Wave   2:   Mean = 6.70;   S.D. = 2.10;
Cronbach A = .50; N = 117.

TABLE C-8
Job Powerlessness—Punishments

Punishments for Doing One's Job Very Poorly	Wave	(1) Ex- tremely Likely (%)	(2) Quite Likely (%)	(3) Some- what Likely (%)	(4) Not Very Likely (%)	Mean
1. You will be fired	1	29.0	19.3	29.0	22.7	2.46
	2	26.3	23.7	26.3	23.7	2.47
2. You won't be promoted or given a better job	1	52.1	23.9	11.3	12.7	1.85
	2	47.0	24.8	14.5	13.7	1.95
3. A report will be put in you personnel file	1	60.1	22.5	10.5	6.8	1.64
	2	57.5	23.0	11.5	7.1	1.74

NOTE: Items reversed for scaling.   SCALE STATISTICS:
             Wave 1: Mean = 9.20; S.D. = 2.30;
      Cronbach A = .63; N = 143.
             Wave 2: Mean = 8.87; S.D. = 2.17;
      Cronbach A = .44; N = 111.

TABLE C-9
Democratic Supervision

Choose the Statement Which You Think is More True	Wave	Percentage Choosing
1. Most people need very little if any supervision on the job	1	31.5
	2	32.5
Most people need supervison to make sure the job gets done and done right	1	68.5
	2	67.5
2. In general, it's much better if one person, say the lead, makes decisions for his group	1	53.5
	2	52.2
It is better when decisions in a section are made by the group as a whole	1	46.5
	2	47.8
3. A supervisor's most important responsibility should be to the company	1	40.7
	2	44.9
A supervisor's most important responsibility should be to the people who work for him	1	59.3
	2	55.1

NOTE: Item 1 reversed for scaling.   SCALE STATISTICS:
             Wave 1: Mean = 4.40; S.D. = 1.10;
      Cronbach A = .40; N = 127.
             Wave 2: Mean = 5.63; S.D. = 1.95;
      Cronbach A = .41; N = 112.

TABLE C-10
Company Attitudes

	Wave	(1) Strongly Agree (%)	(2) Agree (%)	(3) Disagree (%)	(4) Strongly Disagree (%)	Mean
1. This company cares more about money and machines than people	1	7.5	25.4	51.5	15.8	2.75
	2	13.6	26.3	52.5	7.6	2.54
2. All things considered, there is a feeling around here that this is a pretty good place to work	1	22.3	66.2	10.8	22.3	1.90
	2	17.8	68.6	10.2	3.4	1.99
3. It's hard to get people higher up in the company to listen to people at my level	1	28.4	20.6	41.8	9.3	2.32
	2	19.7	34.2	40.2	6.0	2.33
4. I never know what's happening in this company until after it's happened	1	16.5	37.2	42.7	3.4	2.33
	2	14.5	33.3	46.2	6.0	2.44
5. When management says something, you can really believe it is true	1	6.6	45.6	38.2	9.5	2.51
	2	4.3	51.3	38.3	6.1	2.46

NOTE: Items 2 and 5 reversed for scaling.   SCALE STATISTICS:
Wave 1: Mean = 13.00;   S.D. = 2.61;
Cronbach A = .65; N = 145.
Wave 2: Mean = 12.87;   S.D. = 2.53;
Cronbach A = .67; N = 114.

TABLE C-11
Perceived Worker-Management Conflict

	Wave	(1) Strongly Agree (%)	(2) Agree (%)	(3) Disagree (%)	(4) Strongly Disagree (%)	Mean
1. In general, in this company management thinks pretty much one way and workers the other	1	12.7	53.7	30.6	3.0	2.24
	2	14.8	49.6	34.8	.9	2.22
2. I'd say there is a lot of conflict at SI between workers and management	1	13.7	36.7	48.1	3.6	2.40
	2	13.0	39.1	41.7	6.1	2.41

SCALE STATISTICS:
Wave 1:   Mean = 4.60;   S.D. = 1.31;
Cronbach A = .76; N = 141.
Wave 2:   Mean = 4.60;   S.D. = 1.30;
Cronbach A = .71; N = 113.

TABLE C-12
Democratic Values

	Wave	(1) Strongly Agree (%)	(2) Agree (%)	(3) Disagree (%)	(4) Strongly Disagree (%)	Mean
1. If a person wanted to make a speech in this city against churches and religion, he should not be allowed to speak	1 2	8.3 15.4	10.1 19.2	43.1 45.2	38.5 20.2	3.12 2.70
2. If an admitted communist wanted to make a speech in this city favoring communism, he should be allowed to speak	1 2	10.8 14.4	43.2 38.5	18.0 25.0	27.9 22.1	2.63 2.55
3. If a Black Panther were legally elected mayor of this city, he should be allowed to take office	1 2	19.3 17.5	41.3 37.9	18.3 26.2	21.1 18.4	2.41 2.46
4. If a person wanted to make a speech in this city favoring government ownership of railroads and big industry, he should be allowed to speak	1 2	20.7 14.4	62.2 63.5	10.8 14.4	6.3 7.7	2.03 2.15
5. A communist should be allowed to run for mayor of this city	1 2	11.0 9.5	26.6 25.7	23.9 27.6	38.5 37.1	2.90 2.92
6. If a communist were legally elected mayor of this city, people should not allow him to take office	1 2	20.6 18.4	20.6 27.2	38.3 35.0	20.6 19.4	2.59 2.55
7. A member of the American Nazi party should not be allowed to run for mayor of this city	1 2	30.8 28.7	17.8 27.7	36.4 31.7	15.0 11.9	2.35 2.27

NOTE: Items 2–5 reversed for scaling.

SCALE STATISTICS:
Wave 1: Mean = 18.20; S.D. = 4.90; Cronbach A = .84; N = 111.
Wave 2: Mean = 17.57; S.D. = 4.86; Cronbach A = .84; N = 95.

TABLE C-13
Political Activism

Have You Ever Been Involved in the Following Political Activities?	Wave	(1) Yes (%)	(2) No (%)
1. Written letters to public officials	1	28.3	71.7
	2	29.7	70.3
2. Written to newspapers concerning public affairs	1	9.6	90.4
	2	11.0	89.0
3. Talked to public officials or political party leaders	1	26.9	73.1
	2	23.7	76.3
4. Worked in a political campaign	1	16.6	83.4
	2	11.9	88.1
5. Given money to a political campaign	1	12.4	87.6
	2	20.3	79.7
6. Attended political meetings or rallies	1	32.4	67.6
	2	26.3	73.7
7. Tried to persuade someone to vote one way or another	1	31.0	69.0
	2	29.7	70.3
8. Voted for president in 1972	1	42.1	57.9
	2	44.4	55.6
9. Voted for Congress or state officials in 1974	1	31.0	69.0
	2	30.8	69.2

NOTE: Items reversed for scaling.

SCALE STATISTICS:
Wave 1: Mean = 11.30; S.D. = 2.40; Cronbach A = .80; N = 144.
Wave 2: Mean = 11.28; S.D. = 2.33; Cronbach A = .79; N = 117.

TABLE C-14
Srole Anomie Scale

	Wave	(1) Strongly Agree (%)	(2) Agree (%)	(3) Disagree (%)	(4) Strongly Disagree (%)	Mean
1. Most public officials	1	22.2	40.7	33.3	3.7	2.19
really aren't interested	2	21.2	40.4	33.7	4.8	2.22
in the problems of the						
average man						
2. Most people can still be	1	16.7	53.7	25.9	3.7	2.17
depended upon to come	2	10.1	57.6	25.3	7.1	2.29
through in a pinch						
3. It's hardly fair to bring	1	11.7	21.6	44.1	22.5	2.77
children into the world	2	10.4	27.4	47.2	15.1	2.67
with the way things look						
for the future						
4. The average man is	1	19.8	48.6	24.3	7.2	2.19
probably better off today	2	18.1	50.5	27.6	3.8	2.17
than he ever was before						
5. With everything in such	1	14.4	36.0	43.2	6.3	2.41
a state of confusion,	2	4.8	49.5	42.9	2.9	2.44
most people don't know						
where they stand from						
one day to the next						

NOTE: Items 1, 2, and 4 reversed for scaling.   SCALE STATISTICS:
Wave 1:   Mean = 13.10;   S.D. = 2.41;
Cronbach A = .53; N = 114.
Wave 2:   Mean = 12.89;   S.D. = 2.16;
Cronbach A = .46; N = 98.

TABLE C-15
Political Alienation

	Wave	(1) Strongly Agree (%)	(2) Agree (%)	(3) Disagree (%)	(4) Strongly Disagree (%)	Mean
1. Sometimes politics and government seem so confusing that I can't really understand what's going on	1 2	19.8 22.1	47.7 51.9	25.2 20.2	7.2 5.8	2.20 2.10
2. People like me don't have any say about what government does	1 2	16.2 9.5	21.6 33.3	42.3 39.0	19.8 18.1	2.66 2.66
3. There is no way other than voting that people like me can influence actions of the government	1 2	12.8 17.6	28.4 36.3	44.0 39.2	14.7 6.9	2.61 2.35
4. I believe public officials don't care much what people like me think	1 2	13.8 9.6	37.6 41.3	40.4 43.3	8.3 5.8	2.43 2.45

SCALE STATISTICS:
Wave 1:   Mean = 9.91;   S.D. = 2.41;
Cronbach A = .51; N = 113.
Wave 2:   Mean = 9.58;   S.D. = 1.95;
Cronbach A = .37; N = 99.

TABLE C-16
Normlessness

	Wave	(1) Strongly Agree (%)	(2) Agree (%)	(3) Disagree (%)	(4) Strongly Disagree (%)	Mean
1. The trouble with the world today is that people really don't believe in anything	1	14.5	32.7	34.3	18.2	2.56
	2	11.3	41.5	38.7	8.5	2.44
2. With everything in such a state of confusion, most people don't know where they stand from one day to the next	1	14.4	36.0	43.2	6.3	2.41
	2	4.8	49.5	42.9	2.9	2.44
3. Everything changes so quickly these days that I often have trouble deciding which are the right rules to follow	1	7.1	26.8	45.5	20.5	2.79
	2	2.9	35.3	45.1	16.7	2.75
4. I often feel my life is very confusing	1	4.5	23.4	45.0	27.0	2.95
	2	1.0	26.0	52.9	20.2	2.92

SCALE STATISTICS:
  Wave 1:   Mean = 10.70;   S.D. = 2.51;
Cronbach A = .71; N = 114.
  Wave 2:   Mean = 10.63;   S.D. = 2.09;
Cronbach A = .68; N = 100.

TABLE C-17
Rotter's Internal-External Control

Choose the Statement You Feel to be More True	Wave	Percentage Choosing
1. I think we have adequate means for preventing runaway inflation	1 2	64.8 43.7
There is very little we can do to prevent prices from going higher	1 2	35.2 56.3
2. Persons like myself have little chance of protecting our personal interests when they conflict strongly with those of strong pressure groups	1 2	49.5 57.6
I think we have adequate ways of coping with pressure groups	1 2	50.5 42.4
3. A lasting world peace can be achieved by those of us who work for it	1 2	63.0 71.6
There is very little we can do to bring about permanent world peace	1 2	37.0 28.4
4. There's very little persons like myself can do to improve world opinion of the United States	1 2	25.2 22.0
I think each of us can do a great deal to improve world opinion of the United States	1 2	74.8 78.0
5. This world is run by the few people in power, and there is not much the little guy can do about it	1 2	44.9 47.0
The average citizen can have an influence on government decisions	1 2	55.1 53.0
6. It is only wishful thinking to believe that one can really influence what happens in society at large	1 2	33.0 34.7
People like me can change the course of world events if we make ourselves heard	1 2	67.0 65.3
7. More and more I feel helpless in the face of what's happening in the world today	1 2	70.0 71.7
I sometimes feel personally to blame for the sad state of affairs in our government	1 2	30.0 28.3

NOTE: Items 1 and 3 reversed for scaling.   SCALE STATISTICS:
Wave 1:   Mean = 10.1;   S.D. = 2.00;
Cronbach A = .69; N = 110.
Wave 2:   Mean = 10.23;   S.D. = 2.00;
Cronbach A = .71; N = 85.

Notes

CHAPTER 1

1. The best documentation of these events is the HEW task force report, *Work in America* (Cambridge, Mass.: M.I.T. Press, 1973).

2. Warren G. Bennis and Philip E. Slater, *The Temporary Society* (New York: Harper & Row, 1968), p. 4.

3. Arnold S. Tannenbaum, ed., *Control in Organizations* (New York: McGraw-Hill, 1968), p. 32. Note that Tannenbaum defines control in the same way participation and influence are defined here.

4. See, e.g., Robert Michels, *Political Parties*, 1966 ed. (New York: Free Press), pp. 63–77; Robert A. Dahl, *After the Revolution?* (New Haven: Yale University Press, 1970), pp. 40–56; and Bertrand de Jouvenal, "The Chairman's Problem," *American Political Science Review* 55 (1961): 368–73.

5. The work most relevant to our subject is that of Antonio Gramsci; see *Letters from Prison*, 1973 ed. (New York: Harper & Row), pp. 42–45; and *Prison Notebooks*, 1971 ed. (London: Lawrence & Wishart).

6. Carole Pateman, *Participation and Democratic Theory* (Cambridge: Cambridge University Press, 1970).

7. For an interesting comparison, see the discussions by Robert Dahl and Robert Michels in which both argue that competence forms a limit to direct decision making. For Michels the limit is pervasive and rooted in the intellectual and psychological incompetence of the common man, but Dahl sees the limit as much less extensive and, most important, as defined by the rational choices of individuals themselves (Dahl, *After the Revolution?*, pp. 28–39; and Michels, pp. 85–97, 107–16).

8. Hugh Clegg, *Industrial Democracy and Nationalisation* (London: Blackwell, 1951) and *A New Approach to Industrial Democracy* (London: Blackwell, 1960). For an interesting review and critique of Clegg's position, see Paul Blumberg, *Industrial Democracy: The Sociology of Participation* (New York: Schocken, 1969), chap. 7.

9. See, e.g., Rensis Likert, *New Patterns of Management* (New York: McGraw-Hill, 1961) and *The Human Organization* (New York: McGraw-Hill, 1967). For an early, although excellent, review of this literature, see Victor Vroom, *Work and Motivation* (New York: Wiley, 1964), chaps. 6–8. For a recent pessimistic review, see H. Roy Kaplan and Curt Tausky, "Humanism in Organization: A Critical Appraisal," *Public Administration Review* 37 (1977): 171–80.

10. A possible exception to this is provided by Carole Pateman. In both *Participation and Democratic Theory* and, more explicitly, a paper entitled "A Contribution to the Political Theory of Organizational Democracy" (delivered at the 1974 American Political Science Association meeting), she argues that representation will not succeed, implying that direct participation in all decisions is essential.

11. An exception to this is the remarkable project at I.G.P., Inc., a Washington-based insurance company. For a very honest description of that project, see Daniel Zwerdling, "The Day the Workers Took Over," *New Times* (10 December 1976), pp. 40–45. For a review of these projects, see HEW's *Work in America* and David Jenkins' *Job Power* (Baltimore: Penguin, 1973).

12. Fred Emery and Einar Thorsrud, *Form and Content in Industrial Democracy,* 1969 ed. (London: Tavistock).

13. Josip Obradović, "Distribution of Participation in the Process of Decision-Making on Problems Related to the Economic Activity of the Company," *Participation and Self-Management* 2 (Zagreb, 1972): 137–64; and Veljko Rus, "Influence Structure in Yugoslav Enterprises," *Industrial Relations* 9 (1970): 148–60.

CHAPTER 2

1. The exact figures are approximate because sales and profit figures were not directly available, since SI is a subsidiary and not required to release separate financial statements. The information presented here was obtained in conversations with managers at SI throughout the time covered by this study.

2. Likert, *New Patterns of Management,* chap. 8.

3. Also involved in this discussion was the realization that such a structure could be technically classified as "support and domination" by management of a company union and would violate section 8.2 of the Taft-Hartley Act. This became irrelevant when we learned that almost anything we wanted to do was in violation of this clause. Under present interpretations, not only this project but almost every other project in the United States is in violation of the Taft-Hartley Act.

4. For the first year, three of the original steering committee members were retained on the Planning Council. I also sat on the council as a nonvoting member.

5. Surprisingly, the eight-vote rule was never exercised. Even when the council was defining its participation in the various aspects of wage and benefit decisions, majority rule was used. Perhaps more significantly, very few votes relative to decisions were taken. Approximately 80% of the decisions were finally reached by unanimous agreement.

6. The order of the working agenda was established by first listing major issues that any member wanted to discuss. Each item on the list was then discussed for an average of twenty to thirty minutes. The items were then put in priority order by a voting procedure allocating each member twelve votes which could be distributed in any fashion, with the exception that a maximum of four votes could be used on any single issue.

7. Usually these task forces consisted of the plant manager (or department heads in office areas), one or two supervisors, the industrial engineer for the plant, Planning Council members from the facility, the director of employee relations, and myself.

8. This occurred early in the project. The group, which volunteered, said they wanted no part in the project if their leadman was not included. Part of their rationale was to protect him from what they misinterpreted as a loss of lead status. Even after this notion was dispelled, they persisted, saying they felt very comfortable under his guidance.

9. The problem of obtaining reliable interviews is more difficult in an organization, because the researcher is invariably associated with management. Although I experienced some of this difficulty, I was at SI three months before any interviewing was done. During this time my position as a neutral third party, not on the company payroll, was made clear on many occasions.

10. The random sample and a combined sample including later interviews have been analyzed separately, but for the main part the combined sample was used. To be conservative, I reported only statistics based on total sample that show no differences at a .20 level of significance. Similarly, whenever possible, the date of interview was entered as an independent variable, to test for possible effects of late interviews.

11. For example, evaluation of supervisors is done by first asking what people think makes a good supervisor and later asking them to rate their own supervisors on the factors they have mentioned. This measure combines both evaluation and intensity, supplies interesting additional information on what people think supervisors should be like, and takes very little time. The idea for this method came from a suggestion by a worker in a pretest interview.

12. Some respondents (10%) took these questionnaires home and did not return them, so the data on these questions are not complete.

CHAPTER 3

1. Harriet Holter, "Attitudes towards Employee Participation in Company Decision-making Processes," *Human Relations* 18 (1965): 300; Arnold Tannenbaum et al., *Hierarchy in Organizations* (San Francisco: Jossey-Bass, 1974), p. 54.

2. Sidney Verba and Norman Nie, *Participation in America* (New York: Harper & Row, 1972), pp. 37, 368–69.

3. Philip E. Converse, "The Nature of Belief Systems in Mass Publics," in *Ideology and Discontent*, ed. David E. Apter (New York: Free Press, 1964).

4. See Angus Campbell et al., *The American Voter* (New York: Wiley, 1964); Verba and Nie; Lester Milbrath, *Political Participation* (Chicago: Rand McNally, 1965); Samuel Stouffer, *Communism, Conformity, and Civil Liberty* (Garden City, N.Y.: Doubleday, 1965); Herbert McClosky, "Consensus and Ideology in American Politics," *American Political Science Review* 5 (1960): 361–83; James W. Prothro and Charles M. Grigg, "Fundamental Principles of Democracy: Bases of Agreement and Disagreement," *Journal of Politics* 22 (1960): 276–89; and Converse.

5. Although SRC surveys indicate that levels of political interest, knowledge, and activism were basically unchanged from 1952 to 1972, there is evidence that tolerance for democratic norms has increased. See James C. Davis, "Communism, Conformity, Cohorts, and Categories: American Tolerance in 1954 and 1972–73," *American Journal of Sociology* 81 (1975): 491–513, and John F. Witte and Charles Whitmore, "Democratic Values, Civic Virtue, and Liberal Democracy" (1976; unpublished ms.).

6. Robert Michels, *Political Parties: A Sociological Study of the Oligarchic Tendencies of Modern Democracy* (New York: Free Press, 1966).

7. I am thinking specifically of the ITU and the relatively high level of union participation engendered by their two-party system of competition. See Seymour M. Lipset, James S. Coleman, and Martin Trow, *Union Democracy* (Garden City, N.Y.: Doubleday, 1962).

8. See Verba and Nie, pp. 41–42; also John Anderson, "Local Union Participation: A Re-Examination," *Industrial Relations* 18 (1979): 18–31.

9. Lipset et al., chap. 8; Arnold S. Tannenbaum and Robert L. Kahn, *Participation in Union Locals* (Evanston, Ill.,: Row, Peterson, 1958), pp. 88–94, 96–97; and Anderson, p. 25.

10. Tannenbaum and Kahn, p. 130.

11. Holter, pp. 301, 307–15.

12. Nancy Morse, *Satisfactions in the White Collar Job* (Ann Arbor, Mich.: Survey Research Center, 1953), p. 9.

13. Daniel Katz, "Satisfactions and Deprivations in Industrial Life," in *Industrial Productivity*, ed. A. Kornhauser et al. (Madison, Wis.: Industrial Relations Research Assn., 1951), p. 91.

14. See Arnold S. Tannenbaum, "The Concept of Organizational Control," *Journal of Social Issues* 12 (1956): 50–60; and "Control in Organizations"; Tannenbaum and Kahn; and Tannenbaum et al., *Hierarchy in Organizations*, esp. chap. 3. I should reiterate that Tannenbaum uses what we might call a "soft" definition of control akin to my use of the terms *participation* and *influence*. He is thus able to argue that control is not a zero-sum situation where there is only so much to be distributed.

15. Due to the timing of the interviews, there may be some bias in these measures. There had been some prior discussion of worker participation in terms of a memo and group meetings. Also, in some cases, respondents had voted for Planning Council representatives. Any bias must be assumed to be in the direction of stimulating greater desire for participation.

16. I tested for response bias throughout the interview by randomly assigning respondents to one of two card sets. For a series of questions that had the same responses, the subject

was given a card that listed the responses. The order of the answers were mirror images on the two separate card sets. Difference-of-means tests never break the .40 probability level on any of the items where different card sets were used.

17. Tannenbaum et al., *Hierarchy in Organizations,* p. 178.

18. Statistically, difference-of-means tests are significant at the .05 level for only four of these decisions: planning the new facility, job assignments, selecting supervisors, and wages.

19. Tannenbaum et al., *Hierarchy in Organizations,* pp. 174–75. However, Frank Heller's study of pairs of managers reverses this finding; for managers, the subordinate sees himself as having more influence than the boss thinks he has (see Frank A. Heller, *Managerial Decision Making* [London: Tavistock, 1971], pp. 72–76).

20. All information on the Bolivar project comes from an unpublished report entitled "The Bolivar Project of Joint Management-Union Determination of Change According to Principles of Security—Equity—Individualism—Democracy, May 1973–January 1974," submitted 15 February 1974 by the Upjohn Institute for Employment Research and the Harvard Project on Technology, Work, and Character.

21. I am particularly suspicious of the large difference on the decision about promotions. As will be demonstrated below, ambition is correlated with the desire for participation and is the most significant variable predicting activism in the program. Ambitious individuals may also be more willing to volunteer for an interview. At SI, during the three weeks of interviews, five people asked to be interviewed. When I agreed, I discovered they all had one thing in common: they were ambitious people who had been frustrated in their desire to be promoted. These interviews were excluded from the sample.

22. In the surveys of two large eastern cities, I discovered that 55% and 53%, respectively, agreed that workers should be represented on corporate boards. Even more surprising was the fact that between 48% and 53% also agreed that employees should own some portion of their companies. See John F. Witte, "A Preliminary Study of Attitudes toward Workers' Participation," Ph.D. qualifying examination paper, Yale University, March 1974.

23. Ideally, questions asking the respondent how much money or time at SI he would be willing to give up would be a better means of measuring these trade-offs. We were concerned, however, that respondents might wrongly interpret such questions as a signal of impending sacrifices as a result of participation. For this reason, the question was framed in terms of a hypothetical choice at another company.

24. These findings are in very close agreement with a recent national quality of employment survey. In the 1977 survey conducted by the University of Michigan Survey Research Center, when workers were asked if they would trade a 10% pay raise for various changes in employment conditions, exactly 17% said they would give up the raise for "more freedom to decide how to do your work." The job facets in which workers were more willing to make trade-offs were better retirement benefits (54%), improved medical coverage (47%), more vacation days (48%), and a better chance for promotion (41%). See Robert P. Quinn and Graham L. Staines, *The 1977 Quality of Employment Survey* (Ann Arbor, Mich.: Institute for Social Research, 1979), table 4.11, p. 57.

25. Responses in this latter category make no reference to a person's job and are usually general in nature. Typical examples are "I guess we're just trained to do what we're told"; "It's just automatic; after awhile you don't even think about it."

26. Peter Blau, *Bureaucracy in Modern Society* (New York: Random House, 1956), p. 76.

27. Zwerdling, p. 44.

28. As the reader has undoubtedly noticed, I am consistently utilizing interval-level statistical techniques with ordinal data. Support for utilizing these more powerful techniques can be found in John Tukey and Robert Abelson, "Efficient Conversion of Nonmetric Information into Metric Information," in *The Quantitative Analysis of Social Problems,* ed. Edward Tufte (Reading, Mass.: Addison-Wesley, 1970), pp. 407–17. Whenever possible I have created scales in order to increase the range of variables, thus reducing the

potential bias in measurement error. In addition, for all dichotomous dependent variables in this study, a Probit analysis was done in addition to the standard least-squares multiple regression. As is usually the case, Probit findings were very similar to the multiple regressions in terms of explained variance and the independent variables that proved to be significant.

29. See Stouffer, *Communism, Conformity, and Civil Liberty;* Prothro and Grigg, pp. 276–89; and Witte and Whitmore.

30. A number of other external influences, notably the SRC political alienation scale and the Srole anomie scale, were originally included but dropped because they had no appreciable effect in any configuration on the dependent variables and produced severe multicollinearity. I might add, as indicated in app. C herein, that the reliability of the SRC and Srole scales is suspect with Cronbach A's of .61 and .51, respectively. Dropping items proved futile in attempting to improve the reliabilities.

31. See Holter, op. cit.

32. See Melvin Seeman, "Alienation and Engagement," in *The Human Meaning of Social Change,* ed. Angus Campbell and Philip Converse (New York: Russell Sage, 1972), pp. 467–527, and "Alienation Studies," *Annual Review of Sociology* 1 (1975): 91–123.

33. In fact these concepts were studied for three levels of authority: usually lead, supervisor, and superintendent (or department head in white-collar areas). The lead responses are a somewhat distorted measure, in that in many cases leads are not really viewed as superiors and are much closer to the workers than to management. At the other extreme, very few people had enough contact with superintendents to make judgments. Only 25% of the sample could answer questions about superiors above their supervisor.

34. Missing data in this analysis were corrected in scales by substituting sample means if less than 33% of the variables comprising the scale had missing values. Since for about 20% of the sample entire scales were missing because respondents failed to return a take-home questionnaire, I have created estimated values for crucial independent variables, using regression techniques. In the analysis to follow, I estimated scores for twenty-nine respondents on the "belief in democratic values" and "job attributes" scales, using the following regression predictions that were highly significant for the rest of the sample.

Job attributes = 10.65 + .094*alienation in work − .577*authority + .435*job
        classification

Belief in democratic values = 22.26 + .313*Education − .094*age + .40*political
        activism

This technique is recommended by Milton Dagenais in "The Use of Incomplete Observations in Multiple Regression Analysis," *Journal of Econometrics* 1 (1973): 317–28.

35. Ted R. Gurr, "A Comparative Study of Civil Strife," in *Violence in America,* ed. H. D. Graham and Ted R. Gurr (New York: New American Library, 1969); Douglas A. Hibbs, Jr., "Industrial Conflict in Advanced Industrial Societies," *American Political Science Review* 70 (1976): 1033–58; and Joel Seidman, ed., *Trade Union Government and Collective Bargaining: Some Critical Issues* (New York: Praeger, 1970), esp. the chapters by Willard Wirtz and Jack Barbash.

36. James C. Davis, "The Curve of Rising and Declining Satisfactions as a Cause of Some Great Revolution and Contained Rebellion," in *Violence in America,* ed. Graham and Gurr.

CHAPTER 4

1. We can be quite specific about these effects. For example, if we consider the choice of running for the Planning Council (table 2) as a probability ranging from 0 to 1, for each additional political activity, chances increase 3.2% for a total across the full range of 25.6% (.032 × 8). The effect across the range of the democratic values scale is even greater, at 38% (.019 × 20). Assuming a 95% confidence interval ($t = 1.6$), the standard errors indicate a

range in the estimated effect for political participation of 7.7%–43.5%. For democratic values the range is 12.4%–63.6%. The effects are very similar when the dependent variable is the four-point participation index.

2. If we considered all the variables in the previously discussed models, the question whether belief in participation is significant would be moot, because in chap. 3 I have demonstrated that 40% of the variance in that variable could be explained by a linear combination of these other variables. However, even when those variables most significantly related to predicting belief are excluded and only those most strongly related to activism included (political participation, democratic values, job attributes, ambition, and supervisor evaluation), the t value of the b for the desire-for-participation scale is only .53.

3. It could be argued that this conclusion is unwarranted because my activism measures rely only on participation on joint committees which consider higher-level decisions, while the belief-in-participation scale includes a much broader range of decisions. To test this, I created a subscale of the belief-in-participation scale that included only the "plantwide" decisions listed in table 2. The items included profit reinvestment, management hiring and firing, management salaries, and selection of supervisors. When this scale is used in place of the seventeen-item belief-in-participation scale, the same waffle effect results from a comparison with factors predicting activism. In fact the bivariate correlations between the plantwide decisions subscale and the activism measures are .01 and .02, less than with the overall belief in the participation index.

4. George Strauss and Lipset, Coleman, and Trow found that union leaders and activists were more likely to aspire to being managers or union officials. On the other hand, Tannenbaum and Kahn found the reverse (see Leonard Sayles and George Strauss, *The Local Union* [New York: Harper & Row, 1953]; Lipset et al., p. 174; and Tannenbaum and Kahn, p. 100).

5. See Robert A. Dahl, *Who Governs?* (New Haven: Yale University Press, 1961), pp. 223–29.

6. See Robert K. Merton and A. S. Rossi, "Contributions to the Theory of Reference Group Behavior," in Robert Merton, *Social Theory and Social Structure* (Glencoe, Ill.: Free Press, 1957), pp. 275–80. They stress that people may tend to conform to the norms of groups of which they are not members, thus becoming nonconformists within their groups of origins.

7. Holter, pp. 309–13.

8. Sayles and Strauss; and Lipset et al., p. 174, n. 12.

9. Emery and Thorsrud, *Form and Content in Industrial Democracy*, p. 75.

10. Josip Obradović, J. R. P. French, and Willard Rogers, "Worker Councils in Yugoslavia: Effects of Perceived Participation and Satisfaction of Workers," *Human Relations* 5 (1970): 468.

11. National Institute of Industrial Psychology, *Joint Consultation in British Industry* (London: Staples, 1951), p. 47.

12. Selig Perlman, *A Theory of the Labor Movement*, 1949 ed. (New York: Kelley), pp. 7, 166–67, 191.

13. Tannenbaum et al., *Hierarchy in Organizations*, table 1, p. 84; p. 64.

CHAPTER 5

1. Clegg, *Industrial Democracy and Nationalisation* and *A New Approach to Industrial Democracy*.

2. Adolph F. Sturmthal, *Workers Councils: A Study of the Workplace Organization on Both Sides of the Iron Curtain* (Cambridge, Mass.: Harvard University Press, 1964).

3. Jiri Kolaja, *Workers' Councils: The Yugoslav Experience* (London: Tavistock, 1965); and Obradović. For a later replication of the Kolaja study, see Ichak Adizes, "The Effect of Decentralization on Organizational Behavior: An Exploratory Study of the Yugoslav Self-Management System," Ph.D. Dissertation, Columbia University, 1968.

4. The official grievance procedure at SI is similar to that of most nonunion companies. If an employee has a grievance, he must first discuss it with his supervisor. If not satisfied, he can go up the chain of command, first to the superintendent, then to the plant manager, etc., all the way to the president of the company.

5. There was a problem of management coercion in some meetings, but this was characteristic of only one or two managers.

6. Of the forty-four meetings, I failed to analyze six. Two were not recorded. I missed the first two meetings of the original council because the tapes were reused before I could complete my analysis. Two recordings were unintelligible because of mechanical difficulties.

7. The drawback of the Obradović study is that, as of this writing, only the analysis of "economic" discussions by worker councils had been published.

8. The one exception is Factory B in the Kolaja study. He explains this peculiarity as a function of two highly skilled technicians who were considered workers in his statistics and who participated at a much higher rate than their comrades (p. 46).

9. That the ratios for the time of participation are higher than for frequency of participation is an interesting phenomenon typical of both the experience at SI and the companies studied by Obradović. The reason is quite simply that managers tend to make more speeches. This is partly because managers answer more questions, give more reports (at SI thirty-nine to nine for workers), and have acquired the loquacity born from greater exposure to group discussion.

10. Clegg, Emery and Thorsrud, and Abraham Shuchman, relying more on deduction or interviews, reported similar problems in experiments in Great Britain, Norway, and Germany. See Clegg, *A New Approach to Industrial Democracy;* Emery and Thorsrud, *Form and Content of Industrial Democracy;* and Abraham Shuchman, *Codetermination: Labor's Middle Way in Germany* (Washington, D.C.: Public Affairs, 1957).

11. The incentives are based on the fact that, first, with more money available it is easier for managers to use wage increases as motivation and a mechanism for increasing loyalty. Second, and common to many companies, salaried wage increases are almost always tied to hourly increases. In many large corporations, salary increases are directly tied to negotiated union contract increases. Thus, at companies like AT&T and GM, white-collar workers follow negotiations just as closely (and hopefully) as union members.

12. For this reason, Sturmthal recommends that decisions "in the work process itself," such as scheduling, standards, physical arrangements, hours, vacations, and most important, discipline are best adapted to joint committees (*Workers Councils,* pp. 189–90).

13. Only one worker, an alternate on the first council, carried over to the second year. Thus the learning effect essentially occurred for two separate groups.

14. In the second quarter of the first council, managers gave six reports to none for workers. In the second year the count was nine to nothing.

15. A graphic example of this difference was provided by a lead in the furniture factory who was a member of the first Planning Council. When I interviewed him, he evaluated his chances of getting ahead as excellent. His overall evaluation of his job was positive: "I like it; I mean there are some things that get to you, but it's not bad. [Pause] I wouldn't want it for the rest of my life, mind you, but I enjoy it now." Six months later, he quit the company after coming very close to being selected for supervisor. I interviewed him at home with a tape recorder. I asked him about his experience on the Planning Council, and he answered in terms of a comparison with his job: "I don't know why, but it was a more constructive atmosphere in the Planning Council. Easier people to deal with. It was a very good experience. Probably those experiences kept me there until the point I did." Witte: "And the other atmosphere?" He responded, "I found it very frustrating, *very frustrating;* that's why I had to quit. Sheer frustration. I couldn't stand to go in there another day."

16. In fact the relationship between combinations of ambition and expectations and measures of satisfaction with the job and company is closer to an S-shaped pattern in which the combination of high ambition and low expectations produces the least satisfaction, high

ambition and high expectations the most satisfaction, with the remaining combinations in the middle.

17. Substituting the measure of long-range ambition (see p. 44) made almost no difference in the results. All of the differences reported below were significant for this measure of ambition as well. Additionally, selecting the cut point for defining "low" on expectations as 1–3 rather than 1 and 2 made the results more extreme. The cut point shown in the figure was used because it provides for more equal cell sizes.

18. As can be seen from the percentages in box 1, expectations by themselves are only slightly related to activism. The correlation was approximately −.05. All attempts to include expectations in the regression model above not surprisingly proved futile.

19. These questions had to do with attitudes toward how a work group should be run. They were forced-choice questions. For details, see table C-12, app. C.

20. The lead described in n. 15 above provides a good example of this situation.

CHAPTER 6

1. In an unpublished study of a Canadian experiment at a nonunion company called Supreme Aluminium, the problem with grievances was also evident. Attempting to alleviate the inadequacy of their management grievance procedure, management established a joint worker-management governing body (very similar to the SI Planning Council), as part of the formal grievance mechanism. The governing body lacked credibility in this role, and only two formal grievances were filed. The primary reason was the same as at SI: "Many workers will not file a grievance for fear of getting in their boss's bad books." Without the security and protection of a union, I doubt that any committee could gain the confidence of most workers: it is preferable to muddle through than to risk your job. See Jacquelynn Mansell, "Supreme Aluminium Industries Limited—a Case Study in Workers' Participation," paper presented at the People for Self-Management Conference, Cornell University, Ithaca, N.Y., June 1975.

2. The third year (1977), the same thing happened, but with an interesting twist. Again the council became involved too late to have any real impact in formulating the initial policy. However, in July the SI president's staff suggested changing the formula for yearly wage increases from a flat percentage for everyone to an increase based solely on supervisory evaluations of performance. The council, including the first-line supervisors, reacted vehemently. They did not argue against performance-based increases, which most favored, but, rather, against the fact that not everyone would get a base increase. They wanted merit increases in addition to a base increase for the current year. The staff withdrew their plan and accepted the council proposal. However, to date no formal committee has been established on the question of wages.

3. The problem of pay as it related to sharing productivity or profit gains was apparently an important factor in the decline or termination of two of the best known U.S. experiments in workers' participation—the General Foods plant at Topeka and the Prudential experiments carried out in the late 1940s. For General Foods, see "Stonewalling Plant Democracy," *Business Week* (28 March 1977), pp. 78–82; for Prudential, see Everett Reimer, "Creating Experimental Social Change in an Ongoing Organization," paper presented at the meeting of the American Psychological Association, New York, September 1954, p. 11.

4. According to Mansell (pp. 11–13), this mechanism is the one used at Supreme Aluminium. The key pay questions are decided in a subcommittee which is fully dominated by managers.

5. Blumberg, chap. 7.

6. In Kolaja's early study of Yugoslavia, he also emphasizes the lack of a strong union as a problem. "If the workers had an organization of their own, as management has its collegium, there would be more balanced relationship between the men who manipulate concepts and the men who manipulate things. Yugoslav theory, on the other hand, sought rather to decrease the management-labour dichotomy" (p. 72).

7. The comments of one long-time supervisor in an interview will describe this action orientation, which is recognizable to most people who have been closely involved with production. I naively asked the supervisor how he went about making decisions on the job. His response was sophisticated and quite accurate. "I'm not even sure what I do can be described as 'making decisions.' I fix things. . . . When problems come up, I fix them. Most of the time, it's not like sitting down and thinking about alternatives, and all that college boy stuff. [Laughs] You try something; if it works, fine. If not, you change it. If nothing works, you go to your boss, and he tries something. I mean, you make decisions; but you can't really say when you make them."

8. Obradović and his colleagues came to a similar conclusion for the Yugoslav case. "Theoretically, the Workers' Councils were established to provide power to the workers, but the data suggest that in practice workers have much less influence than the factory manager and those in supervisory levels. The effect on the worker who has been elected to the Workers' Council could well be a feeling of frustration; he has been elected to the body with the greatest ideal and perceived influence on the management of the factory, only to find himself subordinated to the same personnel who hold powerful roles in the ordinary factory hierarchy" (Obradović et al., p. 469).

9. A good example of this latter situation was provided by participation in the new facility design. It was agreed that the same process used in office areas, essentially doing a full layout from scratch, would be done in areas of the furniture factory that were small, self-contained, office-type areas. Since I had been responsible for coordinating participation in the office areas, it was assumed that I would coordinate the meetings in the factory areas. However, when I left in June 1976, the coordination of the program was dropped, and several areas were designed with negligible worker input.

10. The relationship between special-purpose committees and the regular hierarchy was somewhat better than that between the hierarchy and the Planning Council. Because of their narrowly defined and clearly stated goals, the organization could adjust to them fairly easily. Although jealousies arose occasionally, there was nothing of the turmoil that surrounded Planning Council actions.

11. In March 1977, in an effort to resolve some of the problems experienced by the Planning Council, four subcouncils were established in each facility. After six months of operation, these councils found communication a central concern as well. Employees wanted every work group represented so they "could find out what was going on in those meetings." This was not done because the meetings would have been too large. Thus, even with decentralization, communication remained a serious problem.

12. Mansell, p. 23; Kolaja, p. 71; and National Institute of Industrial Psychology, p. 153.

13. The rest of the discussion was led by several antiunion workers, with management remaining fairly impartial. The council decided to have the representative ask the individuals specifically what their problems were and report back to the council. She reported at the next meeting that they had withdrawn their request.

14. In the first election, interest was openly stimulated by the employee "election committees" described earlier. This stimulus was provided in the second election by the council members, but they may not have been so effective. At best, however, this explains only part of the decline.

15. For Great Britain, see the thorough study of joint consultations by the National Institute of Industrial Psychology, pp. 64–65, 84–85, 211. See also Elliott Jacques, *The Changing Culture of a Factory* (London: Tavistock, 1951), for evidence of the strong opposition of workers to joint consultation committees at the British Glacier Metals Company. For Yugoslavia, see Kolaja; Rus, pp. 156–57; and Blumberg, pp. 227–29. For Norway, see Holter, pp. 304–5; Emery and Thorsrud, *Form and Content in Industrial Democracy*, esp. chap. 2; and Einar Thorsrud and Fred Emery, *Democracy at Work: The Report of the Norwegian Industrial Democracy Program* (Canberra: Australian National University, 1974), pp. 31, 56, 73. For Canada, see Mansell. For Germany, see Adolph F. Sturmthal,

"Unions and Industrial Democracy," *Annals of the American Academy of Political and Social Science* 431 (1977): 18.

CHAPTER 7

1. See G. D. H. Cole, *Guild Socialism Restated* (London: Parsons, 1920) and *Self-Government in Industry* (London: Bell, 1919).

2. The two examples that come immediately to mind are HEW's *Work in America;* and Jenkins' *Job Power*. Both of these books present glowing reviews on a wide range of American projects, including some like those at Proctor & Gamble, where no formal studies have ever been released to the public.

3. Several workers were also added to the group after it began functioning. In these cases, the workers already on the line had a chance to interview prospective members before they joined the group.

4. My information on the employee relations project was mostly indirect. Here I only attended two meetings. I did, however, have a very close relationship with members of the department. My wife, who worked in the credit union, attended meetings for almost a year. In addition, I worked very closely with the director of employee relations on the QWL program. I also interviewed many of the people in the department, although, because of turnovers, I was only able to complete two interviews with three project members.

5. This outcome was a surprise and disappointment to the director of employee relations. When the meeting was over, he came into my office, very dejected. "They don't want any part of it," he said. "They want [supervisor's name] and I to do it all . . . on what we think is merit. We're sure not getting very far with this thing." I urged him not to be too discouraged. A logical method of solving distributive problems in a group is to submit the case to a qualified judge. As long as the judge is perceived as legitimate, potential conflict within the group is avoided.

6. This intriguing experiment was only tried with one person. The woman involved felt it was a failure, because the old lines of communication to the Employee Relations Department were never severed, and she therefore felt underutilized. While there may be partial truth in this, the workers clearly did not respond well to the woman involved. Her personality was as important as any other factor.

7. Job-training matrices were charts that displayed the skills required in the work procedure on one axis and individual names on another. It provided a graphic display of individual and group deficiencies for each procedure.

8. Emery and Thorsrud are also well aware of the problem of maintaining linkages between a work group and its surrounding environment. They are particularly concerned about the changing role of supervisors. However, in answer to their own rhetorical question, "What will [more autonomous work groups] eventually mean for supervisors?" they write, "We cannot give any definite answer to that question on the basis of our field experiments." Although they go on to speculate on four or five possibilities, they emphasize the need for a great deal more research and more highly educated supervisors (*Democracy at Work*, pp. 116–17).

9. This woman's development was a result partly of her interaction in the work group and partly of the training program for lead development. Early in the project, she learned of her reputation among her fellow workers for impatience and exerting too much pressure. She was deeply hurt and began to change almost immediately. The experiment failed in its attempt to operate without a lead, but it succeeded admirably in fostering a democratic style of leadership within the group.

CHAPTER 8

1. Pay schemes and bonus systems have been critical and controversial in many shop floor experiments. All four of the Norwegian experiments reported by Emery and Thorsrud

incorporated such systems, and the authors imply that in several of the experiments the pay system was the key issue dealt with (*Democracy at Work,* esp. pp. 33–44, 77, 91–92). Similarly, the Rushton Mines experiment in Rushton, Pennsylvania, was stopped by vote of the union when the membership objected to the higher wages being paid to the experimental groups. See National Quality of Working Life Center, *The Quality of Work Program: The First Eighteen Months, April 1974–October 1975* (Ann Arbor, Mich., 1975), pp. 37–43. Similarly, the work improvement program at Bolivar has revolved for three years around the concept of "earned idle time." Under this scheme, workers who completed a daily standard could leave the plant and still receive a full day's pay. This situation led to a reduction in teamwork, cheating on counts, and severe hostility on the part of workers who could not take advantage of the scheme. These problems were confirmed in an internal report at Bolivar by Robert Duckles, "The Development of Earned Idle Time," April 1975. See also Joseph Lelyveld, "The Gone-Fishing Syndrome," *New York Times Magazine* (29 May 1977), p. 62.

2. The best example of this form of optimism is given by Bennis and Slater.

3. See, e.g., Fred E. Emery and Eric L. Trist, "Socio-Technical Systems," in *Systems Thinking,* ed. Fred E. Emery (London: Penguin, 1969); Louis E. Davis and Eric L. Trist, "Improving the Quality of Working Life: Sociotechnical Case Studies," in *Work and the Quality of Working Life,* ed. James O'Toole (Cambridge, Mass.: M.I.T. Press, 1974); and Eric L. Trist, G. W. Higgins, H. Murray, and A. B. Pollock, *Organizational Choice* (London: Tavistock, 1963).

4. For the best short review to date of this literature, see Kaplan and Tausky.

5. Ibid., p. 173.

6. A dramatic example of this profit orientation occurred at the work humanization conference briefly described at the beginning of this book. At one point, in a mass meeting of all those attending (from 150 organizations), a personnel manager from the CRYOVAC division of W. R. Grace, Inc., addressed several professors who had been expounding on the virtues of job enlargement and participative management. He said forcefully, "Look: at CRYOVAC, and I'm sure at the companies here, we are interested in the bottom line. Let's be honest; we don't usually say it, but the bottom line is what counts. And you fellows haven't talked much about that." He was immediately supported by managers from Ralston Purina and Texas Instruments. At that point, I asked the audience how many managers disagreed with his statement. One or two raised their hands. A woman from Banker's Trust explained what may have been the position of many of the managers: "It's not necessarily what we want; it's what we have to do. In the long run, if we can't relate all this to profits, eventually some high-level manager will call it quits."

7. See Charles Perrow, *Complex Organizations* (Glenview, Ill.: Scott Foresman, 1972), p. 175; and J. Richard Hackman, "The Design of Self-managing Work Groups," Technical Report no. 11, Yale University School of Organization and Mangement, December 1976, p. 25. Similarly, Bennis and Slater (p. 5), while arguing that complex work environments are inevitable, admit the limits of participation for simple work environments.

8. For an example of this type of authority, see the definition used by Harold D. Lasswell and Abraham Kaplan in *Power and Society* (New Haven: Yale University Press, 1950), p. 133.

9. Herbert A. Simon, *Administrative Behavior* (New York: Free Press, 1945), p. 125.

10. See, e.g., Robert A. Dahl and Charles E. Lindblom, *Politics, Economics, and Welfare* (Chicago: University of Chicago Press, 1953), chap. 4; and Simon, pp. 133–40.

11. A dramatic example occurred in the L606 project, when a woman joined the line after having been unsuccessful on several previous lines. Since she was a probationary employee, the L606 line was her last chance. After about a month of extreme patience by the team and the supervisor, it became apparent that she lacked the skills required to function at even half the expected rate on any of the jobs. As the work group began to realize this and discussion about what should be done took place on the line, three or four women became extremely

nervous. They told me privately that they wanted nothing to do with firing the woman. In the words of one of the older ones, "That's management's job, not ours. They get paid for having to do that." In the end, the supervisor transferred the woman to a job in another part of the plant; but she quit four weeks later.

12. The Norwegian experiments reported by Emery and Thorsrud again support these conclusions. "Some experiences we have had indicate a tendency for members to leave the difficult and dangerous things to the leading hand [of the foreman], 'because that is what he is paid for'" (*Democracy at Work,* p. 117).

CHAPTER 9

1. John Tukey, *Exploratory Data Analysis* (New York: Addison-Wesley, 1977). See also Donald R. McNeil, *Interactive Data Analysis: A Practical Primer* (New York: Wiley, 1977), pp. 6–8, for a description and computer program to construct box plots.

2. Of the original sample of 145, 27 left the company before they could be reinterviewed. Tests comparing terminated employees with those remaining produced significant differences on only four variables. Those who left the company were on the average five years younger, had more education (one year), felt they had less control over the rewards associated with their jobs, and experienced more participation in decisions on their jobs. The potential effects of these differences will be discussed as appropriate.

3. There is a lengthy, confusing, and contradictory literature on the proper analysis of change studies. However, most experts agree that nonequivalent designs can only be analyzed within treatment groups and not compared across these groups. See Frederick Lord, "A Paradox in the Interpretation of Group Comparisons," *Psychological Bulletin* 74 (1967): 304–5; and Lee J. Cronbach and Lita Furley, "How We Should Measure 'Change'—or Should We?" ibid. 68 (1970): 68–80, for arguments favoring limitation of comparison to within-group tests. For a counterargument, see David A. Kenny, "A Quasi-experimental Approach to Assessing Treatment Effects in the Nonequivalent Control Group Design," ibid. 82 (1975): 345–62.

4. The formulas used for these computations are derived from Cronbach and Furley, p. 72. The basic structure of the formula is

$$\hat{x}_i = w_1 x_i + w_2 y_i + c_x;$$
$$\hat{y}_i = w_3 x_i + w_4 y_i + c_y,$$

where x_i, y_i are observed scores at times 1 and 2; $\hat{x}_i$, $\hat{y}_i$ are estimated true scores at times 1 and 2; and w_1, w_2, w_3, w_4, c_x, and c_y are constants. The more reliable the initial measures (x_i and y_i), the less they are "corrected" by drawing them toward the mean. Thus, as the reliability of x_i increases, w_1/w_3 increases and c_x is reduced; and as the reliability of y_i increases, w_4/w_3 increases and c_y is reduced.

5. Since almost the same percentage of activists left the company as nonactivists, the fact that terminated employees had higher levels of initial participation probably had little effect on the differences between activists and nonactivists. However, across the whole sample, the loss of respondents with higher levels of participation on their jobs also contributes to understating the level of participation at time 2.

6. The initial experiment at Harwood Mills is reported in Lester Coch and J. R. P. French, Jr., "Overcoming Resistance to Change," *Human Relations* 1 (1948): 512–32. The book describing Harwood's takeover and subsequent change in management practices at the Weldon Company is Alfred J. Marrow, David G. Bowers, and Stanley E. Seashore, *Management by Participation* (New York: Harper & Row, 1967). For the Prudential experiment, see Nancy C. Morse and Everett Reimer, "The Experimental Manipulation of a Major Organizational Variable," *Journal of Abnormal and Social Psychology* 52 (1956): 120–29; and for one of the few reports on the extensive long-range project at Non-linear Systems in San Diego, begun and terminated by its owner, see Erwin L. Malone, "The Non-linear

Systems Experiment in Participative Management," *Journal of Business* 48 (1975): 52–64.

7. See Emery and Thorsrud, *Democracy at Work,* for reports on the Norwegian projects; Lelyveld; and Duckles for the Bolivar Project.

8. See Marrow et al., pp. 181–82.

9. My specific concern is with the work of Rensis Likert, particularly in his second book, *The Human Organization,* where he relies on evidence from a study of insurance salesmen and on the results of the Weldon Company transformation. The difficulties have been described with remarkable accuracy by Perrow (*Complex Organizations,* pp. 128–37).

10. I did not have direct access to the profit statements at SI, because it was a wholly owned subsidiary. However, during the time I spent at SI, I knew from conversations with top management that sales were setting records and that the company was responsible for an increasing share of the parent company's profits.

11. Subsequent communication with managers at SI confirmed that the upward trend in productivity continued over the next two quarters.

12. Those workers placed in the frustrated ambitious category based on the first wave of interviews (see fig. 1, p. 29) were significantly more alienated from their work than the rest of the sample on the second wave of interviews. The difference in change scores was significant at the .01 level.

13. In the interviews I asked workers their chances of getting ahead at SI. When they answered, I asked them why they felt the way they did. Of those respondents who felt their chances were not good, 83% explained this by some reference to the limited number of openings available. Pyramids are simple figures to understand, especially when one is looking up from the inside.

CHAPTER 10

1. See Dahl, *Polyarchy* (New Haven: Yale University Press, 1971), esp. chaps. 1 and 2.

2. I emphasize the word *healthy*. One of the most unfortunate occurrences for the industrial democracy movement is the recent trend of workers attempting to buy or take over companies about to close. As might be expected, most of these companies fail and industrial democracy is given part, if not the lion's share of the blame. In truth, of course, most of these companies would have failed under any conditions.

3. See Simon; Richard M. Cyert and James G. March, *The Behavioral Theory of the Firm* (Englewood Cliffs, N.J.: Prentice-Hall, 1963); James G. March and Herbert A. Simon, *Organizations* (New York: Wiley, 1958); and James D. Thompson, *Organizations in Action* (New York: McGraw-Hill, 1967).

4. The term *operative goal* was first introduced by Charles Perrow in "The Analysis of Goals in Complex Organizations," *American Sociological Review* 26 (1961): 854–65.

5. James K. Dent, "Organizational Correlates of the Goals of Business Management," *Journal of Personnel Psychology* 12 (1959): 365–93.

6. See, e.g., Cyert and March, pp. 40–43.

7. See, e.g., Simon, pp. 133–34; and Dahl and Lindblom, esp. pp. 106–10.

8. Douglas McGregor, *The Human Side of Enterprise* (New York: McGraw-Hill, 1960), pp. 33–34.

9. Bennis and Slater, p. 17.

10. The most forceful statement of this position is in Arthur F. Bentley, *The Process of Government,* 1967 ed. (Cambridge, Mass.: Harvard University Press, Belknap Press). He renounces the idea of the state as "intellectual amusement" (p. 263) and ridicules notions of the "public interest" and the "social whole" as having no meaning (pp. 220, 222, 240). To varying degrees, the later writings of Schumpeter, Truman, and Dahl and Lindblom follow in this tradition, without Bentley's flamboyant overstatement. See Joseph P. Schumpeter, *Capitalism, Socialism, and Democracy,* 1947 ed. (New York: Harper & Row), pp. 250–56, 269–73; David B. Truman, *The Governmental Process* (New York: Knopf, 1951), pp. 50–51 (but also see p. 515 for something of a reversal); and Dahl and Lindblom, pp. 350, 501.

11. These basic assumptions are very close to the philosophy and attitudes that characterize Israeli kibbutz plants. For the best data to date on the kibbutzim, see Tannenbaum et al., *Hierarchy in Organizations*.

12. Tannenbaum and his colleagues found both of these conditions to be true for kibbutz plants relative to plants in the United States, Austria, Italy, and Yugoslavia (ibid., pp. 18, 59).

13. Frederick Jackson Turner, *The Frontier in American History* (New York: Holt, 1921).

14. Tannenbaum et al., *Hierarchy in Organizations*, pp. 213–14.

15. Ichak Adizes, *Industrial Democracy: Yugoslav Style* (New York: Free Press, 1971).

16. Tannenbaum et al., *Hierarchy in Organizations*, p. 183.

17. Likert, *New Patterns of Management*, p. 112.

18. Adolph A. Berle and Gardiner C. Means, *The Modern Corporation and Private Property* (New York: Macmillan, 1934).

19. Juroslav Vanek, *Participatory Economy* (Ithaca, N.Y.: Cornell University Press, 1971) and *General Theory of the Labor Managed Economy* (Ithaca, N.Y.: Cornell University Press, 1970).

20. See, e.g., G. D. H. Cole, *Social Theory* (London: Methuen, 1920), and *Guild Socialism Restated*.

Bibliography

Adizes, Ichak. "The Effect of Decentralization on Organizational Behavior: An Exploratory Study of the Yugoslav Self-Management System." Ph.D. dissertation, Columbia University, 1968.

———. *Industrial Democracy: Yugoslav Style.* New York: Free Press, 1971.

Anderson, John. "Local Union Participation: A Re-examination." *Industrial Relations* 18 (1979): 18–31.

Bavelas, Alex. "Communication Patterns in Task Oriented Groups." In *The Policy Sciences,* edited by Daniel Learner and Harold Lasswell. Stanford, Calif.: Stanford University Press, 1951.

Bennis, Warren G., and Slater, Philip E. *The Temporary Society.* New York: Harper & Row, 1968.

Bentley, Arthur F. *The Process of Government.* 1967 ed. Cambridge, Mass.: Harvard University Press, Belknap Press.

Berle, A. A., and Means, Gardiner C. *The Modern Corporation and Private Property.* New York: Macmillan, 1934.

Blau, Peter. *Bureaucracy in Modern Society.* New York: Random House, 1956.

Blumberg, Paul. *Industrial Democracy: The Sociology of Participation.* New York: Schocken, 1969.

Campbell, Angus; Converse, P. E.; Miller, W. E.; and Stokes, D. E. *The American Voter.* New York: Wiley, 1964.

Clegg, Hugh. *Industrial Democracy and Nationalisation.* London: Blackwell, 1951.

———. *A New Approach to Industrial Democracy.* London: Blackwell, 1960.

Coch, Lester, and French, J. R. P., Jr. "Overcoming Resistance to Change." *Human Relations* (1948): 512–32.

Cole, G. D. H. *Guild Socialism Restated.* London: Parsons, 1920.

———. *Self-Government in Industry.* London: Bell, 1919.

———. *Social Theory.* London: Methuen, 1920.

Converse, Philip E. "The Nature of Belief Systems in Mass Publics." In *Ideology and Discontent,* edited by David E. Apter. New York: Free Press, 1964.

Cronbach, Lee J., and Furley, Lita. "How We Should Measure 'Change'—or Should We?" *Psychological Bulletin* 68 (1970): 68–80.

Cyert, Richard M., and March, James G. *The Behavioral Theory of the Firm.* Englewood Cliffs, N.J.: Prentice-Hall, 1963.

Dagenais, Milton. "The Use of Incomplete Observations in Multiple Regression Analysis." *Journal of Econometrics* 1 (1973): 317–28.

Dahl, Robert A. *After the Revolution?* New Haven: Yale University Press, 1970.

———. *Polyarchy.* New Haven: Yale University Press, 1971.

———. *Who Governs?* New Haven: Yale University Press, 1961.

——— and Lindblom, Charles E. *Politics, Economics, and Welfare.* Chicago: University of Chicago Press, 1953.

Davis, James C. "Communism, Conformity, Cohorts and Categories: American Tolerance in 1954 and 1972–73." *American Journal of Sociology* 81 (1975): 491–513.

———. "The Curve of Rising and Declining Satisfactions as a Cause of Some Great Revolution and Contained Rebellion." In *Violence in America,* edited by H. D. Graham and Ted R. Gurr. New York: New American Library, 1969.

Davis, Louis E., and Trist, Eric L. "Improving the Quality of Working Life: Sociotechnical Case Studies." in *Work and the Quality of Working Life,* edited by James O'Toole. Cambridge, Mass.: M.I.T. Press, 1974.

De Jouvenal, Bertrand. "The Chairman's Problem." *American Political Science Review* 55 (June 1961): 368–73.

Dent, James K. "Organization Correlates of the Goals of Business Management." *Journal of Personnel Psychology* 12 (1959): 365–93.

Duckles, Robert. "The Development of Earned Idle Time." Report for the Harman International Work Improvement Program, Bolivar, Tennessee, April 1975.

Emery, Fred E., and Trist, Eric L. "Socio-Technical Systems." In *Systems Thinking,* edited by Fred E. Emery. London: Penguin, 1969.

—— and Thorsrud, Einar. *Form and Content in Industrial Democracy.* London: Tavistock, 1969 ed.

Gramsci, Antonio. *Letters from Prison.* 1973 ed. New York: Harper & Row.

———. *Prison Notebooks.* 1971 ed. London: Lawrence & Wishart.

Gurr, Ted R. "A Comparative Study of Civil Strife." In *Violence in America,* edited by H. D. Graham and Ted R. Gurr. New York: New American Library, 1969.

Hackman, J. Richard. "The Design of Self-managing Work Groups." Technical Report no. 11, Yale University School of Organization and Management, December 1976.

Heise, George A., and Miller, George. "Problem Solving in Small Groups Using Various Communication Nets." *Journal of Abnormal Social Psychology* 46 (1951): 327–35.

Heller, Frank A. *Managerial Decision Making.* London: Tavistock, 1971.

Hibbs, Douglas A., Jr. "Industrial Conflict in Advanced Industrial Societies." *American Political Science Review* 70 (1976): 1033–58.

Holter, Harriet. "Attitudes towards Employee Participation in Company Decision-making Processes." *Human Relations* 18 (1965): 297–319.

Jacques, Elliott. *The Changing Culture of a Factory.* London: Tavistock, 1951.

Jenkins, David. *Job Power.* Baltimore: Penguin, 1973.

Kaplan, H. Roy, and Tausky, Curt. "Humanism in Organizations: A Critical Appraisal." *Public Administration Review* 37 (1977): 171–80.

Katz, Daniel. "Satisfactions and Deprivations in Industrial Life." In *Industrial Productivity,* edited by A. Kornhauser et al. Madison, Wis.: Industrial Relations Research Association, 1951.

—— and Kahn, Robert. *Social Psychology of Organizations.* New York: Wiley, 1966.

Kenny, David A. "A Quasi-experimental Approach to Assessing Treatment Effects in the Nonequivalent Control Group Design." *Psychological Bulletin* 82 (1975): 345–62.

Kolaja, Jiri. *Workers' Councils: The Yugoslav Experience.* London: Tavistock, 1965.

Lasswell, Harold D., and Kaplan, Abraham. *Power and Society.* New Haven: Yale University Press, 1950.

Lelyveld, Joseph. "The Gone-Fishing Syndrome." *New York Times Magazine* (29 May 1977), p. 62.

Likert, Rensis. *The Human Organization.* New York: McGraw–Hill, 1967.

———. *New Patterns of Management.* New York: McGraw–Hill, 1961.

Lipset, Seymour M.; Coleman, James S.; and Trow, Martin. *Union Democracy*. Garden City, N.Y.: Doubleday, 1962.

Lord, Frederick. "A Paradox in the Interpretation of Group Comparisons." *Psychological Bulletin* 74 (1967): 304–5.

McCloskey, Herbert. "Consensus and Ideology in American Politics."; *American Political Science Review* 5 (1960): 361–83.

McGregor, Douglas. *The Human Side of Enterprise*. New York: McGraw–Hill, 1960.

McNeil, Donald R. *Interactive Data Analysis: A Practical Primer*. New York: Wiley, 1977.

Malone, Erwin L. "The Non-linear Systems Experiment in Participative Management." *Journal of Business* 48 (1975): 52–64.

Mansell, Jacquelynn. "Supreme Aluminium Industries, Limited—a Case Study in Workers' Participation." Paper presented at the People for Self-management Conference, Cornell University, Ithaca, New York, June 1975.

March, James G., and Simon, Herbert A. *Organizatons*. New York: Wiley, 1958.

Marrow, Alfred J.; Bowers, David G.; and Seashore, Stanley E. *Management by Participation*. New York: Harper & Row, 1967.

Merton, Robert K., and Rossi, A. S. "Contributions to the Theory of Reference Group Behavior." In Robert K. Merton, *Social Theory and Social Structure*. Glencoe, Ill.: Free Press, 1957.

Michels, Robert. *Political Parties: A Sociological Study of the Oligarchical Tendencies of Modern Democracies*, 1966 ed. New York: Free Press.

Milbrath, Lester. *Political Participation*. New York: Rand McNally, 1965.

Morse, Nancy. *Satisfactions in the White Collar Job*. Ann Arbor, Mich.: Survey Research Center, 1953.

———— and Reimer, Everett. "The Experimental Manipulation of a Major Organizational Variable." *Journal of Abnormal and Social Psychology* 52 (1956): 120–29.

National Institute of Industrial Psychology. *Joint Consultation in British Industry*. London: Staples, 1951.

National Quality of Working Life Center. *The Quality of Work Program: The First Eighteeen Months, April 1974–October 1975*. Ann Arbor, Mich.: 1975.

Obradović, Josip. "Distribution of Participation in the Process of Decision-Making on Problems Related to the Economic Activity of the Company." *Participation and Self-Management* 2 (1972): 137–64.

————; French, J. R. P.; and Rogers, Willard. "Worker Councils in Yugoslavia: Effects of Perceived Participation and Satisfaction of Workers." *Human Relations* 5 (1970): 459–71.

Pateman, Carole. "A Contribution to the Political Theory of Organizational Democracy." Paper presented at the meeting of the American Political Science Association, Chicago, September 1974.

————. *Participation and Democratic Theory*. Cambridge: Cambridge University Press, 1970.

Perlman, Selig. *A Theory of the Labor Movement*. 1949 ed. New York: Kelley.

Perrow, Charles. "The Analysis of Goals in Complex Organizations." *American Sociological Review* (1961): 854–65.

————. *Complex Organizations*. Glenview, Ill.: Scott Foresman, 1972.

Prothro, James W., and Grigg, Charles M. "Fundamental Principles of Democracy: Bases of Agreement and Disagreement." *Journal of Politics* 22 (1960): 276–89.

Quinn, Robert P. and Staines, Graham L. *The 1977 Quality of Employment Survey*. Ann Arbor, Mich.: Institute for Social Research, 1979.

Reimer, Everett. "Creating Experimental Social Change in an Ongoing Organization." Paper presented at the meeting of the American Psychological Association, New York, September 1954.

Rus, Veljko. "Influence Structure in Yugoslav Enterprises." *Industrial Relations*
9 (1970): 148–60.

Sayles, Leonard, and Strauss, George. *The Local Union.* New York: Harper &
Row, 1953.

Schumpeter, Joseph P. *Capitalism, Socialism, and Democracy.* 1947 ed. New
York: Harper & Row.

Seeman, Melvin. "Alienation and Engagement." In *The Human Meaning of Social Change,* edited by Angus Campbell and Philip Converse. New York: Russell Sage, 1972.

———. "Alienation Studies." *Annual Review of Sociology* 1 (1975): 91–123.

Seidman, Joel, ed. *Trade Union Government and Collective Bargaining: Some
Critical Issues.* New York: Praeger, 1970.

Shuchman, Abraham. *Codetermination: Labor's Middle Way in Germany.*
Washington, D.C.: Public Affairs Press, 1957.

Simon, Herbert A. *Administrative Behavior.* New York: Free Press, 1945.

"Stonewalling Plant Democracy." *Business Week,* 28 March 1977, pp. 78–82.

Stouffer, Samuel. *Communism, Conformity, and Civil Liberty.* 1965 ed. Garden
City, N.Y.: Doubleday.

Sturmthal, Adolph F. "Unions and Industrial Democracy." *Annals of the American Academy of Political and Social Sciences* 431 (1977): 12–22.

———. *Workers Councils: A Study of the Workplace Organization on Both Sides
of the Iron Curtain.* Cambridge, Mass.: Harvard University Press, 1964.

Tannenbaum, Arnold S. "The Concept of Organizational Control." *Journal of
Social Issues* 12 (1956): 50–60.

———. "Control in Organizations: Industrial Adjustments and Organizational
Performance." *Administrative Science Quarterly* 7 (1962): 236–57.

Tannenbaum, Arnold S. and Kahn, Robert L. *Participation in Union Locals.*
Evanston, Ill.: Row, Peterson, 1958.

Tannenbaum, Arnold S., ed. *Control in Organizations.* New York: McGraw–Hill,
1968.

———; Kavcic, B.; Rosner, M.; Vianello, M.; and Wieser, G. *Hierarchy in
Organizations.* San Francisco: Jossey-Bass, 1974.

Thompson, James D. *Organizations in Action.* New York: McGraw–Hill, 1967.

Thorsrud, Einar, and Emery, Fred. *Democracy at Work: The Report of the
Norwegian Industrial Democracy Program.* Canberra: Australian National
University, 1974.

Trist, Eric L.; Higgins, G. W.; Murray, H.; and Pollock, A. B. *Organizational
Choice.* London: Tavistock, 1963.

Truman, David B. *The Governmental Process.* New York: Knopf, 1951.

Tukey, John. *Exploratory Data Analysis.* New York: Addison-Wesley, 1977.

——— and Abelson, Robert. "Efficient Conversion of Non-metric Information
into Metric Information." In *The Quantitative Analysis of Social Problems.*
Edited by Edward Tufte. Reading, Mass.: Addison-Wesley, 1970.

Turner, Frederick Jackson. *The Frontier in American History.* New York: Holt,
1921.

Upjohn Institute for Employment Research and the Harvard Project on Technology, Work and Character. "The Bolivar Project of Joint Management–Union
Determination of Change According to Principles of Security—Equity—Individualism—Democracy, May 1973–January 1974," Washington, D.C., 15
February 1974.

U.S. Department of Health, Education, and Welfare. *Work in America*. Cambridge, Mass.: M.I.T. Press, 1973.

Vanek, Juroslav. *General Theory of the Labor Managed Economy*. Ithaca, N.Y.: Cornell University Press, 1970.

————. *Participatory Economy*. Ithaca, N.Y.: Cornell University Press, 1971.

Verba, Sidney, and Nie, Norman. *Participation in America*. New York: Harper & Row, 1972.

Vroom, Victor. *Work and Motivation*. New York: Wiley, 1964.

Witte, John F. "A Preliminary Study of Attitudes toward Workers' Participation." Ph.D. qualifying examination paper, Yale University, 1974.

———— and Whitmore, Charles S. "Democratic Values, Civic Virtue, and Liberal Democracy." Unpublished manuscript, 1976.

Zwerdling, Daniel. "The Day the Workers Took Over." *New Times*, 10 December 1976, pp. 40–45.

Index

Adizes, Ichak, 73, 165
Alienation in work: changes in, 144–48, 155, fig. 5; concern for, 1; expected effect of industrial democracy on, 6; measurement of, 43–44, tables C-4 to C-8; related to belief in workers' participation, 43–47, 53, table 9; related to worker activism, 53–54, 56, tables 10–12
Ambition: measurement of, 44; related to belief in workers' participation, 45–47, 53, table 9; related to failure of industrial democracy, 7; related to worker activism, 52–60, tables 10–12
—frustrated: effect of, on alienation, 146–47; effect of, on joint decision making, 76, 82–85, fig. 2; future effects of, 169
Apathy: in joint decision making, 104–7, 154–55, 165; in work projects, 116, 122
Authority: and authoritarianism, 41; effect of joint decision making on, 95–97; hierarchical form of, in corporations, 158–59; problem of, in work projects, 115, 122–24, 129–32; related to responsibility, 129–32; workers' acceptance of, 38–40, 132–33

Bennis, Warren, 160
Bentley, Arthur, 160 n.10
Berle, Adolph, 166
Blau, Peter, 39–40
Blumberg, Paul, 91, 105 n.15
Bolivar, automotive parts plant, 31–32, 126 n.2, 141, table 4

Clegg, Hugh, 6, 8, 61, 73 n.10
Cole, G. D. H., 109 n.1, 167 n.20
Coleman, James, 56 n.4
Communication: changes in, 140–41; general problem of, 154–55; problem with, in joint decision making, 98–100
Community, sense of, 168–69
Competence: definition of, 5–6; and learning by workers, 78–82, table 16; workers', in

decision making, 5, 70, 74–76, 153
Control, definition of, 2–3
Co-optation, 6, 8–9; defined, 61; in joint decision making, 61–85; related to belief in workers' participation, 47; related to worker activism, 57, 59
Cyert, Richard, 156, 157 n.6

Dahl, Robert, 5 n.7, 56, 57
Decision making, 157–58; definition of democratic, 3; method at SI, Inc., 94 n.7; policy, versus procedural, 19–20
Democracy: constraints on, 3–7; definition of, 3; illusion of, xi, 61–62, 107–8, 153; principles of, 166–67. *See also* Industrial democracy; Workers' participation
—norms supporting: conflict of, with meritocratic norms, 156, 159–65; effect of, on joint decision making, 79, 84–85; related to ambition, 84–85, fig. 1; related to belief in workers' participation, 42, 45, table 9; related to worker activism, 49, 52–54, 56–57
Dual hierarchies, 91–97. *See also* Joint worker-manager committees
Duckles, Robert, 126 n.1

Education, 10; effects of, on workers' participation in future, 85; effects of, on joint decision making, 81–82, 85; level of, at SI, Inc., 11; related to belief in workers' participation, 42, 45, table 9; related to worker activism, 52, 54, table 12
Efficiency, 127–28. *See also* Productivity
Emery, Fred, 8, 58, 73 n.10, 105 n.15, 120 n.8, 126 n.1
Equality: in kibbutz, 164; as norm of democratic organizations, 160–62; of opportunity, 163; political, xi, 156, 160–61; of rewards, 162, 164, table 18
Expectations: for advancement, effects of, 84–85, fig. 2; and apathy, 106–7; related to belief in workers' participation, 45, 47.

213